THE
PRESIDENT AND CONGRESS
IN
POSTAUTHORITARIAN CHILE

Peter M. Siavelis

THE
PRESIDENT AND CONGRESS
IN
POSTAUTHORITARIAN CHILE

INSTITUTIONAL CONSTRAINTS
TO
DEMOCRATIC CONSOLIDATION

The Pennsylvania State University Press
University Park, Pennsylvania

Library of Congress Cataloging-in-Publication Data

Siavelis, Peter.
    The president and congress in postauthoritarian Chile : institutional constraints
to democratic consolidation / Peter M. Siavelis.
        p.   cm.
    Includes bibliographical references (p.   ) and index.
    ISBN 0-271-01947-6 (cloth : alk. paper)
    ISBN 0-271-01948-4 (pbk. : alk. paper)
    1. Separation of power—Chile.   2. Executive power—Chile.   3. Legislative
power—Chile.   4. Constitutional history—Chile.   5. Democracy·—Chile.
6. Political stability—Chile.
JL2619.S56 2000
320.483'04—dc21   98-54921
                                                                                    CIP

It is the policy of The Pennsylvania State University Press to use acid-free paper for
the first printing of all clothbound books. Publications on uncoated stock satisfy the
minimum requirements of American National Standard for Information Sciences—
Permanence of Paper for Printed Library Materials, ANSI Z39.48–1992.

CONTENTS

LIST OF TABLES

ACKNOWLEDGMENTS

Many personal and intellectual debts were incurred in the course of writing this book, which I gratefully acknowledge. I would like to thank the Fulbright-Hays Commission, which provided the financial support for this study, and the Center for Latin American Studies at Georgetown University for providing travel support for the exploratory fieldwork. The research and publication fund at Wake Forest University also provided editorial support in the course of this project.

The bulk of research for this study was undertaken while I was a visiting scholar and researcher at the Institute of Political Science at the Pontificia Universidad Católica de Chile. I am indebted to the Institute's director, Oscar Godoy, and to the entire faculty of the Institute for making my stay intellectually and personally enjoyable.

I owe a great debt to Eusebio Mujal-León and John Bailey, who carefully read very early versions of this study. Arturo Valenzuela's thoroughgoing knowledge of Chilean politics, and his intellectual and personal support during the course of this project, immeasurably improved its quality and made it more interesting to undertake.

I am also grateful for the support of friends and colleagues in the United States and in Chile whose personal views and insights on Chilean politics helped to improve this study. These include Alvaro Jara Bucarey, Joan Caivano, Alejandro Foxley Tapia, Fernando Acuña, Ricardo Pino Matus, Marcela Pacheco, Alfredo Rehren, Andrés Allamand, Katty Kauffman, and Carlos Jiménez Seguín.

Thanks are also due to Mark Jones and Michael Coppedge, who critically and carefully read and critiqued an earlier version of this book. Many of their suggestions are incorporated throughout. Any errors contained in the manuscript are, of course, my own.

I would also like to acknowledge the many Chileans in the government and academic community who agreed to be interviewed for this study. Their commitment to enhancing the quality and functioning of Chilean democracy was truly inspirational. César Ladrón de Guevara Pardo, of the Ministry of the General Secretary of the Presidency, went well out of his way to provide crucial insights, support, and data during every phase of this project. I owe him a special debt of gratitude for his help and kindness. Carlos Carmona Santander and Patricio Zapata, also of the Ministry of the General Secretary of the Presidency, were indispensable in helping me understand the intricacies of interbranch relations in Chile. Discussions with and help from Eugenio Guzmán Astete of the Instituto Libertad y Desarrollo helped to sharpen analysis of the binomial electoral system. Gisela von Muhlenbrock was also quite generous with her time, and very helpful. The Center for Legislative Studies (CEAL) at the Catholic University of Valparaíso, particularly Amelia Dondero and Fernando Parada, provided crucial help in securing interviews with legislative leaders.

Many legislators made special efforts to spend a great deal of their valuable time with a young researcher interested in the National Congress. The many hours spent with them immeasurably improved this study. These include Arturo Alessandri, Carlos Bombal, Olga Feliú, Carmen Frei, Antonio Horvath, José Miguel Ortiz, Arturo Longton, Eugenio Ortega, Mario Papi, Jaime Rocha, William Thayer, and Andrés Zaldívar. Many legislative advisors were of crucial help in understanding the real functioning of the legislature as an institution. Eduardo Barros González and Leon Guzmán Gatica were enthusiastic about discussing legislative affairs and provided very instructive insights based on their crucial role as advisors within the legislative process.

A preliminary version of this study previously appeared in very abridged format as a chapter in *Presidentialism and Democracy in Latin America*, edited by Matthew Shugart and Scott Mainwaring (Cambridge: Cambridge University Press, 1997). A section of Chapter 3 also appeared in an article published in *Comparative Political Studies*, vol. 30 (1997). I thank the respective presses for their permission to reproduce portions of these works.

I owe a special debt of gratitude to my colleagues in the Politics Department at Wake Forest University, who are without fail supportive and encouraging.

Finally, the unquestioning and constant support of my parents, Joan Siavelis and William Siavelis, has been indispensable both to my intellectual growth and to bringing this project to fruition.

This work is dedicated with deepest appreciation to Colleen Galvan, who made this work possible, and to Alexander and Marissa Siavelis, who made it worth undertaking.

INTRODUCTION

In March 1990, Chile's seventeen-year interregnum of authoritarian rule ended. In a ceremony in the country's newly constructed National Congress in the port of Valparaíso, former authoritarian leader Augusto Pinochet Ugarte passed the presidential sash to the popularly elected Christian Democrat, Patricio Aylwin Azocar. With the transfer of power, Chileans inherited a new government and, at the same time, a transformed institutional framework for democracy. This study analyzes the significance this new framework has given the social and political realities of postauthoritarian Chile.

Chile's military coup of 11 September 1973 brought an end to one of the longest periods of democratic rule in Latin America. The country's legislative branch was an essential element of Chile's relative success with democracy when compared with other countries in the region. Virtually in continuous operation from 1823 to 1973, the Chilean National Congress was one of the strongest legislative bodies on the continent. In global political terms, it served as an arena for negotiation in a highly divided political system, encouraging interbranch and interparty bargaining, compromise, and consensus.[1] Chile's proportional representation (PR) electoral system permitted the widespread participation of the country's numerous and ideologically dispersed political parties in Congress. Through a combination of pork barrel politics, interparty negotiation, and clientelistic relationships, members of Congress successfully performed their interest-representation functions, channeling demands in Chile's centralized political system and ultimately contributing to the overall

---

1. Though he does point to some of the ways the legislature is "impaired" in carrying out its constitutional role, Gil, more than other authors, also underscores the efficacy of the Chilean legislative branch. See Federico Gil, *The Political System of Chile* (Boston: Houghton Mifflin, 1966), and especially 106–22. For a more explicit discussion of the importance of the Chilean legislative branch, and particularly the Senate, during this period, see Weston H. Agor, *The Chilean Senate* (Austin: University of Texas Press, 1971).

success of democracy.[2] In spite of a fragmented and ideologically polarized party system, presidents were able to legislate (albeit not always smoothly) through the structuring of working coalitions in Congress.[3]

Despite Chile's relative success with democracy from a comparative regional perspective, the military intervention brought a violent end to the legislative regime that had helped sustain Chilean democracy for decades. The 1970 election of Marxist president Salvador Allende Gossens with a minority of the popular vote and lacking a majority in Congress proved to be a recipe for governmental ineffectiveness. Allende's administration was characterized by almost constant deadlock between the branches of government at a time of national conflict concerning the most basic questions of economic and social organization. Already suspicious of the country's political parties and politicians, military leaders pointed to the Allende administration as additional evidence of the bankruptcy of Chile's long-standing governmental institutions.[4] On 24 September 1973, a decree was issued dissolving Congress and transferring all legislative functions to the new military junta.[5]

During military rule, governing authorities embarked on a concerted strategy to shape the postauthoritarian political order in an effort to limit the political forces that they viewed as the root causes of Chile's institutional crisis of democracy. A new constitution drafted by the authoritarian government was approved in a national plebiscite in 1980 and still governs Chile today.

The 1980 constitution established an institutional framework for a limited democracy characterized by executive domination and an electoral system designed to limit party-system fractionalization and provide benefits for the parties of the Right.[6] The Chilean presidency is one of the strongest in Latin America and the world and has broad powers to control the legislative

2. See Arturo Valenzuela, *Political Brokers in Chile: Local Government in a Centralized Polity* (Durham, N.C.: Duke University Press, 1977).

3. For an accounting of these coalitions from 1932 to 1989, see Arturo Valenzuela, "Party Politics and the Crisis of Presidentialism in Chile," in *The Failure of Presidential Democracy*, 2 vols., ed. Juan Linz and Arturo Valenzuela (Baltimore: Johns Hopkins University Press, 1994).

4. For a discussion of the corrective and foundational aspirations of the Chilean military, see Manuel Antonio Garretón, *The Chilean Political Process* (Boston: Unwin Hyman, 1989), 45–67, and Genaro Arriagada, *Pinochet: The Politics of Power* (Boulder, Colo.: Westview Press, 1988). For a useful, albeit dated, general discussion of the political roles of Latin American militaries, see Abraham Lowenthal, ed., *Armies and Politics in Latin America* (New York: Holmes and Meier, 1976).

5. Decree Law No. 27, published in the *Diario Oficial de la República de Chile*, No. 28.658, 24 September 1973.

6. Genaro Arriagada provides an excellent analysis of what he calls "autocratic neo-presidentialism" in Chile. Genaro Arriagada, "El sistema político chileno: Una exploración del futuro," *Colección estudios CIEPLAN* 15 (December 1984): 171–202.

process.[7] What is more, given its majoritarian characteristics, the legislative electoral law has the potential to limit the congressional representation of the full range of Chile's numerous political parties.

Thus, this study explores a fundamental paradox. The defeat of General Pinochet in the plebiscite of October 1988 and the subsequent formation of the first democratic governing coalition vividly demonstrated the ability of Chilean parties to cooperate and unite in a common effort across party lines, indicating a significant change within Chile's notoriously polarized and competitive party system. The center-left Concertación de Partidos por la Democracia (known simply as the Concertación) forged a consensus alliance that successfully navigated a complex democratic transition, and it has governed Chile since the return of formal democracy.

Economic transformations that occurred during the military regime have fundamentally altered the socioeconomic structure of the country and provided a context of attenuated social and class conflict. The scope of the labor movement has narrowed, and labor activism has significantly decreased. Survey data have demonstrated that there is increased consensus concerning the most important problems facing Chilean society and the role that should be played by the state. International and domestic transformations have also produced moderation in the ideological tendencies of elites and the electorate, and there has been a drastic reduction in the ideological scope of the party system. Finally, the democratic transition consistently demonstrated that the authoritarian experience was accompanied by a process of political learning that increased sensitivity to the need for cooperation.

However, despite this transformed socioeconomic and political context, and the new way of doing politics in Chile, the 1980 constitution imposes

7. Constitutional reforms in 1989 and 1991 limited some of the powers originally granted to the president according to the 1980 constitution (most notable was the elimination of the executive's ability to dissolve the Chamber of Deputies). However, the Chilean presidency remains one of the most powerful in Latin America and in the world. Shugart and Carey's cross-national study ranks Chile among the most presidential of systems in terms of nonlegislative powers, with only Paraguay scoring higher. See Matthew Shugart and John Carey, *Presidents and Assemblies: Constitutional Design and Electoral Dynamics* (New York: Cambridge University Press, 1992). In terms of legislative powers, the presidency is also quite strong, though Shugart and Carey underestimate its strength in their power-measuring schema (see Chapter 1 of this work for a discussion). Similarly, Mainwaring and Shugart's comparative study of Latin American presidents also places the Chilean presidency among the strongest, along with Colombia, Argentina, and Ecuador, in the "potentially dominant" category in terms of legislative powers. See Scott Mainwaring and Matthew Shugart, eds., *Presidentialism and Democracy in Latin America* (New York: Cambridge University Press, 1997). For an analysis of the constitutional reforms of 1989, see Carlos Andrade Geywitz, *Reforma de la Constitución Política de la República de Chile* (Santiago: Editorial Jurídica de Chile, 1991).

strict limits on the very elites and parties that led the way in establishing a pattern of political behavior characterized by moderation and cooperation. The cornerstone of the entire institutional framework is control: presidential control of the legislative process, a majoritarian electoral law designed to control the number of parties with access to Congress, and additional checks to ensure military tutelage and veto power over the decisions of civilian authorities. Thus, the constitution imposes rigidities that limit the scope of action of the same political actors who were successful in building upon social transformations to create a new consensus and dynamic of political interaction. Although Chile's democratization is based on cooperation, its constitutional system includes institutional restrictions that mitigate against the maintenance and reproduction of this dynamic of cooperation.

This paradox raises questions that this study seeks to analyze: Will strong presidentialism prove a workable option for Chile, given the socioeconomic, political, and party-system transformations that have occurred during the past two decades? What are the consequences of legislative weakness in a country historically characterized by a relatively strong, influential, and effective legislature? Will strong presidentialism affect Chile's long tradition of conflict resolution through interbranch and interparty negotiation centered in the legislative branch? Will the parliamentary electoral system help to reduce the number of political parties? And what consequences will it have for the representative capacity of the political system? In short, was the military successful in designing an institutional framework for long-term democratic governability, or will the institutional framework inherited by democratic leaders prove a hindrance to full democratic consolidation?

The thesis of this study is that exaggerated presidentialism and the institutional, electoral, and legal framework that supports it are detrimental to governability and long-term political stability for two important reasons. First, despite the profound transformations within society, Chile still has many underlying structural economic difficulties, enduring socioeconomic divisions, and important pending social questions to resolve. The country's profound neoliberal economic transformation has created a number of complex new problems whose resolution demands a responsive and representative political system. The withdrawal and shrinking of the Chilean state has severed citizens' traditional connections to political and state institutions.

What is more, despite some of the changes in the party system outlined above, the military has been unable to transform fundamentally the multiparty nature of political competition. Though the ideological distance between Chilean parties has decreased and the incentives for coalition formation are certainly greater, individual parties are still relatively strong and well developed, with distinct programmatic commitments.

In this context, the mediation of conflict and the resolution of controversial problems require negotiation and compromise within democratic institutions that represent all segments of Chilean society and all significant political parties. In the past, Congress effectively provided an arena for negotiation between parties and between the executive and legislative branches. In contrast to other nations in the region, in Chile negotiation between the branches of government was the axis for the resolution of wider social conflict.[8] Contemporary congressional weakness limits both the representative capacity of the legislature and its ability to act as an arena for cooperation and interbranch negotiation. Given the many winner-take-all characteristics of Chilean presidentialism and the reality that political power is concentrated in a single office, those who are not partisans of the president are left without an effective institutional voice. This is aggravated by the exclusionary characteristics of the parliamentary electoral system that has the potential to significantly underrepresent important parties in Congress. These realities pose serious obstacles to conflict resolution in a country in which no single party is able to garner a majority. Further, the emasculation of the legislature produces few incentives for executive/legislative cooperation because Congress lacks the tools to extract concessions from the executive branch or to engage the president effectively in negotiations.

Second, beyond the imbalance of power between the executive and legislative branches, given the perseverance of Chilean multipartism, additional institutional variables undermine the already limited incentives for executive/legislative cooperation. The potentially volatile and exclusionary characteristics of the parliamentary electoral law, the timing and sequencing of elections, and related electoral legislation all make the election of minority presidents more likely, providing an additional impediment to interbranch cooperation. Finally, the existence of a number of institutions not subject to the control of civilian authorities undermines the ability of the president and Congress to resolve conflict effectively within the bounds of democratically elected institutions.

<hr/>

8. See Federico Gil, *The Political System of Chile*, 106–22, and Arturo Valenzuela and Alexander Wilde, "Presidential Politics and the Decline of the Chilean Congress," in *Legislatures in Development: Dynamics of Change in New and Old States*, ed. Joel Smith and Lloyd Musolf (Durham, N.C.: Duke University Press, 1979), 189–215, for a discussion of the multifunctional contribution of the legislature to Chile's democratic legitimacy and governability.

During Chile's long history with democracy, the formula for the resolution of conflict was negotiation between the president and a relatively strong and well-institutionalized Congress. The Congress also provided an important arena for negotiations among Chile's numerous parties. In contemporary Chile, exaggerated presidentialism and the complete institutional framework in which it is embedded undermine the incentives for interbranch and inter-party cooperation, and ultimately pose a threat to democratic legitimacy, political efficacy, and the quality and durability of Chilean democracy.

Students of Chilean politics may take issue with many of these conten-tions, given the exemplary conduct of executive/legislative relations during the first postauthoritarian administrations. During Patricio Aylwin's (1990–94) and Eduardo Frei's (1994–2000) terms as president, executive/legislature rela-tions have been characterized by cooperation, consensus, and compromise. There has been a willingness on the part of both branches of government to engage in give-and-take in an attempt to negotiate agreements that will confront the challenges posed by the transition to democracy, including the resurrection of political institutions, the problematic legacies inherited from the previous regime, and the deepening of democracy at the regional and municipal levels.

However, this work contends that the legislative success of the Aylwin and Frei governments was due in large part to the contextual features of the democratic transition itself, and to its effect on the party system, incentive structure, and decisions made by governing elites, which tempered the nega-tive drives associated with exaggerated presidentialism and electoral majori-tarianism. It will be argued that in the post-transitional setting, exaggerated presidentialism, the emasculation of the Congress, and the negative character-istics of the electoral system will undermine the so-far cooperative dynamic of interbranch and interparty relations.

Without institutional and electoral reforms aimed at reinforcing the leg-islative branch as an arena of accommodation for Chile's multiparty system, the potential for interbranch and interparty conflict is greatly enhanced, along with the attendant problems of democratic governability and limited political efficacy.

Theoretical Approach and Significance

Traditional analyses of democracy in Latin America often focused on the economic or cultural preconditions necessary for the emergence of stable democratic systems. Authors like Seymour Martin Lipset argued that a certain level of capitalist development and national wealth was necessary to sustain a democratic regime.[9] Other scholars, without establishing as direct a relationship, have also pointed to the high correlation between economic development and political democracy.[10]

Another traditional approach to the question of the requisites of democracy focused on political culture. Scholars employing this approach argued that the values of developing societies were antithetical to the establishment of stable democratic systems. Lucian Pye and Sidney Verba's work posited a strong relationship between the so-called traditional values of the populations of developing nations and the types of nondemocratic political systems that emerged.[11] Later work more particularly focused on the political systems of Latin America built on Pye and Verba's framework to argue that the Catholic, elitist, patrimonial, and hierarchical political tradition of Latin America was a strong impediment to the establishment of stable political democracies.[12]

However, events of the 1970s and 1980s in Latin America pointed to the implausibility of uni-causal economic and cultural explanations for the development and breakdown of democracy. During the 1970s, it was precisely the countries with relatively high levels of per capita gross domestic product (GDP), good educational opportunities, and other positive measures of cultural "modernity" and economic development like Argentina, Chile, and Uruguay that experienced protracted and harsh periods of authoritarian rule. Moreover, the redemocratization of the region during the 1980s reinforced intellectual dissatisfaction with these types of arguments. It was difficult to sustain the belief that the widespread return of democracy in Latin America was a result of the transformation of the political culture of

9. Seymour Martin Lipset, "Some Social Requisites of Democracy: Economic Development and Political Legitimacy," *American Political Science Review* 53 (March 1959): 69–105.

10. See, for example, Robert Dahl, *Polyarchy* (New Haven: Yale University Press, 1971), and Samuel Huntington, "Will More Countries Become Democratic?" *Political Science Quarterly* 99 (Summer 1984): 193–218.

11. Lucian Pye and Sidney Verba, eds., *Political Culture and Political Development* (Princeton: Princeton University Press, 1965).

12. These works include Robert Scott, "Mexico: The Established Revolution," in *Political Culture and Political Development*, ed. Lucian Pye and Sidney Verba (Princeton: Princeton University Press, 1965); Richard Morse, "The Heritage of Latin America," in *Politics and Social Change in Latin America*, ed. Howard Wiarda (Amherst: University of Massachusetts Press, 1974); and Howard Wiarda, "Toward a Framework for the Study of Political Change in the Iberic-Latin Tradition: The Corporative Model," in *Corporatism and National Development in Latin America,* ed. Howard Wiarda (Boulder, Colo.: Westview Press, 1981).

the region. Further, though the return of democracy in Brazil and Chile was preceded by a marked improvement in economic performance, other countries such as Argentina and Peru experienced democratic transitions within a context of economic deterioration, making the already shaky theoretical connection between prosperity and democratic politics even more tenuous.

The less than complete explanatory power of traditional approaches has led scholars in recent years to focus more upon discrete political factors as important determinants of breakdown, democratization, and democratic stability.[13] Studies employing this approach better capture the complexity of these processes by underscoring the importance of the actions and decisions of elites embedded in distinct historical, political, and institutional contexts and of the incentive structure created by them.

An important component of the literature focusing on political variables has dealt specifically with institutions and the formal/legal rules of democracy.[14] Recent theoretical and comparative work has suggested that political arrangements, including the electoral regime, the configuration of executive/legislative relations, and the incentive structures they produce, can have a powerful influence on the prospects for cooperation and democratic governability.[15]

Studies of the Chilean breakdown and subsequent comparative work on other Latin American presidencies have led scholars to focus on institutional arrangements, and particularly the structure of executive/legislative relations, as crucial variables that determine the incentives and prospects for cooperation among political elites. Some authors have suggested that parliamentarism is a more appropriate type of institutional arrangement in multiparty systems. Juan Linz, Arturo Valenzuela, and others have argued that parliamentary systems are more flexible and are better able to avoid the problems

13. See Guillermo O'Donnell and Phillipe Schmitter, eds., *Transitions from Authoritarian Rule: Tentative Conclusions About Uncertain Democracies* (Baltimore: Johns Hopkins University Press, 1986); Juan Linz, *The Breakdown of Democratic Regimes: Crisis, Breakdown, and Reequilibration* (Baltimore: Johns Hopkins University Press, 1978); Arturo Valenzuela, *The Breakdown of Democratic Regimes: Chile*; Larry Diamond, Juan Linz, and Seymour Martin Lipset, eds., *Politics in Developing Countries: Comparing Experiences with Democracy* (Boulder, Colo.: Lynne Rienner Publishers, 1990).

14. For example, see K. Shepsle and B. Weingast, "Institutionalizing Majority Rule: A Social Choice Theory with Policy Implications," *American Economic Review* 73 (1983): 357–72, and James March and John Olsen, "The New Institutionalism: Organizational Forces in Political Life," *American Political Science Review* 78 (1984): 734–49.

15. See Juan Linz and Arturo Valenzuela, eds., *The Failure of Presidential Democracy*; Oscar Godoy, ed., *Hacia una democracia moderna: La opción parlamentaria* (Santiago: Ediciones Universidad Católica de Chile, 1990); and Comisión Andina de Juristas, *Reformas al presidencialismo en América Latina: Presidencialismo vs. parlamentarismo* (Caracas: Editorial Jurídica Venezolana, 1993).

of minority presidencies and the dual legitimacy produced by having two agents of the electorate.[16] Fundamentally, according to this view, parliamentary systems are better able to produce incentives for executive/assembly cooperation within the context of multiparty systems.

This important literature helped to establish a fresh focus on the institutional dimensions of democracy that had been overlooked during the period of the paradigmatic prevalence of economic and cultural approaches. Nonetheless, at the same time, much of this literature focused on the configuration of interbranch relations without sufficient attention to other important components of the institutional equation. Specifically, more recent literature on democratic institutions has departed from a focus on the simple configuration of executive/legislative relations to concentrate more on the significance of particular institutional combinations. Thus, a discussion of the attributes of presidential systems per se is not valid without reference to the type of legislative electoral system, the formula for electing the president, the timing of elections, and other institutional variables.

Matthew Shugart and John Carey, for example, have argued that certain types of presidential systems may be more likely than others to produce problems of democratic governability, depending on the balance of constitutional powers between the branches of government and a number of other variables, including the method of electing the president, the timing and sequencing of presidential and parliamentary elections, and the nature and extent of presidential cabinet authority.[17]

Scott Mainwaring and Matthew Shugart's findings relative to the Latin American cases are similar. They argue that weaker executives are less likely to find themselves in crisis situations, given that presidents are forced to deal with Congress and, thus, are less likely to attempt to bypass it. Mainwaring and Shugart also stress the importance of finding mechanisms that help to ensure presidents a majority or near majority in Congress. They find that non-concurrent elections tend to contribute to party-system fragmentation, which in turn makes the formation of presidential majorities in Congress difficult.[18]

Thus, in addition to the type of presidential system, its accompanying institutions, and the relative power of the presidents, electoral laws have

16. Discussions of the significance of each of these problems in various presidential regimes appear throughout Linz and Valenzuela, eds., *The Failure of Presidential Democracy*.

17. Shugart and Carey, *Presidents and Assemblies*.

18. Mainwaring and Shugart, eds., *Presidentialism and Democracy in Latin America*. For a comprehensive discussion of electoral laws throughout the Americas, see Mark Jones, "A Guide to the Electoral System of the Americas," *Electoral Studies* 14 (1995): 5–21.

xx   Introduction

also been recognized as a fundamental determinant of the potential success of presidential systems. Mark Jones's cross-national study, for example, focused specifically on the effects of electoral formulas, convincingly demonstrating their importance to the functional dynamic and potential success of presidential systems. He found that the majority runoff presidential election formula and nonconcurrence between legislative and presidential elections discourage the formation of coherent legislative majorities or near majorities for presidents.[19] This, of course, makes it difficult for presidents to govern.

All of these findings concerning institutional interrelationships are quite relevant to the Chilean case, given the combination of institutional features created by the 1980 constitution. Chile's institutional framework is characterized by an extremely strong president, a majority runoff presidential electoral system, and nonconcurrent elections. Also problematic (though less analyzed due to the paucity of applicable cases) is the coexistence of a legislative electoral system with strong majoritarian tendencies and a fractionalized multiparty system. Thus, in many ways Chile is a country with perhaps the most problematic institutional structure in Latin America in terms of the findings of this study and those of the theorists discussed here.

Another important vein in the institutional literature deals with the significance of societal variables in regard to the functioning of democratic institutions. For theorists employing this approach, it is erroneous to speak of the "superiority" of certain types of institutional arrangements without referring to the type of party system; ideological divisions; and the breadth and intensity of social, ethnic, and religious cleavages.[20]

These theoretical discussions of the importance of institutions, and the social contexts in which they are embedded, have certainly been fruitful in terms of bringing the significance of these issues to the fore. However, while many studies have focused on the importance of complete institutional packages, or on the significance of the social dimensions of institutional performance, few have systematically combined these approaches for particular cases.[21] This work will attempt to do so by suggesting that the functional

19. Mark Jones, *Electoral Laws and the Survival of Presidential Democracies* (South Bend, Ind.: University of Notre Dame Press, 1995).
20. See, for example, Donald Horowitz, "Democracy in Divided Societies," *Journal of Democracy* 4 (October 1993): 18–38, and Arend Lijphart, "Constitutional Choices for New Democracies," *Journal of Democracy* 2 (Winter 1991): 72–84.
21. This is, of course, understandable, given the difficulties in operationalizing social differences across distinct cases.

dynamic of institutional packages is distinct depending on the sociopolitical context of different societies.

First, evidence from the Chilean case confirms and builds upon recent theoretical findings that the difficulties often associated with presidentialism are not functions of its mere existence. There are distinct types of presidentialism and parliamentarism. The functional dynamic of each institutional arrangement depends on its specific properties and on how these properties interact with other institutional features of the political system. This interactive combination helps to determine the effectiveness of presidential and parliamentary government. The workability of presidentialism depends on the relative strength of the president and the institutional components of the entire framework for democracy.[22] The scope of presidential prerogatives, areas of exclusive initiative, veto powers, and the legislative capacity of presidents all serve to differentiate the operational dynamics of presidential systems. What is more, the parliamentary electoral system, the timing and sequencing of elections, and the existence of institutional bodies outside the legislative and executive branches affect the workability of distinct presidential systems. This study will analyze the implications of both the relative strength of the branches of government and the impact of additional electoral, institutional, and legal variables for interbranch cooperation, conflict resolution, and democratic governability.

Second, this case study suggests how crucial it is to analyze the relationship between distinct institutional arrangements and the socioeconomic and political characteristics of the societies in which they operate, and the importance of the *congruence* between them, for democratic governability.[23] Congruence refers to the appropriateness of distinct types of institutions given discrete political phenomena like the nature and competitive dynamic

22. Matthew Shugart and John Carey certainly have made clear the need to underscore the differences between types of presidential systems. However, their approach is cross-national and focuses primarily on the formal-legal powers of presidents. This study proposes to explore these issues in greater detail as they apply to a particular case while introducing an analysis of the functional powers of the president that are not rooted in legal precepts. See Shugart and Carey, *Presidents and Assemblies.*

23. There is an important body of literature that considers the issue of congruence. Harry Eckstein, in his study of Norway, for example, deals with the issue of congruence as it pertains to political culture, and with its relationship to the institutional features of the political system. The description of congruence presented in the text parallels Arend Lijphart's analysis of consolidated democracies. However, the issue of fit and congruence has not been sufficiently analyzed as it relates to nascent and transitional democracies in Latin America or in the Third World in general. See Harry Eckstein, *Division and Cohesion in Democracy: A Study of Norway* (Princeton: Princeton University Press, 1966); and Arend Lijphart, *Democracy in*

of the party system and socioeconomic and political divisions. These variables may aggravate or attenuate the problematic features of certain of the
institutional combinations discussed here.

In essence, exaggerated presidentialism, a majoritarian electoral system,
and a system with nonconcurrent elections may indeed be functional and
encourage democratic stability in a society characterized by few divisions,
consensus, and a nonideological two-party system. However, in a society
like Chile's, characterized by latent but still-existing conflict, significant
socioeconomic divisions, and a complex multiparty system, this institutional
combination creates important impediments to interbranch cooperation.
This study contends that it is the entire institutional framework of exaggerated Chilean presidentialism within the post-transitional socioeconomic and
political context, rather than presidentialism per se, that has the potential to
cause problems of political efficacy and long-term democratic governability.

Organization of the Study

The study is divided into four broad thematic sections. One of its major
assumptions is the difficulty of disentangling the functional dynamics of
institutions from the societies in which they operate. The characteristics of
individual societies affect how institutions function, and these institutions, in
turn, shape the forms of social and political action employed by citizens and
political elites. Because of the interconnectedness of institutions and society
that the study seeks to capture, there is an overlap of themes in each section.

Chapters 1 and 2 analyze the institutional and formal-legal structure of
Chilean democracy as outlined in the 1980 constitution and provide a preliminary evaluation of the system's functioning. Chapter 1 begins by analyzing
the historical evolution of exaggerated presidentialism in Chile, underscoring how the scope of presidential power has consistently been widened
throughout Chile's modern experience with democracy. It goes on to analyze presidential power in postauthoritarian Chile. The chapter then turns
to Chile's unique, two-member district parliamentary electoral system and

Plural Societies: A Comparative Exploration (New Haven: Yale University Press, 1977),
Democracies: Patterns of Majoritarian and Consensus Government in Twenty-One Countries
(New Haven: Yale University Press, 1984), and Electoral Systems and Party Systems: A Study
of Twenty-Seven Democracies 1945–1990 (New York: Oxford University Press, 1994).

its consequences for the party system and the incentive structure of government leaders. It suggests some of the difficulties and disincentives to cooperation created by exaggerated presidentialism and the parliamentary electoral law, given the nature of Chilean society, but leaves their in-depth analysis for later chapters. The chapter ends with an overview of the institutions established to give the armed forces a tutelary role over civilian authorities, and points to the significance of these structures and laws in affecting the relative power of the branches of government and the legislative process.

Chapter 2 analyzes the first postauthoritarian administration. Despite the negative picture of the institutional framework suggested in the first chapter, the administration of Patricio Aylwin was really quite successful in managing interbranch relations. What is more, it was one of the most stable and successful governments in Chilean history. However, the chapter seeks to dispel the notion that the success of the Aylwin administration was a function of successful constitutional design on the part of military authorities and their civilian supporters. Again stressing the importance of context in helping to determine how institutions function, the chapter argues that the political conditions of the democratic transition and the consociational elements it produced helped to mitigate many of the potential difficulties the current institutional framework has the capacity to produce. The chapter goes on to contend that, with the fading of the urgency of the immediate postauthoritarian context, the special characteristics that helped to make the Aylwin administration a success will be less influential. A necessarily tentative discussion of the Frei administration concludes the chapter, which observes that many of the consensual dynamics of the Aylwin government continue to be significant, albeit to a lesser extent.

Given the study's focus on the importance of congruence between institutions and the characteristics of society, Chapters 3 and 4 seek to set out the socioeconomic and political context of contemporary Chile. Chapter 3 argues that, though there have been important changes in both the socioeconomic and political realms, some pressing unresolved issues and latent social conflict remain and will be difficult to resolve given many of the features of the current legal institutional framework, and particularly its limited representative capacity.

In recognition of the profound importance of political parties, both to Chilean society and to the context in which executive/legislative relations are structured, Chapter 4 analyzes the current competitive dynamic of the party system. It argues that despite some important changes and a less ideological party system, multipartism is alive and well in Chile and will continue to be for the foreseeable future—with important consequences for the workability of the presidential system. This is not to suggest that Chile's party system has not changed in some important respects due to both the experience of authoritarian rule and the reformed electoral system. Undoubtedly the incentives for coalition formation have been enhanced. The chapter will explore the significance of this continuity and change within the party system for democratic governability.

Chapters 5 and 6 bridge the first two sets of chapters by analyzing the interplay between society and institutions. They argue that the current institutional structure fails to provide a framework for the resolution of still-existing social and political conflict, given the limited representative capacity of the political system and the lack of incentives for interbranch cooperation. Chapter 5 emphasizes how exaggerated presidentialism limits the capacity of legislators to undertake their functions as lawmakers and agents of interest representation, and in the process undermines the ability of Congress to act as an arena for negotiation and compromise.

However, the relative strength of the branches of government is not the only variable that affects the conflict-dampening capacity of democratic institutions. Chapter 6 underscores how, given the endurance of Chilean multipartism, other institutional and legal variables produce additional obstacles to interbranch cooperation and threaten the prospects for democratic governability. The most important are the potentially volatile and exclusionary characteristics of the parliamentary electoral system, and the timing and sequencing of elections. The chapter concludes by analyzing the significance for the legislative process of the so-called autonomous powers not subject to civilian authority.

Finally, Chapter 7 attempts to make some generalizations concerning the future of Chilean democracy and comments on the theoretical significance of the study's findings. Chapter 7 proposes reforms to the current institutional structure to remedy some of the difficulties analyzed throughout the study. Institutional and legal changes are suggested to enhance both the representative capacity of the democratic system and the incentives for interbranch cooperation and conflict resolution. The chapter argues that through the strengthening of Congress, a reform of the electoral system, and the implementation of additional but limited institutional reforms, presidentialism can be a workable option for Chile. The chapter also underscores the features that helped to make the Aylwin administration a success, and argues that institutionalization of these features can further enhance the workability of Chilean presidentialism. Chapter 7 concludes with a review of some of the theoretical insights provided by the case study in terms of the comparative examination of presidentialism and potential avenues for future research.

1

THE 1980 CHILEAN CONSTITUTION AND THE
FRAMEWORK FOR LIMITED DEMOCRACY

Exaggerated Presidentialism and
Electoral Majoritarianism

The 1980 Chilean constitution is a legal reflection of the military government's negative view of the capacity of democratic political processes to solve the most pressing problems facing Chilean society.[1] The role of the president, the scope of presidential power, and the parliamentary electoral system were elements incorporated within a broader agenda of social control characterized by significant limitations on civilian political authorities.

The political model inherited by democratic authorities was designed both to protect the economic legacy of the government of Augusto Pinochet and to prevent the reemergence of the dynamic of polarization and instability that characterized the early 1970s. Military authorities contended that the succession of events leading to the military coup provided ample evidence of the irresponsibility of civilian leaders. This problem was compounded by a proportional representation (PR) electoral system that was entirely too

---

1. For an analysis of the historical evolution of the political thought of the Chilean military, see Genaro Arriagada, *El pensamiento político de los militares* (Santiago: CISEC, 1981), and Augusto Varas, Felipe Aguero, and Fernando Bustamante, eds., *Chile: Democracia, fuerzas armadas* (Santiago: FLACSO, 1980). The foundational and corrective aspirations of the Chilean military regime are analyzed in Manuel Antonio Garretón, *The Chilean Political Process* (Boston: Unwin Hyman, 1989).

permissive in its representation of parties, and produced a situation in which the country could be held hostage to the interests of self-serving political parties. According to regime officials, party leaders used their leverage as elected officials to mobilize popular support, resulting in the ideological polarization of Chilean society and the corruption of democratic institutions.[2] The goal of constitutional reform was to design a constitution in which restrictions on the power of civilian elites and political parties would prevent the recurrence of similar phenomena.

Strong presidentialism was the cornerstone of this formula for control. Military leaders contended that the positive economic legacy of the authoritarian government could be better guaranteed by turning over the political and economic administration of the country to a president with a wide range of powers and the Central Bank. This would prevent the Congress from falling victim to the excesses of populism and personalism. What is more, by creating an electoral system that would ostensibly lead to party-system integration and the moderation of party platforms (given the centripetal competitive tendencies often imputed to small magnitude systems[3]), military leaders believed they could limit what they perceived as the many negative and divisive features of the political party system.

This chapter begins with an analysis of the elements of the institutional framework that this study hypothesizes are the most important obstacles to democratic consolidation in Chile. First, given that executive/legislative relations formed the core of wider conflict resolution in the past, the question of the relationship between the branches of government is crucial to Chile's political future. The 1980 constitution provides for the weakest Congress of any period in Chile's modern political history. Thus, much of this chapter is devoted to a discussion of the roles of the president and Congress according to the constitution of 1980 and their significance for long-term governability and democratic consolidation. Initially, an outline of the historical evolution of presidential power in Chile is provided, followed by a brief review of the intellectual underpinnings and the views of the designers of the 1980 constitution in regard to the need for a strong presidency. Subsequently, the extraordinary powers of the Chilean president as a co-legislator and the driving

2. These attitudes are clear both in the statements issued by the military immediately following the coup outlining their motives for assuming power and in the declaration of principles made by the governing junta the following March. See República de Chile, *El Pronunciamiento Militar del 11 de Septiembre de 1973*, and the *Declaración de Principios de la Junta de Gobierno*, March 1974.

3. Those with a small number of representatives per district.

force within the legislative process are described, and the limited capabilities of Congress to act as a check on executive power are analyzed. Some suggestions are made regarding the potential difficulties created by Chile's exaggerated presidential system, but complete analysis of these difficulties is left for later chapters.

Second, given the continued existence of multipartism in Chile (a reality discussed at length in Chapter 4), the remainder of the first chapter is devoted to a discussion of the military government's exercise in electoral engineering. This analysis provides the context for later discussion of the significance of the combination of electoral majoritarianism and a consolidated multiparty system, both in terms of interbranch relations and in terms of long-term democratic governability.

Finally, the chapter underscores how exaggerated presidentialism and electoral majoritarianism are embedded in a wider framework for control that goes beyond the interbranch balance of power and electoral politics but affects the incentive structure of elites and how the political system and legislative processes function.

The Genesis of the 1980 Constitution and Exaggerated Presidentialism

Critics of the 1980 constitution point to its uniquely authoritarian nature. However, in terms of presidential power it fits quite well within the historical evolution of executive powers in Chilean constitutional law.[4] Since 1925, the response of leaders to problems of governability has been to consistently increase the latitude of executive authority through constitutional reform.[5]

---

4. For a comprehensive discussion of the genesis and characteristics of the 1980 Chilean constitution, see José Luis Cea Egaña, *Tratado de la Constitución de 1980: Características generales, garantías constitucionales* (Santiago: Editorial Jurídica de Chile, 1988).

5. Arturo Valenzuela and Alexander Wilde have underscored how attempts to increase the latitude of executive authority have been the consistent response to problems of governability and party domination of the political system in Chile. See Arturo Valenzuela and Alexander Wilde, "Presidential Politics and the Decline of the Chilean Congress," in *Legislatures in Development: Dynamics of Change in New and Old States*, ed. Joel Smith and Lloyd Musolf (Durham, N.C.: Duke University Press, 1979). On this point, see also Bernardino Bravo-Lira, *De Portales a Pinochet* (Santiago: Editorial Jurídica de Chile, 1985), especially 104–5, and Arturo Valenzuela, "Party Politics and the Crisis of Presidentialism in Chile," in *The Failure of Presidential Democracy*, vol. 2, ed. Juan Linz and Arturo Valenzuela (Baltimore: Johns Hopkins University Press, 1994), 138.

The 1980 constitution represents the next logical step in this process, by creating a presidency with a wider scope of powers than at any time since 1925.[6]

The tradition of exaggerated executive authority also has roots that predate the 1925 constitution. However, in the period from independence to the promulgation of the 1925 constitution, the scope of presidential power varied. There have been eight Chilean constitutions (including the 1980 document), all of which provide for presidential forms of government.[7] In three of these constitutions, those of 1818, 1822, and 1833, the president is clearly the dominant actor, at least according to the original texts of the documents. Under these constitutions, the president had a wide range of decree authority, a number of areas of exclusive initiative, and almost complete control over the budgetary process. The president also had the right to appoint and remove ministers as well as a wide range of other judicial, diplomatic, and local officials.

The constitutions of 1823 and 1828, and the original text of the 1925 document (before the reforms of 1943 and 1970), though unquestionably presidential, provided for greater equilibrium between the branches of government, clearly delineating executive and legislative authority and distinct and real attributes for each of the branches of government.

Though the relative power of the presidency and Congress varied throughout Chilean history, depending on the constitution and the nature and direction of constitutional reforms, executive/legislative conflict has been an

6. Presidential power is variable and multidimensional. A distinction must be made between the partisan powers and the constitutional powers of presidents. Partisan powers are those that presidents can rely on given the party composition of the Congress. Here, the author refers to the powers of presidents outlined in the constitution and those resulting from the relative position of the president within the overall institutional framework. Certain scholars have contended that the legislative powers of the president have decreased in Chile. This is an incorrect interpretation, as the discussion presented below suggests. According to the constitution of 1980, the president retains all of the powers granted to the executive by the 1925 constitution. In addition to these powers, the 1980 constitution widens the range of presidential authority by granting an increased scope of implied powers, by designating more areas in which the president has exclusive initiative, by granting increased urgency powers, and by increasing the number and type of officials that the president has the power to name.

7. This analysis draws heavily from José Luis Cea Egaña, "Presidencialismo reforzado. Críticas y alternativas para el caso chileno," in *Cambio de régimen político*, ed. Oscar Godoy (Santiago: Ediciones Universidad Católica de Chile, 1992), 102–16, and especially 106–7. For other useful analyses of Chilean constitutional law, see Cristián Bulnes Ripamonti, *Relaciones y conflictos entre los órganos del poder estatal* (Santiago: Editorial Jurídica de Chile, 1967), and Fernando Campos Harriet, *Historia constitucional de Chile* (Santiago: Editorial Jurídica, 1969). Bernardino Bravo-Lira provides an excellent analysis of the tradition of authoritarian presidentialism in *De Portales a Pinochet*.

enduring reality. Despite the establishment of an extremely powerful presidency in the 1833 constitution,[8] the advent of a series of Liberal governments in the 1870s, accompanied by a spirit of democratic reformism, led to the gradual increase of the powers of the legislative branch at the expense of the president. The most important were the Liberal constitutional reforms of 1873–76.[9]

With the gradual erosion of presidential power, presidents became increasingly frustrated with what was perceived as the interference of Congress in the efficient conduct of government. Liberal president José Manuel Balmaceda's election in 1886 set the stage for the most significant conflict between the branches of government in Chilean history.[10] Scholars on the left have traced the roots of this conflict to an intransigent Conservative Congress repeatedly stymieing Balmaceda's reform efforts. In reality, it was the frustrated reform efforts of Conservatives that sowed the seeds for conflict. Since the early 1870s, the Conservatives had attempted to wrest control of the electoral process from presidential and Liberal Party domination through suffrage expansion. Unlike their European counterparts, the Chilean Conservatives realized that they had much to gain from the elimination of restrictions on the democratic franchise. Members of the party, many of whom were large landowners themselves, could rely on their aristocratic allies to influence the voting behavior of rural populations, which depended on elites for subsistence. It was Balmaceda's unwillingness to negotiate with the Conservative-controlled Congress in reaching an agreement on electoral reform and the very issue of the scope of congressional authority that led to conflict between the branches of government.[11]

Employing increasingly tyrannical tactics, Balmaceda ultimately announced the closing of the Congress by executive decree on 11 February 1891. After an

8. The scope of presidential power was extremely wide, according to the original version of the 1833 constitution. On presidential power according to this constitution, see Sergio Villalobos R. et al., *Historia de Chile* (Santiago: Editorial Universitaria, 1974), 532–33.

9. For their discussion, see Campos Harriet, *Historia constitucional*, 342.

10. For a discussion of this period, see Fernando Pinto Lagarrigue, *Balmaceda y los gobiernos seudo-parlamentarios* (Santiago: Editorial Andrés Bello, 1991); Hernán Ramírez Necochea, *Balmaceda y la contrarrevolución de 1891* (Santiago: Editorial Universitaria, 1969); and Julio Heise González, *Historia de Chile. El período parlamentario, 1861–1925* (Santiago: Editorial Andrés Bello, 1974).

11. For this interpretation and the convincing evidence supporting it, see Samuel Valenzuela, *Democratización vía reforma: La expansión del sufragio en Chile* (Santiago: Ediciones del IDES, 1985). For a discussion of Conservative strategies for suffrage expansion, see Timothy Scully, *Los partidos del centro y la evolución política chilena* (Santiago: CIEPLAN, 1992), chap. 2.

eight-month civil war between forces supporting the president and Congress (dominated by an odd alliance of Conservatives and Radicals), Balmaceda was eventually deposed and had committed suicide by the end of that year. Thus, executive/legislative conflict in Chile had been carried to the point of war.

The victory of the congressional forces in 1891 inaugurated a period known as the "Parliamentary Republic," which would last until 1924.[12] Despite its name, the Parliamentary Republic lacked many of the characteristics normally associated with parliamentary government. While Congress could act to dissolve presidential cabinets, the president did not have the corresponding ability to dissolve the Chamber of Deputies and call for new elections. Given this unique and unquestionably awkward arrangement, cabinet instability became the defining feature of this period. Even if new cabinets named by presidents upon assuming power are not included, 489 cabinet positions were vacated and filled between 1891 and 1925, with an average cabinet lasting 133 days.[13] The cabinet instability and deadlock that resulted from this unique institutional arrangement ultimately led again to Congress being closed following a military coup in September 1924.

The 1925 constitution was a reaction to the perceived excesses encouraged by the wide scope of legislative power that characterized the Parliamentary Republic. Arturo Alessandri Palma, who most influenced the drafting of the constitution, was an ardent proponent of strong presidential government. Though the president was still the dominant actor according to the constitution of 1925, and became increasingly so with subsequent reforms, certain realities granted more de facto power to the legislative branch than analysts have suggested.

Despite the instability that characterized the Parliamentary Republic, the centrality of the Congress throughout the period helped to deepen its institutionalization, producing a tradition and quality of parliamentary politics as yet unseen on the continent. The Congress and parliamentarians had become accustomed to playing a more important role than their counterparts in other Latin American countries, and Congress was relatively more influential in terms of concrete outcomes.

---

12. Certain scholars have argued correctly that the parliamentary aspects of the political system began to develop before 1891. See, for example, two works by Julio Heise González, *Historia de Chile. El período parlamentario, 1861–1925* (Santiago: Editorial Andrés Bello, 1974), and *El período parlamentario* (Santiago: Editorial Universitaria, 1982). However, the political system was at its most "parliamentary" between 1891 and 1924.

13. IDEAS, *Manual del Congreso Nacional: Historia, funciones y atribuciones* (Santiago: IDEAS, n.d.).

But more important, many of the de facto powers of the legislature were rooted in partisan powers and the norms that developed as a result of the necessity of legislating in a multiparty environment. The advent of Chile's modern party system produced innovations that made the Congress an important axis of the political system. The consistent inability of presidents to garner legislative majorities forced them to deal and negotiate with Congress in the interests of coalition and cabinet formation and stability. Between 1932 and the fall of Allende, the only time a president has enjoyed a majority coalition in both chambers of Congress was between 1961 and 1963.[14] In order to secure passage of their legislation, presidents were forced to cobble together working alliances. Thus, presidents negotiated with parties, which in turn had to make programmatic peace with each other in order to coexist within the same working coalition. This granted the Congress increased influence, making it the locus of negotiation where agreements between parties were hammered out.

What is more, while the 1925 constitution eliminated ministerial responsibility to Congress, presidents still depended on congressional and party leaders during the process of cabinet formation. Congress retained the ability to censure ministers, a right extensively employed during the tenure of most contemporary presidents. Though presidents were vested with the power to name ministers, their decisions were not independent of party authorities. Indeed, party leaders maintained a great deal of influence over the process of cabinet formation, given the requirement that candidates first obtain party permission (what was known as "pase") before assuming office. Presidents were forced to deal and bargain with party central committees in order to piece together cabinets that were acceptable to all members of a coalition.[15] This process foreshadowed and paralleled in an interesting way the process of cabinet formation adopted by the postauthoritarian Concertación alliance that has governed Chile in the post-Pinochet era.

Given this historical party context, and the exigencies of cabinet formation, the president's need to secure legislative and party approval produced a politics of give-and-take. The president was also more apt to yield to congressional demands. This was the case both for legislation with a bearing on national policy and for the particularistic demands of individual legislators.

14. For a discussion of this reality, as well as a detailed account of the extent of congressional support for all presidents since 1932, see Arturo Valenzuela, "Party Politics and the Crisis of Presidentialism in Chile," 122–25.

15. For a discussion of this point, see Arturo Valenzuela, "Party Politics and the Crisis of Presidentialism in Chile," 120.

Presidents often allowed amendments to bills in the form of pensions and personal favors and in response to the demands of individual members in the name of political expediency and in order to achieve victory on larger legislative issues.[16]

The ability of legislators to extract concessions gave increased authority to individual members of Congress and the legislature as an institution. It also produced a proliferation of personalism and pork. Jorge Tapia Valdés cites law No. 10.343 as an example of the extent to which personalistic legislative proposals became tacked on to presidential initiatives. The law, which consists of 215 articles, deals with twenty-eight separate issues ranging from a municipal loan for the town of Talca, to whale oil production, the creation of a journalism school, and a tax exemption for firemen. Valdés estimates that between 1938 and 1958, more than 55 percent of legislation dealt with such particularistic issues.[17]

Perceived abuse of personalistic legislation led to demands for reforms in the powers of Congress in 1943.[18] In that year, constitutional revisions proscribed parliamentary initiative for proposals dealing with the political and administrative division of the country, job creation, and salaries and benefits in the public sector. Congress was empowered only to accept, reject, or reduce expenditures in relation to such legislation.

However, the wording of restrictions was not sufficient or specific enough to limit the proposal of personalistic spending. Part of the difficulty with the 1943 reforms in the eyes of advocates of increased presidential power was that legislators retained the right to initiate legislation dealing with tax exemptions, social policy, and setting wages in the private sector. In addition, limitations were not instituted on congressional initiatives dealing with pensions and widows' and retirement benefits. What is more, these types of legislation could be proposed, voted on, and promulgated without designating the sources of revenue for implementation.

16. Valenzuela and Wilde, "Presidential Politics and the Decline of the Chilean Congress," 201. Note that although the terms *personalistic* and *particularistic* are often used interchangeably, there is a difference. Particularistic legislation deals with the particular interests of a city, congressional district, small group, or individuals, and generally does not apply to the country as a whole or all citizens. Personalistic legislation, on the other hand deals with the personal interests of individuals (pensions, benefits, employment, etc.). Both types of legislation served as the currency of negotiation between the executive branch and legislators.

17. Jorge Tapia Valdés, *La técnica legislativa* (Santiago: Editorial Jurídica, 1966), 42–47.

18. Francisco Cumplido provides a useful synopsis of the constitutional reforms of 1943 and 1970 in "Análisis del presidencialismo en Chile," in *Cambio de régimen político*, ed. Oscar Godoy (Santiago: Ediciones Universidad Católica de Chile, 1992), 117–40.

Despite these efforts to limit the latitude of legislative authority, the continued necessity of coalition formation and maintenance after 1943 provided incentives for both branches of government to continue to bypass even the limited restrictions imposed by the reforms. Both branches of government had something to gain from the politics of particularism, despite their negative public pronouncements concerning the practice. This allowed for the continued profusion of personalistic initiatives in the form of "indications" attached to presidential bills. In addition, the ability of members of Congress to present bills related to remunerations in the private sector served to undercut the ability of the president to control and set wages in the public sector and to manage the economy as a whole. Parties often encouraged the politics of *reajuste*, by which certain groups were granted wage concessions immediately preceding appeals for popular support.

The functional weakness of the 1943 reforms in limiting particularistic spending, and the inflationary pressures generated by the politics of *reajuste*, led to additional proposals for constitutional revisions in the mid-1960s. Christian Democratic (PDC) president Eduardo Frei Montalva (1964–70) proposed stronger limitations on the spending capabilities of Congress.[19] For Frei and the Christian Democrats, these reforms were part of a comprehensive development plan known as *"revolución en libertad,"* which sought to create a modern, reformist and developmentalist state that would undermine the revolutionary appeal of the Left. The party's overarching strategy was to portray itself as a modern, technocratic party not steeped in the traditional way of doing politics but poised to confront vigorously the challenges posed by the social transformations occurring in Chile.

To achieve these goals, the party sought to modernize the state and enhance the efficiency of policy-making by streamlining the legislative process. The Christian Democrats also sought to consolidate presidential wage-setting authority, contending that the inflationary pressure produced by the politics of *reajuste* was the main impediment to economic stability and the long-term growth of the Chilean economy. Only by eliminating congressional interference in wage policy could inflation be halted and the party's project of transformation be realized.

Ultimately approved in 1970, Frei's reform measures explicitly proscribed congressional proposal of any *"asuntos de gracia"* (personal favors),

---

19. Frei initially proposed a much wider series of limitations on congressional power in 1964, but they languished as a result of the limited incentives for passage in the Congress. The constitutional reforms of 1970 constituted watered-down versions of the original reform proposals.

including pensions and other social benefits, and disallowed amendments not germane to the "*idea matriz*"(central concept) of the proposal at hand. This would put an end to particularistic "indications" on presidential bills.

In addition, the president was granted exclusive initiative for proposals dealing with salaries and benefits within both the public and private sectors, putting an effective end to the politics of *reajuste*. As an additional measure to control spending excesses, the reforms strengthened the wording of the 1943 reforms by definitively establishing exclusive initiative for the president in the creation of new state services and jobs in the public sector.[20] Finally, the president was granted the ability to employ executive decrees with only superficial involvement of the legislature.

In addition to the party's agenda of modernization, short-term political considerations were also factored into the Christian Democrats' desire for reform. A spectacular increase in the party's level of support during the mid-1960s led leaders to perceive that they had finally succeeded in the unprecedented formation of a majority party in Chile. Party leaders sought to provide a framework within which they would be better able to undertake their own political project of transformation, given the expectation that the party would win the presidency in 1970 and hold it for a number of years to come. The PDC sought to create an executive branch from which it could successfully and forcefully promote its reform agenda and formulate economic and social policy unfettered by Congress and the fiscal difficulties that particularistic spending entailed. The Christian Democrats were able to extract support for the reforms from the National Party on the Right, given that the Nationals assumed it would be their candidate, Jorge Alessandri, who would become the next president, and, thus, the inheritor of a strengthened presidency.

As it turned out, the real beneficiary of increased presidential powers following the 1970 elections was Socialist Salvador Allende, who in constitutional terms assumed office with the widest latitude of executive authority of any president since 1925. The Christian Democrats had no idea that their framework for strong presidentialism would be inherited by the very revolutionary forces they sought to undermine. What is more, much to their despair, the presidency was inherited by leaders who would be guilty of precisely the excesses and type of inflationary spending that the Christian Democrats believed a strong presidency could help to limit.

20. For comprehensive discussions of the constitutional reforms of 1970, see Eduardo Frei et al., *Reforma constitucional 1970* (Santiago: Editorial Jurídica, 1970), and Guillermo Piedrabuena R., *La reforma constitucional* (Santiago de Chile: Ediciones Encina, 1970).

Though a "Statute of Democratic Guarantees" negotiated between Allende's Unidad Popular (Popular Unity [UP]) coalition and the Christian Democrats limited the president's spheres of action, Allende set out to vigorously employ the wide range of presidential authority granted him in an effort to undertake the UP's program of social and economic transformation. Nonetheless, Allende's status as a minority president, in both electoral and legislative terms, made the use of presidential faculties difficult. Indeed, Allende often exceeded the limits of the already wide range of powers that were constitutionally at his disposal, bypassing Congress and the judiciary in a clear abuse of executive authority. Thus, Allende's strong constitutional powers were undermined by a lack of partisan powers, and he was forced to resort to the use of extraconstitutional power.[21] What is more, the Christian Democratic reforms had so weakened Congress that it no longer had the capacity to play its constructive role as an arena for negotiation, and it was reduced to simply rejecting presidential proposals.

The Allende administration is consistently cited as a source of important lessons for constitutional analysts and engineers. However, one of the most overlooked lessons (and most important, given its relevance for Chile's contemporary institutional framework) is the potential consequences of the contradiction between a president with strong constitutional and weak partisan powers. While most analysts point to the weakness of the Allende administration, in reality his constitutional strength was as much a source of his undoing as his partisan weakness. The latter forced him to exploit the former.

Military Politics and the Consolidation of Presidential Strength

Thus, the 1980 constitution represents the culmination of a historical process involving the gradual expansion of presidential powers. However, the personalities, events, and circumstances of the military government also influenced the eventual scope of presidential power set down in the document and the qualitative characteristics of the presidency.

21. On the distinction between constitutional and partisan powers, and its significance, see Scott Mainwaring and Matthew Shugart, "Introduction," in their edited volume *Presidentialism and Democracy in Latin America*, ed. Scott Mainwaring and Matthew Shugart (New York: Cambridge University Press, 1997).

First, the ethos of military officers and their civilian allies helped set the stage for establishment of exaggerated presidentialism in Chile. There was a widespread negative view of legislative politics among the military in general.[22] The behavior of the legislature throughout the 1960s and 1970s was seen as the very epitome of the excesses of political leaders, who sought to ensure their positions through popular mobilization and the granting of favors. When assembling the team for institutional design, military leaders also relied extensively on civilian conservative jurists like Jaime Guzmán and Enrique Ortuzár, who shared their views concerning the need for strong and decisive presidential leadership.

Second, both the Frei (1964–70) and Allende (1970–73) administrations were pivotal to the formative political education of military leaders. The 1973 coup was not an isolated case of civil/military conflict, but rather the culmination of a gradual deterioration in civil/military relations that began a decade earlier. During the 1960s, military leaders felt ignored and undervalued as resources were transferred from military budgets to finance the reform projects of progressive politicians.[23] In addition, despite the personal enmity of military leaders toward Allende, his administration provided striking evidence of how even a constitutionally strong president could be held hostage by a hostile Congress dominated by party leaders.[24]

Third, the ultimate model for exaggerated presidentialism took shape as a result of discussions and the interchange of proposals between President Pinochet, regime moderates, and conservative jurists. There is strong evidence that Pinochet himself wanted to institutionalize a permanent authoritarian

22. The tradition of disparaging the Congress as an institution did not begin with the Pinochet era but has a long history in Chile that predates the authoritarian regime. See H. E. Bicheno, "Anti-parliamentary Themes in Chilean History: 1920–1970," *Government and Opposition* 7 (Summer 1972): 351–88.

23. For an elaboration of this point, see Pamela Constable and Arturo Valenzuela, *A Nation of Enemies* (New York: Norton, 1991), 47–52. The most visible representation of military discontent during the Frei administration was Army General Roberto Viaux's seizing of the Tacna tank regiment on 21 October 1969. Though the rebellion was eventually condemned by other military leaders, it was part of an overall dynamic of increasing civil/military tension during these years. Thus, military discontent was not solely a reaction to the actions of the Allende administration, as is often suggested.

24. A member of the Chamber of Deputies from the center-right Renovación Nacional Party pointed to a "fundamental contradiction" in the military's view of the Congress as an institution. The constitution imposed by the authoritarian regime effectively eliminated the power of one of the institutions that was most opposed to Allende. This deputy pointed to the irony of the military regime's effort to limit the prerogatives of Congress, which he called the "gran enemigo de Salvador Allende" (great enemy of Salvador Allende). Off the record interview, Valparaíso, 13 May 1993.

solution for governing Chile that would perpetuate a supervisory role for military authorities.[25] The process of negotiation ultimately served to water down Pinochet's extreme proposals, though his plan for a "protected" democracy is still evident in the constitution. Thus, the presidential system that ultimately resulted grew out of the incomplete imposition of Pinochet's model for longer-term authoritarian rule.

Finally, as Genaro Arriagada has stressed, dictatorship is "by definition the extreme concentration of power in the chief of state."[26] Military authorities viewed the Pinochet regime, characterized by executive domination, as a workable option when setting down the institutional framework for a limited democracy.[27]

The powers of the executive branch were also designed to benefit those whom military leaders saw as the likely democratic heirs to the legacy of the authoritarian government, and to serve the short-term political interests of Pinochet and his supporters on the Right. Though Pinochet was opposed to the 1988 plebiscite, which was imposed on him as negotiations with regime moderates played out, he believed that he would be victorious.[28] This would allow him to remain in power until 1997, but he would be assuming the mantle of a president who had withstood the test of a popular election. Following the plebiscite, Pinochet had no desire to be hamstrung by an uncooperative Congress.

For all of these reasons, and taking into account the historical evolution of presidential power in Chile, the designers of the 1980 constitution contended that the president should be vested with a great deal of power to allow the executive to rise above petty political squabbles and to initiate policy forcefully and efficiently without the interference of a legislative branch dominated

25. Evidence of Pinochet's desire for a permanent authoritarian solution is presented in Arturo Valenzuela, "The Military in Power: The Consolidation of One-Man Rule," in *The Struggle for Democracy in Chile*, rev. ed., ed. Paul W. Drake and Iván Jaksic (Lincoln: University of Nebraska Press, 1995), 50–54. In particular, Valenzuela points to the interchange of documents and discussions between Pinochet and former Uruguayan President José María Bordaberry concerning the latter's unsuccessful proposal for a restricted democracy with a permanent supervisory role for the armed forces.

26. Genaro Arriagada, "Después de los presidencialismos ... ¿Qué?" in *Cambio de régimen político*, ed. Oscar Godoy (Santiago: Ediciones Universidad Católica de Chile, 1992), 68. Translation by the author.

27. For a discussion of the Pinochet government, see Genaro Arriagada, *Pinochet: The Politics of Power* (Boulder, Colo.: Westview Press, 1991), and Augusto Varas, *Los militares en el poder: Régimen y gobierno militar en Chile, 1973–1986* (Santiago: FLACSO, 1987).

28. For a valuable discussion of the 1988 plebiscite, see Constable and Valenzuela, *A Nation of Enemies*, 307–11.

by self-interested party leaders. In the view of military reformers, a strong presidency would better guarantee the economic legacy of the authoritarian regime by squelching the personalism, populism, and party-politicking that had led to the corruption of Chile's democratic institutions.

Presidential Strength and Legislative Weakness in Postauthoritarian Chile

The Chilean political regime has all of the characteristics normally associated with presidential systems. The chief executive is directly elected and there are fixed terms for the assembly and the executive that are not contingent on mutual confidence. The president chooses cabinet ministers independently and is vested with constitutionally granted lawmaking authority.[29]

In their cross-national study of presidential systems, Shugart and Carey contend that the constitution of 1980 weakened the legislative powers of the president compared with earlier periods in Chilean history, while expanding nonlegislative powers. However, a number of oversights in their interpretation lead them to underestimate the legislative power of the president.[30] What is more, there are other constitutional and statutory prerogatives not considered within Shugart and Carey's schema that make for a more powerful president than they suggest.

Shugart and Carey provide an excellent framework for comparing presidential systems. In their appraisal of the legislative powers of presidents, they rate executives on a scale from 0 to 4, with a score of 4 reflecting a great deal of presidential power in regard to six separate faculties.[31] Thus, presidents' legislative powers can conceivably range from 0 to 24. Nonetheless, most of the scores are relatively low, with the highest-ranked case

29. This definition is consonant with that of Shugart and Carey, *Presidents and Assemblies*, 19. The authors call the Chilean regime "super-presidential"(129), providing support for the contentions of this study. Although part of the reason they characterize it as such is based on the president's ability to dissolve the Chamber of Deputies once during his or her term, that prerogative was eliminated by the constitutional reforms of 1989. Nonetheless, as shown below, the extraordinary power of the president in other areas certainly makes the term "super-presidential" appropriate.

30. These observations are subject to distinct interpretations and should not be construed as criticisms that detract from the overall quality of Shugart and Carey's study.

31. These are package veto/override, decree, budgetary powers, partial veto/override, exclusive introduction of legislation, and proposal of referenda.

scoring a 12. The average score for all cases considered is 2.86. Shugart and Carey contend that the current Chilean president scores a 5.[32]

However, in terms of their scores for exclusive initiative for certain types of legislation, Shugart and Carey give the Chilean president a score of 1, because Congress has the ability to amend or reject presidential initiatives altogether. While this is true for some types of legislation, there is a nuance not captured by this score. In certain areas (i.e., creation of new public services, remunerations, salaries, loans, benefits, social security, expenditures), the Congress may only accept, reduce, or reject presidential proposals. Congress cannot amend presidential initiatives or redistribute or increase expenditures in any of these areas.[33] Thus, the Chilean president should probably score a 2 in this area. In addition, in terms of budgetary power, Shugart and Carey give the Chilean president a score of 2 (because the president "sets upper limit on total spending, within which the assembly can amend"[34]). Nonetheless, Article 64 of the constitution states that the National Congress "may only reduce the expenditures contained in the Budgetary Law Bill," and members of Congress cannot propose the transfer of funds between budget items. Thus, in this area, the president should receive a score of 3, which Shugart and Carey categorize as the "assembly may reduce, but not increase the amount of budgetary items." Finally, Shugart and Carey give the president a 0 in the area of proposal of referenda. However, the Chilean president can propose plebiscites in cases where he or she vetoes a constitutional reform approved by Congress and Congress overrides the veto. Thus, the president should actually receive a 2, or "restricted referenda" powers. These important distinctions grant the president more power than Shugart and Carey suggest and, if considered, would push the Chilean presidency up significantly on the scale of power, making it one of the most powerful (from a score of 5 to a total score of 9).[35] While individually the presidential prerogatives discussed here are not unique to the Chilean presidential system, their combined effect makes for a formidable executive branch and transforms the president into the most important legislator in the country.

32. The highest-scoring presidency in terms of legislative powers was the Chilean presidency following the 1969 reforms of the 1925 constitution, which Shugart and Carey scored at twelve. The average cited here includes only constitutions in force as of the publication of Shugart and Carey's study (33 of the 44 cases). See Shugart and Carey, *Presidents and Assemblies*, 155.

33. *Constitución Política de la República de Chile*, Article 62.

34. Shugart and Carey, *Presidents and Assemblies*, 155.

35. For a complete discussion and the comparative "scoring" of presidential systems, see Shugart and Carey, *Presidents and Assemblies*, 148–66.

What is more, a number of other realities not considered in many schemata measuring presidential authority make the Chilean president more powerful than might appear to be the case at first glance. Indeed, throughout interviews with members of both the Chamber and the Senate, the presidency was often described as "exaggerated," "authoritarian," and even "imperial."

Areas of Exclusive Initiative

One of the most important powers of Chilean presidents is the wide range of areas in which they have exclusive initiative. Article 62 of the constitution states: "[the] President of the Republic holds the exclusive initiative for proposals of law related to changes in the political or administrative division of the country, or to the financial or budgetary administration of the state." The same article goes on to specify in detail a series of areas in which the executive shall have exclusive initiative, including "establishing, amending, granting or increasing remunerations, retirement payments, pensions," and "widows' and orphans' allowances" (No. 4); "establishing the norms and procedures applicable to collective bargaining and determining the cases where bargaining is not permitted" (No. 5); and "establishing or amending the norms on or regarding social security of both the public and the private sector" (No. 6). Each of these stipulations further extends the reach of the legislative power of the president, compared with earlier constitutions.

The president has almost exclusive control over the budgetary process.[36] The president must submit the budget at least three months before it is to become effective, at which point the Congress may only reduce or approve the expenditures contained in the budgetary law. It may not increase or redistribute them. If the budget law is not approved by both chambers within sixty days, the president's proposal enters into force, granting the president effective decree power in budgetary matters. These limitations on Congress were designed to prevent budgetary immobilization and the proliferation of clientelistic and individualistic legislation and coterminous spending excesses. However, these measures also impose important limitations on the latitude that assembly members have on questions with a bearing on policy-making at the national level.

36. For a discussion of the constitutional and related legal aspects of the budget law, see Iván Maurico Obando Camino, "Observaciones acerca de la regulación de la ley de presupuesto en la Constitución Política de 1980 y sus normas complementarias," *Jornadas de derecho público* 23 (1993): 120–55.

Respect for the limitations on the spheres of action of assembly members is enforced by the Constitutional Tribunal, which possesses broad powers to determine the constitutionality of proposals at any point in the legislative process. Once the tribunal rules on a particular proposal, the president of either chamber of Congress may be removed from office if he or she "permits the voting of a motion which is declared openly contrary to the Political Constitution of the State."[37] The tribunal has in several instances declared initiatives unconstitutional based on Article 62 of the constitution, resulting in their immediate withdrawal.

In Latin America, it is not unusual for presidents to have areas of exclusive initiative. However, most constitutions that contain exclusive introduction clauses also have provisions for a low veto override threshold to introduce a greater degree of legislative control. This is the case, for example, in the absolute majority override provisions of the Colombian and Brazilian constitutions. However, unlike these and other cases, in Chile these faculties are not counterbalanced by a low threshold for veto overrides. A two-thirds majority is necessary to override a presidential veto.[38]

Presidential Urgencies and Extraordinary Sessions

Another source of executive strength and legislative limitation lies in the ability of the president to control the legislative process and to set the agenda through the use of declared executive "urgencies." The president of the republic may declare a proposal urgent in any one or all stages of its consideration, regardless of its branch of origin. Congress then must act on the measure within thirty, ten, or three days, depending on whether the proposal is designated as a "*simple urgencia*," as a "*suma urgencia*," or for "*discusión inmediata*," respectively.[39] If a proposal is declared urgent, consideration of all pending proposals is put on hold. The urgent proposal is then considered in accordance with its level of urgency and the amount of time remaining until it and other declared urgencies are due to expire. This applies both to proposals in committee and to those pending discussion and approval by the general assemblies of the chambers.

Though designed as a measure to be employed in extraordinary circumstances to ensure the passage of key legislation, the use of the faculty has

37. *Constitución Política de la República de Chile*, Article 57.
38. For a discussion of this point, see Mainwaring and Shugart's introduction in their edited volume *Presidentialism and Democracy in Latin America*.
39. *Constitución Política de la República de Chile*, Article 71.

become something of a standard operating procedure in order for presidents to expedite the consideration and approval of proposals. Though during the first democratic administration, President Aylwin was often willing to give the Congress additional time to consider proposals by rescinding urgencies or by withdrawing and reiterating them, the faculty was used at some point in the approval process in 59 percent of the proposals that were sent to Congress by the president.[40] One deputy went so far as to contend that the use of presidential urgency had become the "forma permanente de legislar en Chile" (the permanent way of legislating in Chile).[41] A high-level official in the Ministry of the Presidency contended, on the other hand, that without the president decisively declaring urgencies the legislative process would come to a screeching halt. In his view, the Congress has a tendency to "study and debate legislation that has little importance on the national level" and that has more to do with the personal interests of deputies.[42]

Because the designation of urgency by the president means that there must be immediate discussion of the proposal, consideration of other pending bills, most often those sponsored by legislators (who lack the ability to declare urgencies) is delayed.[43]

The president's control of the legislative agenda is further reinforced by the ability to call the legislature into extraordinary session. During these sessions, the Congress can only consider proposals introduced by the executive.[44] In each of the four congressional periods of the Aylwin administration,

40. Proyecto de Modernización, Congreso Nacional de Chile, *Proceso legislativo chileno: Un enfoque cuantitativo* (Valparaíso: Proyecto de Modernización, Congreso Nacional de Chile, 1995), 15. For an empirical discussion of the legislative difficulties presented by the president's urgency powers, see "Diputados pesimistas por número de proyectos que alcanzarán a tratar," *El Mercurio*, 8 October 1992, C2. Despite the 59 percent figure, it is difficult to effectively measure the number of proposals that have passed with the use of executive urgencies, because they are sometimes withdrawn. An advisor in the Judicial/Legislative Division of the Ministry of the General Secretary of the Presidency stated that the executive branch has attempted to keep the number of pending proposals declared urgent at any one time at or under 20 percent of the total. Even if this 20 percent figure is taken into consideration, executive urgency is clearly not an "extraordinary measure," given that it was used at some point in the consideration of almost 60 percent of the president's initiatives. Interview with César Ladrón de Guevara Pardo, advisor, Judicial/Legislative Division of the Ministry of the General Secretary of the Presidency, Santiago, 28 April 1993.
41. Interview with Deputy Juan Antonio Coloma, Santiago, 12 April 1993.
42. Off the record interview, Santiago, 7 May 1993.
43. For a discussion of the effect of urgencies in terms of the success rate for the passage of legislation, see Peter Siavelis, "Exaggerated Presidentialism and Moderate Presidents" (paper presented at the symposium, Legislaturas en América Latina: Perspectivas Comparadas, Centro de Investigación y Docencia Económicas, Mexico City, 6–7 February 1998).
44. *Constitución Política de la República de Chile*, Article 52. If the president does not convoke an extraordinary session, the Congress may do so, during which time any type of proposals

and during the first four years of the Frei administration, the Congress was called into extraordinary session by the president.

The executive's ability to declare legislation urgent, combined with the ability to convoke extraordinary sessions, grants the president powerful agenda-setting power throughout the legislative process. In addition to ensuring that it will be their proposals that have priority, presidents can also use these faculties to "bottle up" the legislative process and prevent consideration of congressional initiatives. While Presidents Aylwin and Frei both exercised their faculties with a relative amount of flexibility (see Chapter 2), there is nothing to ensure that future presidents will be as charitable in their use.

Other Constitutional Sources of Presidential Power

Though the president must seek congressional approval to declare states of siege, the executive can declare states of constitutional exception, emergency, and catastrophe without congressional approval.[45] The original text of the 1980 constitution allowed the executive to employ forced exile and prohibit the entrance or exit of certain individuals from the national territory and to suspend the guarantees of freedom of association and the press during states of siege. However, according to the reforms of 1989, the president may restrict only freedom of movement, association, and the press during such times.[46]

As in most presidential systems, the Chilean president has a right to veto legislation. Though the executive does not have what is normally understood as a line-item veto, he or she can make specific comments about or changes to legislation, as long as they are "related to the central or fundamental ideas of the bill."[47] Therefore, the president does have the power to change major aspects of bills before returning them to Congress. If the Congress disapproves of presidential comments, it may *insistir* (insist). With a vote of two-thirds of the members of both chambers the proposal becomes law. However, despite the power Congress has to override presidential vetoes, there was only one case during the first four legislative sessions after the return of democracy in which a bill became law without the president's signature.

---

may be discussed. In addition, the president may also decide to allow the discussion of bills proposed by the members of Congress during an executive-declared extraordinary session.

45. *Constitución Política de la República de Chile*, Article 40.
46. Ibid., Article 41, No. 3.
47. Ibid., Article 70.

The power of the president as a legislator is not limited to the legislative process itself, but also extends to the actual designation of a portion of the assembly and to the appointment of other authorities that expand the reach of executive influence. In addition to the thirty-eight elected members of the Senate, there are also nine appointed senators, of which the president appoints two. However, because the president also influences the appointment of, and in some instances names, the officials who staff the institutions that designate the remaining appointed senators, executive influence is more far-reaching than it appears.

The president also names the comptroller general of the republic, the commanders of the armed forces, and the judges of the supreme and appellate courts.[48] According to the 1925 constitution, diplomatic appointments by the president were subject to senatorial approval. The 1980 constitution eliminated any role for the Congress in the designation of diplomatic posts.

Finally, the range of the president's implied constitutional powers is quite broad in Chile. The president is granted the right to "exercise statutory authority in all those matters which are not of a legal nature, without prejudice to the power to issue other regulations, decrees or instructions which he may deem appropriate for the enforcement of the law."[49]

Nonstatutory Sources of Presidential Power

There are also a number of nonstatutory elements that skew the balance of power in favor of the executive branch. Though not specifically outlined in the 1980 constitution, and therefore not technically constitutional powers of the president, they do result from the overall framework of presidentialism set out in the document and grant the president increased influence and lawmaking capabilities. The visibility of the president, the importance of the tradition of presidential government, and the role of the president as a symbol of the nation all grant the president authority and esteem. This contrasts sharply with the public's view of assembly members, who are often seen as venal, corrupt, overpaid, and self-interested.[50]

---

48. The president's power of appointment is limited by certain restrictions that determine the pool from which candidates may be chosen. The most common limitation is the seniority or rank of potential candidates.

49. *Constitución Política de la República de Chile,* Article 32, No. 8.

50. See Chapter 4 for public-opinion data on the negative view of the Congress. As simultaneously the head of state and head of government, the president is often seen as the embodiment of the nation. However, at the same time the president is a party leader. For a discussion

However, the most important nonstatutory source of presidential power lies in the unequal balance of staff and access to information. The executive branch can rely on a vast network of attorneys, experts, and advisors within each of the ministries who are charged with particular subject areas, enabling it to elaborate proposals of a much higher quality than the legislative branch. Because the ministries are divided along functional lines, the staffs tend to be expert in the subject area for which they are drafting legislation. They have a better understanding of the structure and day-to-day functioning of the institutions administered by the ministries, and of the problems that proposed legislation should address.

On the other hand, most deputies and senators have relatively small staffs that consist of a secretary and one or two advisors, often family members. While legislators with more resources, or those with additional outside occupations such as a partnership in a law firm, may have larger staffs, most have little access to expert information and advisors.[51] In interviews with members of the Chamber of Deputies during the Aylwin administration, 94.4 percent of government members and 83.3 percent of opposition members sampled agreed that they had insufficient legislative assistance and too few advisors to adequately perform their most basic lawmaking and representative functions.

At the same time, because assembly members are involved in such a broad range of legislative activity, they must attempt to become experts on legislation that can range from defense policy to fishing regulations to issues involving social welfare. Though congressional committees are ordered along the same functional lines as the ministries, there is no permanent team of experts to advise committee members.

There are independent "think tanks," a Library of Congress, and an Office of Information for both chambers. However, the types of materials and information provided by these institutions deal more with legislation from a broad perspective. They do not provide the individualized or specialized information services often necessary for members who have specific interests or concerns related to the effect of legislation on their districts.[52]

---

of these conflicting roles, see Juan Linz, "Presidential or Parliamentary Democracy: Does It Make a Difference?" in *The Failure of Presidential Democracy*, 2:24–26.

51. Interview with Eduardo Barros González, Valparaíso, 2 April 1993. The lack of personnel was a recurrent theme in several interviews with congressional staff members. For example, because of budgetary constraints, during the 1990–94 legislative period five Radical Party deputies shared a single secretary who had a corresponding number of telephones on her desk.

52. Officials in think tanks across the party spectrum made similar contentions related to misunderstandings concerning the role of these organizations. Interviewees in think tanks

What is more, both deputies and senators consistently complained about the level and speed of the services offered by the Offices of Information. One deputy complained that it could take "hours, or even days" for the offices to answer even the most basic questions.[53] In addition, unlike ministerial staff, members of the Chamber and the Senate must also concern themselves with the demands of their constituency and reelection (with the exception of designated senators), which limit the time and resources that can be devoted to the study and formulation of legislative proposals.

In accordance with a process of legislative modernization and decentralization undertaken by the military regime, a costly new building to house the Congress was constructed in the port of Valparaíso. Several members of Congress contended that the real goal was to keep Congress "off the back of the executive," not decentralization. Moving the Congress outside of Santiago was, for one official, "a system devilishly designed to have a weak Congress physically removed from the seat of government."[54] But, more important, the location of the Congress has created a series of complications and time limitations that have made it more difficult for legislators to do their jobs. Members of Congress are perpetually traveling, often large distances given Chile's geography, in an effort to maintain simultaneous contact with Congress, constituents, and the ministries in Santiago. In addition to the time and money spent, communication between the branches of government, both formal and informal, is complicated by the location of the Congress. Several legislative proposals to move the Congress back to the capital have been made by members. Nonetheless, many deputies and senators, particularly those on the Right, oppose returning Congress to the capital, arguing that it would be a waste of the US$200 million it cost to construct the massive structure.

An additional component of the process of legislative modernization undertaken by military authorities provided senators and deputies with the most up-to-date computer hardware and software packages. Nonetheless, a legislative aide to a Concertación deputy contended that, in his estimation, 50 percent of the computers being used at any given time in the Congress building are running "the most advanced computer games" rather than being employed

contended that deputies and senators often misconstrued their organizations as sources of specialized information. Interviews with Juan Enrique Vega, executive director, Programa de Asesoría Legislativa, 17 March 1993, and Eugenio Guzmán, associate, Instituto Libertad y Desarrollo, 1 June 1993.
53. Off the record interview with an opposition deputy, Santiago, 26 April 1993.
54. Off the record interview with a high-level Ministry of Justice official, 23 June 1993.

for purposes of communication and data handling.[55] Part of the reason for computer misuse lies in the absence of resources and time to train underpaid legislative aides. It is also the result of the lack of an overarching network for the computer system in Congress. This means that it is often difficult for untrained staffers to find and successfully retrieve any data that does exist.

This imbalance in staff and access to information, complicated by time limitations on members of Congress, transfers a tremendous amount of power to the executive branch in terms of its capacities to initiate legislation.[56] It is difficult for members of the assemblies to draft legislation approaching the quality of that produced by the executive, in terms of both substantive content and legislative technique. This makes the already limited chances for the approval for legislative initiatives even less likely.

In possessing these broad powers to formulate and propose legislation and control the legislative agenda, the president is not merely a "co-legislator," as students of the Chilean presidency often contend, but the most important legislator in the country. During the first eight legislative periods of the democratic government, few initiatives originating in one of the two assemblies succeeded in being transformed into law. On the other hand, the executive branch has been quite successful in seeing its proposals become laws of the republic.[57] Table 1.1 summarizes all of the laws passed and promulgated during the first two postauthoritarian democratic governments, based on whether the bill was presented by the president or by a member of one of the two chambers of Congress. The table demonstrates clearly that the Congress has been less than successful in securing the approval of congressional initiatives, though the situation appears to be improving. As Table 1.1 shows, only 8.2 percent of the laws passed during the Alywin administration originated in the legislative branch.

The imbalance in the origin of proposals is not a result of a lack of initiatives by Congress. For example, during the Aylwin government, 529 initiatives

55. Off the record interview, Valparaíso, 2 April 1993.
56. The infrastructure and resources of the Chilean Congress are far superior to those of nearby countries like Argentina and Uruguay, not to mention poorer countries like Bolivia and Paraguay. Nonetheless, being a legislator in a technologically advancing society like Chile's requires a great deal more infrastructure, both physical and intellectual, than is currently available to members of the Congress.
57. A few congressional initiatives are in fact "hidden" in these laws originating in the executive branch, because of the willingness of the president to include certain congressional proposals in his legislative packages. Nonetheless, this reality demonstrates the importance of executive sponsorship in ensuring the passage of legislation and further underscores the dominant role of the president as the country's most important legislator.

Table 1.1. Laws promulgated during the first two postauthoritarian governments (numbers and percentages by origin)

Aylwin Administration (1990–1993)			
Session	Total Laws	Executive Origin	Legislative Origin
1990	153	139	14
1991	123	110	13
1992	112	105	7
1993	52	50	2
Total	440	404	36
% total	100	91.8	8.2

Frei Administration (1994–1997)			
Session	Total Laws	Executive Origin	Legislative Origin
1994	77	61	16
1995	70	49	21
1996	52	40	12
1997	54	40	14
Total	253	190	63
% total	100	75.1	24.9

SOURCE: Congreso Nacional de Chile.

were proposed by assembly members, and 637 originated in the executive branch.[58] However, of the 637 initiatives presented by the president, 447 completed the entire legislative process. Of these, 404 (92 percent) became law. Alternatively, the legislators succeeded in having only 69 (13 percent) of the 529 initiatives they presented considered. What is more, only 36 (52 percent) of the few proposals that were considered became law.[59]

Furthermore, of the few congressional initiatives approved during the first legislative period, most have had to do with insignificant matters. Of the laws originating in Congress, 14 (39 percent) had to do with erecting monuments to important national or regional figures, declaring holidays, or granting honorary citizenship to non-Chileans. Two of these laws, or about 5 percent, were statutes delegating authority to ministers or the president. Thus, 44 percent of this already limited number of legislative initiatives

58. Congreso de Chile. See Table 2.3 for a complete summary of laws and their origins.
59. Unfortunately, complete parallel data on the Frei administration are not yet available.

were really insignificant. The other 66 percent did have to do with issues of national scope, but most were relatively minor changes to the penal or other codes. One of the few significant bills that originated in the Congress lowered the legal age of adulthood.

During the second four years of democratic government (1994–97), Congress' record of legislative success was not much better. Though the total percentage of laws originating in Congress increased moderately, the percentage dealing with insignificant matters, as defined above, remained about the same, 41 percent.[60] Once again, most substantive legislative initiatives had to do with minor changes in the penal and civil codes.

Certainly, these data must be analyzed with a great deal of caution. In the study of Latin American presidentialism, there is a tendency to simply compare the branch of origin of legislation, without taking into account the complexity of legislative processes. In employing such data as measures of presidential power, what really matters is the final wording of bills after they have been amended by Congress, and that is difficult to measure effectively. In addition, it is probably correct to assume that, when a president controls a majority coalition in at least one of the two houses, the president will define the legislative program of the government. In this context, many legislative initiatives would come from members of the opposition, and, therefore, would be less likely to be considered.[61]

Nonetheless, it is important to note that, while both presidents were able to rely on a legislative majority coalition, their party, the Christian Democrats, controlled a minority of seats in both houses, and coalition partners did have policy agendas distinct from those of the overall governing coalition. In addition, during the first two years of the Aylwin government, 63.9 percent of legislative initiatives originating in the Chamber were proposed by deputies of the *governing* parties.[62] While these data do not definitively indicate presidential domination, they do at the very least suggest that Frei and, especially, Aylwin were successful in employing their legislative and partisan powers so that they would be able to accomplish their legislative goals, while members of Congress were less successful in securing the passage of legislation not tied to the presidents' initiatives.

60. Congreso Nacional de Chile.
61. The author is grateful to Matthew Shugart and Scott Mainwaring for these insights.
62. Instituto Libertad y Desarrollo, "Análisis cuantitativo del proceso legislativo," *Opinión sector político institucional*, No. P19 (December 1991), 7. Unfortunately, more recent and comprehensive data are not available.

Legislative Prerogatives: A Check on Presidential Power?

Despite the broad range of constitutional, implied, and de facto presidential power in Chile, it would be a mistake to ignore the role of Congress in the legislative process and within the political system as a whole.[63]

One of the most important roles of assemblies in presidential systems, in addition to lawmaking functions, is to act as a check on the executive branch.[64] Article 48 of the constitution establishes that an exclusive attribute of the Chamber of Deputies is the oversight of executive action.[65] Though individual senators may request information from government ministries, the Senate has fewer formal oversight functions than the Chamber of Deputies.

The three most important ways the Chamber of Deputies may exercise its oversight functions are through the formation of commissions to investigate specific acts, the submission of "*oficios*" (official requests for information) to the executive branch, and the initiation of constitutional accusations against the president, ministers of state, or other officials.

The Chamber of Deputies is empowered to form special commissions to investigate acts of the executive branch or irregularities in any area in which state entities have dealings. These commissions are designed both to exercise administrative control of the executive branch and to prevent corruption. They can call on ministers of state and other officials to present testimony when investigating illegalities, fraud, or wrongdoing. Individuals and firms with financial relationships with the state or its agencies can also be investigated or called on by legislative investigative commissions to present testimony.[66]

63. For a comparative discussion of the role of the Congress according to the 1925 and 1980 constitutions, see Alejandro Silva Bascuñán, "El nuevo Congreso Nacional," *Jornadas de derecho público* 20 (Santiago: Edeval, 1990), 103–16. For a review of the legislative and oversight functions of the Chilean Congress according to the 1980 constitution, see Alejandro Ferreiro, "El Congreso chileno," in *Poder legislativo en el cono sur*, vol. 1, ed. Esteban Caballero and Alejandro Vial (Asunción: Centro de Estudios Democráticos, 1994), 125–44.

64. For a general, though dated, discussion of Latin American legislatures, see Weston Agor, ed., *Latin American Legislatures: Their Role and Influence* (New York: Praeger, 1971). On legislatures in the developing world, see George Boynton and Chong Lin Kim, eds., *Legislative Systems in Developing Countries* (Durham, N.C.: Duke University Press, 1975); Joel Smith and Lloyd Musolf, eds., *Legislatures in Development: Dynamics of Change in New and Old States* (Durham, N.C.: Duke University Press, 1979); and Allan Kornberg, Samuel Hines, and Joel Smith, "Legislatures and the Modernization of Societies," *Comparative Political Studies* 5 (1973): 471–91.

65. Stated in Article 54 of *Constitución Política de la República de Chile*, as the "fiscalización de los actos del gobierno."

66. *Reglamento de la Cámara de Diputados*, Articles 297–303.

Since the return of democratic politics, commissions have been formed to investigate allegations of kickbacks made by military industries to relatives of General Pinochet, and financial irregularities at the petroleum refinery of Con-Con and various other state corporations, including DIGEDER (General Directorate of Sports and Recreation), CODELCO (Chilean Copper Corporation), and EMPREMAR S.A. (State Shipping Industry). In addition, and amid great public fanfare, allegations of political espionage have been investigated by legislative special commissions, as have accusations of price gouging in the nation's pharmacies.

Nonetheless, investigative commissions have been of limited usefulness as a tool of oversight and for preventing corruption. Unfortunately, in practice, special commissions have often been used as *"cajas de resonancia"* (sounding boards) to transmit personal or partisan political messages of members.[67] Rather than forming a special commission in order to exercise their oversight functions, opposition members often seek simply to embarrass the government or enhance their own national political prominence or prestige, through vocal and public criticisms of government leaders.

A graphic example of the often political motivations behind the formation of special commissions occurred in April 1993. When debating whether or not to form a special commission to investigate financial irregularities within DIGEDER, a Christian Democrat deputy and a UDI (Unión Demócrata Independiente—Independent Democratic Union) deputy exchanged punches on the Chamber floor (ironically, this immediately followed a unanimous vote to condemn hooliganism and violence in the nation's soccer stadiums). The fistfight erupted as Christian Democratic members questioned the integrity of deputies of the political Right regarding their eagerness to form an investigative commission when none of the financial irregularities of the previous regime had been investigated by the Congress.[68]

Because of the often political motivations behind their formation, commissions have trouble coming to agreement on the final wording of the reports and recommendations they are required to produce. This results in a minority and majority opinion that waters down the contents and perceived validity of the commission's findings. Renovación Nacional (RN—National Renovation) deputy María Angélica Cristi contended: "There is no will [for Congress] to exercise its oversight functions . . . the behavior that the

---

67. This exact wording was used by a number of interviewees in describing legislative commissions.
68. *La Tercera*, 15 April 1993, 9.

Concertación has exhibited in the Chamber and in the investigative commissions is one in which it imposes its majority to produce a report favorable to its political interests, but not that reveals the truth; this, in turn, prevents proposals and arguments of the opposition from becoming known, because only the majority version of the report is officially approved."[69]

Further, special commissions can investigate only alleged improprieties; they have no punitive powers. The simple revelation of irregularities on the part of the administration, when combined with press coverage, may act as a check on executive activities. Nonetheless, the Congress cannot force the executive to take action in accordance with the findings of an investigative commission, nor is the political responsibility of officials appointed by the president affected. Though a constitutional accusation against guilty parties can later be initiated, political concerns and the perfunctory tone of commission reports reduce the effectiveness of special commissions as an avenue for the Chamber to undertake its oversight functions.

An oversight faculty more frequently employed by assembly members is the "*oficio*" (request for information). Members of the Chamber of Deputies may submit two types of oficios. The first type, an *oficio simple*, is simply a request for information directed to a particular ministry. It can be submitted by any deputy subject to the approval of one-third of members present in the Chamber. This type of *oficio* is designed to allow members to exercise oversight of executive action in relation to particular activities being undertaken in a member's district.

The second type, an *oficio de fiscalización*, is designed more precisely as a mechanism for the Chamber as a whole to exercise its oversight and control functions on the executive branch. With the support of the majority of deputies present, members may "adopt agreements or suggest observations which shall be transmitted in writing to the President."[70] The president must then respond through the appropriate minister within thirty days. However, just as in the case of investigative commissions, the agreements or observations made by members of the Chamber in no way affect the political responsibility of the ministers of state, nor is the executive branch obliged to take action on the recommendations contained in the *oficios*. The constitution states: "the Government's obligation shall be understood to be fulfilled simply by delivering its reply."[71]

---

69. Quoted in "Critican acción fiscalizadora de los diputados," *El Mercurio*, 4 May 1998, A1. This article also discusses several of the problems and criticisms of legislative oversight.
70. *Constitución Política de la República de Chile*, Article 48, No. 1.
71. Ibid.

The use of both types of *oficios* has been of limited utility in the exercise of the Chamber's oversight capabilities for a number of reasons. The only legal obligation that the executive branch has is to answer the *oficio* within a thirty-day period. The law says nothing concerning the qualitative or substantive content of the responses to requests for information submitted by the Chamber as a whole, or by individual deputies. Given this reality, responses to *oficios* submitted to the executive branch are often vague or perfunctory or advise the interested party that the matter will be investigated or considered by the corresponding ministry. One Christian Democratic deputy politely described government responses to *oficios* as "más bien difusas" (sort of diffuse).[72]

However, some blame for the ineffectiveness of *oficios* must also be laid at the doors of the Chamber. Most members interviewed for this study agreed that the *oficio* is used excessively as a résumé builder and a mechanism for responding to disgruntled constituents. Many of the issues dealt with in *oficios* should really be referred to lower-level authorities like mayors or town councils.

During the Aylwin administration, 18,532 *oficios* were submitted, and the government succeed in answering about 14,700, or approximately 80 percent of the total.[73] If a member submits an *oficio*, he or she can inform constituents that the problem has been brought to the attention of the appropriate minister and that no further action can be taken by the deputy. At the same time, on his or her résumé and in campaign literature the deputy can point to a long list of actions taken on the behalf of constituents. The Chamber produces a comprehensive chronology of the activities of each member, which lists every time a member has spoken in the Chamber and documents the number and subject of every *oficio* sent. Many deputies simply reproduce this list to provide constituents with a comprehensive list of *oficios*, a purported demonstration of both their concern and the wide range of activities undertaken on behalf of the district they represent.

The abuse of the *oficio* system and the sheer quantity of responses that the executive must generate further encourage superficial responses by the ministries in an effort to get paperwork off their desks. What is more, officials within the Ministry of the General Secretary of the Presidency (SEGPRES)

---

72. Interview with Deputy José Miguel Ortiz Novoa, Valparaíso, 1 April 1993.
73. Official information released by the Ministry of the General Secretary of the Presidency. Though concrete statistics have not yet been assembled for the Frei administration, officials in SEGPRES estimate that the rate of response for the second administration is about the same.

contended that answering often unnecessary *oficios* is a tremendous waste of time, which could be better devoted to working on more substantive issues related to legislation and interbranch relations.[74] A high-level official in the Ministry of Justice pointed to the "poor" quality of congressional *oficios*, calling many of them "downright silly," and contended "There is a difference between oversight and simply asking for information for other purposes."[75]

The final oversight function granted to the Chamber of Deputies is the ability to initiate impeachment proceedings or constitutional accusations against the president for violation of the constitution or the law, or for taking actions "which have gravely affected the honor or security of the nation."[76] Ministers of state, judges, and other government officials can also be subject to constitutional accusations for legal wrongdoing, dereliction of duties, or abuse of power.[77] Although impeachment proceedings have been undertaken, and succeeded in the case of one high-level judicial official, the use of constitutional accusations as an oversight function is really limited to extreme and extraordinary cases of legal wrongdoing or gross violations of the constitution. Also, and again according to most legislators interviewed, the effectiveness of this avenue of oversight was limited principally because of the political motivations behind the initiation of such proceedings.

The most illustrative example of the politicization of oversight authority through the use of impeachment proceedings was the constitutional accusation launched against General Pinochet in early 1998 (discussed in more detail in Chapter 3). The general was accused of "disgracing" the nation during his tenure as commander in chief of the armed forces and undermining the honor and endangering the security of the state through his actions. One of the most serious rifts in the governing coalition emerged as the Left

---

74. Interview with César Ladrón de Guevara Pardo, advisor, Judicial/Legislative Division of the Ministry of the General Secretary of the Presidency, Santiago, 28 April 1993.

75. Off the record interview, Santiago, 23 June 1995.

76. *Constitución Política de la República de Chile*, Article 48, No. 2.

77. The Chamber of Deputies may also initiate constitutional accusations against judges of the Superior Court, the *Contralor General de la República* (controller general), generals or admirals of the armed forces, provincial *intendentes*, and regional governors. The initiation of a constitutional accusation against the president requires the vote of a majority of sitting deputies. For other officials, at least ten, but no more than twenty, members of the Chamber may initiate a constitutional accusation (*Constitución Política de la República de Chile*, Article 57). Once an accusation has been approved by the Chamber, the Senate acts as a jury and declares whether the accused is guilty. In the case of the president, two-thirds of sitting senators must concur with the guilty verdict in order to approve a constitutional accusation. In other cases, a majority of sitting senators must concur. A guilty verdict results in the accused's being immediately removed from office and undergoing a ban of five years on accepting any positions, elected or otherwise, in the administration of the state.

lined up behind the accusation, and the Christian Democrats split, with conservative elements in the party accusing even their own *correligionarios* of playing politics with the country's future. Ultimately, the accusation was overturned by the Chamber.

Thus, as is the case with the legislative capacity of the Chamber of Deputies and the Senate, the oversight capabilities of both houses are limited, hampering the ability of the Congress to act effectively as a check on presidential power. Evidence from interviews with members of the legislative branch supports this contention. Only 27 percent of deputies interviewed felt that members effectively carried out their oversight function, with only slight variations occurring when party identification was considered. The most frequently cited reasons for the limited effectiveness of congressional control of executive action were Congress' lack of oversight capabilities, the politicization of oversight activities, Congress' excessive use of the *oficio*, and Congress' inability to deal with wrongdoings committed by the Pinochet government.

The inability of Congress to carry out its oversight functions effectively undermines its role as a check on presidential power. More generally, although Chile is exemplary in terms of the integrity of its public servants compared with other Latin American countries, many members of Congress who were interviewed underscored how a lack of legislative oversight could easily lead to serious problems of corruption. A high-level official in the Ministry of Justice who asked not to be identified contended that there is already much more corruption in Chile than the government realizes, and that neither the executive nor legislative branch is sufficiently aware of or concerned about this growing problem.[78]

Electoral Reform: The Binomial Electoral System

In addition to exaggerated presidentialism, one of the most important facets of the transformational intentions of the military regime was a comprehensive reform of the parliamentary electoral system. Military reformers contended that Chile's historical proportional representation (PR) electoral system aggravated and magnified divisions within society and was instrumental in the creation of a *"partidocracia"* characterized by ideological polarization, given the

78. Off the record interview, Santiago, 23 June 1993.

electoral system's permissiveness in the congressional representation of small parties.

According to the constitution of 1925, congressional seats were allocated in multimember districts based on the proportional d'Hondt formula with open-list ballots.[79] The fifty-member Senate was elected with representatives from ten geographical units composed of between one and six provinces, each of which elected five senators. For Chamber of Deputies elections, twenty-eight multimember districts were established to elect a total of 150 deputies. District magnitude (the number of seats per electoral district) ranged from 1 to 18, for an average district magnitude of 5.36.[80]

The electoral reforms undertaken by the military were designed with two principal goals in mind. First, military leaders sought to design a system that would limit party-system fragmentation and in the process lead to the formation of a two-party system, which they viewed as the most stable, moderate, and desirable option for Chile. While the proposition that low-district magnitude necessarily produces party-system integration is in itself problematic (an issue discussed in detail in following chapters), reformers contended that such a system would help to reduce the number of political parties in the country. With low-district magnitudes, the argument went, parties would be forced to fuse in order to win parliamentary seats. In the process, the electoral system would encourage parties to move toward the ideological center in an effort to attract the widest possible bases of support.[81]

The most obvious choice to achieve these goals, it seemed, would be the adoption of a single-member district system like that employed in the United

---

79. According to the d'Hondt formula, the number of votes received by each candidate is summed and, using a system of successive divisors (1, 2, 3, 4 . . .), seats are allocated to the party with the highest number of votes at each iteration until all the seats have been distributed. For a complete description of the electoral systems employed throughout the Americas, see Mark Jones, "A Guide to the Electoral System of the Americas," *Electoral Studies* 14 (1995): 5–21.

80. The number of deputies varied in the preauthoritarian period, as their number was based on national population. At the time of the coup, there were 150. Federico Gil, in *The Political System of Chile*, provides a detailed description of the Chilean system for electing members of the Chamber of Deputies and Senate. See also Ronald H. McDonald, *Party Systems and Elections in Latin America* (Chicago: Markham, 1971), 131–36.

81. These arguments were, of course, based on some of the prevailing assumptions concerning the party-system effect of electoral systems, which have been vigorously questioned in the theoretical literature. The argument concerning the reductive effect of low district magnitudes is an extension of that elaborated by Maurice Duverger. The argument concerning the ideological centralization of the party system is distinctly Downsian. See Maurice Duverger, *Political Parties: Their Organization and Activity*, trans. Robert and Barbara North (New York: John Wiley and Sons, 1954), 217, and Anthony Downs, *An Economic Theory of Democracy* (New York: Harper and Row, 1957).

States and United Kingdom. However, military reformers were also aware that the parties of the opposition had received roughly 55 percent of the vote in the October 1988 plebiscite on the continued rule of General Pinochet. With a single member-system, they knew that, should the opposition succeed in maintaining a coalition and garnering a similar percentage of the vote in the first democratic congressional elections, it was possible that the parties of the Right would be completely shut out of Congress. Thus, the second goal was to devise an electoral formula that would guarantee representation for parties of the Right, based on the assumption that they would inherit the roughly 40 percent of the vote received by General Pinochet in the 1988 plebiscite.

To balance the goals of party-system integration with the provision of benefits to the parties of the Right, military reformers ultimately decided to adopt a two-member district system, both for the Chamber of Deputies and for the Senate. For the Chamber, 60 new legislative districts were established, for a total membership of 120. Districts were drawn to favor the parties of the Right, which had comparatively more support in rural than in urban areas.[82] The 20 least-populated districts elect forty deputies, while the 7 most-populated districts have roughly the same population but elect only fourteen. Also, the vote-per-seat ratio is low in the areas in which support for the authoritarian government was strong, and high where the opposition performed better in the plebiscite.[83] For the Senate, 19 districts were established, each electing two senators, for a total of 38 (in addition to the nine appointed senators).

However, the most important feature of the electoral system designed to favor the Right is the procedure for allocating seats. In order for a party or coalition to win both seats in a district, it must double the vote of its nearest competitor. Consequently, and assuming there are two coalitions competing in a particular district, a party need only garner 33.4 percent of the vote to obtain one seat, while it must win 66.7 percent of the vote to win two. Hence, if the highest-polling coalition or party wins 66.6 percent of the vote and its nearest competitor receives 33.4 percent, each wins one seat, or 50 percent of the total seats in the district. With a pattern of two-bloc competition, any support a party receives above 33.4 percent but below 66.7 percent

82. This has traditionally been the case in Chile, principally because of consistent growth in Chile's urban population without regular reapportionment. Nonetheless, despite the designation of new congressional districts before the 1989 elections, rural areas are still overrepresented to a greater extent than they have been traditionally. For comparisons of the relative electoral weight of distinct provinces in the preauthoritarian era, see Ronald H. McDonald, *Party Systems and Elections in Latin America*, 130.
83. *La Epoca*, 6 April 1989, 10.

is effectively wasted. Clearly, this seat-allocation system favors the second-largest party or coalition (in this case the parties of the Right) in each district, given the context of party competition in the country.[84] Of course, the threshold varies, depending on the number of parties and coalitions competing. Nonetheless, the system was designed with the presumption that two coalitions would compete in the first elections, and to provide an electoral benefit for the Right given this supposition.

Table 1.2 provides a more concrete example of how the system functions. The results from the Senate race reproduced in the table demonstrate how, given the distribution of the vote, the Right could succeed in reaping benefits that are disproportionate to its level of support. In this election, the winners were Andrés Zaldívar and Jaime Guzmán. Even though Ricardo Lagos received a higher number and higher percentage of the vote than either of his competitors, the Right garnered one seat because the Concertación total list vote was not twice the total votes that the Democracia y Progreso list was able to obtain.

In terms of their short-term goal of overrepresentation of the Right, military reformers succeeded. The most important conservative party, Renovación Nacional, did benefit the most in the 1989 election in terms of the ratio of the percentage of votes to the percentage of seats.[85]

In terms of the long-term transformational goal of the electoral system, its designers were less successful. While it is clear that an incipient bipolar configuration of competition seems to have prevailed in the first parliamentary elections, Chapter 4 provides strong evidence that this may be just a temporary phenomenon.

Although the electoral system does not represent a limitation of congressional authority per se, it does limit the access that certain party sectors have to democratic institutions, given the importance of the electoral thresholds it

84. All electoral systems have certain distorting effects in terms of proportionality. This section does not suggest any normative preference for perfect proportionality. Rather, it seeks to demonstrate that the electoral formula was designed with a clear intent to produce certain results given the known distribution of partisan strength in the country.

85. Proportionality indices and seat-to-vote ratios for all major parties in the 1989 elections appear in Arturo Valenzuela and Peter Siavelis, "Ley electoral y estabilidad democrática: Un ejercicio de simulación para el caso de Chile," *Estudios públicos* 43 (Winter 1991): 25–87. The authors also provide an extensive analysis of the political consequences of the Chilean *binomial* system supported by a series of electoral simulations. For a more in-depth and varied set of simulations that test the performance of a moderate proportional system against the binomial system within the context of a number of coalitional configurations, see Peter Siavelis, "Nuevos argumentos y viejos supuestos: Simulaciones de sistemas electorales alternativos para las elecciones parlamentarias chilenas," *Estudios públicos* 51 (Winter 1993): 229–67.

Table 1.2. Senatorial election results for Circunscripción 7, Metropolitan Santiago, Concertación and Democracia y Progreso Party Lists

Concertación	Total	% Vote
Ricardo Lagos	399,721	30.6
Andrés Zaldívar	408,227	31.3
Total	807,948	61.9
Democracia y Progreso		
Jaime Guzmán	224,396	17.2
Miguel Otero	199,856	15.3
Total	424,252	32.5
Other lists	73,269	5.6

SOURCE: Servicio Electoral de Chile.

establishes. Parties that do not reach the system's effective thresholds can be shut out of Congress or be significantly underrepresented. Despite coalition formation in the first three postauthoritarian parliamentary elections, which allowed for representation in Congress of smaller parties, the fact remains that there are only two congressional seats available in a country characterized by four to five major parties. In this sense, while not limiting the lawmaking capacity of Congress, the law certainly limits the ability of the legislative branch to effectively undertake its mission of interest articulation and representation, because of the distinct possibility that important political sectors in the country can easily be left without representation in Congress. More seriously, the law limits the ability of Congress to serve as an arena for conflict resolution, given that it has the potential to exclude or reduce the influence and voice of relevant political actors. Finally, in that the electoral system did provide concrete benefits to the Right in both chambers, it also provides additional effective limits on the ability of Congress and the executive to reform the institutional framework inherited from the authoritarian regime.

Exaggerated Presidentialism, Electoral Majoritarianism, and the Framework for Controlled Democracy

In order to analyze the consequences of legislative weakness and the parliamentary electoral system fully, it is important also to understand the broader framework in which these two elements of the institutional formula are embedded. If each component of the entire institutional framework is analyzed separately, it is difficult to understand the consequences of their functional interaction. Taken together, they form a complete web of controls on civilian authorities and establish the context in which interbranch relations are conducted.

In addition to expanded presidential authority and electoral reform, other institutional innovations imposed by military leaders affect interbranch relations and the prospects for long-term political efficacy and democratic governability. The 1980 constitution established an institutionalized role for the armed forces in politics, a number of political bodies and individuals not subject to the control of civilian authorities with the ability to affect legislation, and high quorums for passing the most significant legislation.

Power is not fungible, nor is its distribution a zero-sum game. However, the existence and the decision-making latitude of a number of institutions and individuals not subject to civilian control necessarily limit the power of both the executive and legislative branches to a certain extent. Further, given that the Congress is the junior partner in governing Chile, the existence of these bodies dilutes the influence of the legislative branch even more. They also undermine the legitimacy of the political system, given that nonelected authorities can derail the decision-making process or veto legislative agreements structured in democratic institutions.

The Tutelary Role of the Armed Forces

Perhaps the best-known and most controversial aspect of the Chilean democratic transition has been the continuing influence of the armed forces. Rather than boarding a plane for exile in disgrace like many retiring autocrats, Augusto Pinochet simply packed his desk at La Moneda (the presidential palace) and moved across Santiago's main street to the Ministry of Defense. Similarly, even with Chile's return to formal democracy, all of the country's top military officials remained in office.

But beyond ensuring the tenure of serving officials, the designers of the 1980 constitution also created a series of institutional mechanisms in an effort to establish a permanent tutelary political role for the armed forces. Foremost among these mechanisms is the constitutional proscription against the removal of high-level officials by civilian authorities. The currently serving commanders of the army, air force, navy, and national police cannot be removed by the president; neither could Aylwin remove members of the governing junta that continued to serve during his tenure. Though the president is charged with naming commanders in chief, they must be chosen from among the five most senior officers in each of the services and are to be vested with a four-year term, during which they cannot be removed.[86] The military is further insulated from civilian authorities by the organic laws governing promotions, hiring, firing, training, internal affairs, and military justice. According to these laws, responsibility for each of these activities rests squarely within the individual military institutions.

Given that a constitutional amendment would be necessary to transform the status of the armed forces, it is unlikely, at least in the near future, that there will be any significant erosion in the constitutional power of the armed forces.

"Semiautonomous" Institutions and Appointed Senators

In addition to the *inamovilidad* (unremovability) of high-level military officials, the constitution also provides for the existence of a National Security Council, a Constitutional Tribunal, and a number of senators designated by the outgoing authoritarian regime. Critics of the 1980 constitution have characterized these institutions as being completely controlled by the armed forces.[87] However, it is important to recognize that the influence and latitude of military leaders vary in regard to each, as there is limited civilian influence in terms of membership and appointments (see below). What is more, as Pinochet appointees step down, elected presidents will gain increased influence in determining their membership. Nonetheless, there is also undeniably a permanent institutionalized role for the armed forces, given the legal stipulations that determine the pool of candidates from which officials can be chosen.

---

86. According to Article 93 of the *Constitución Política de la República de Chile*, commanders may be called on to retire by the president but only with the expressed consent of the National Security Council. Nonetheless, given the composition of the council (discussed below), it is unlikely, except in extraordinary circumstances, that the president would be successful in any attempt to remove these officers.

87. For a typical error in interpretation of this type that appears often in the press, see Gabriel Escobar, "In Chile, Army Bows to Civil Justice," *The Washington Post*, 1 June 1995, A16. Escobar incorrectly writes, "In contrast to Argentina and Brazil where the military abjured politics in the 1980s, Chile's armed forces are ensured budgetary autonomy, have seats on the national security council and can appoint a number of legislators." While he is correct in most regards, the military does not appoint legislators. Rather, the president appoints them from a field of senior members of the military.

The National Security Council is empowered to convene in times of crisis and to "make known" its concerns to the government with respect to any "event, act, or subject matter, which in its judgement gravely challenges the bases of the institutional order or could threaten national security."[88] According to the original text of the 1980 constitution, voting members of the council included the president of the republic, the president of the Senate, the president of the Supreme Court, and the four commanders in chief of the armed forces and the national police.[89] Given its composition, military officers had the required absolute majority to make decisions and adopt agreements. Constitutional reforms in 1989 increased the council's membership to eight by adding to its ranks the comptroller general of the republic. This innovation provided that the military would require the vote of at least one civilian member in order to ratify agreements.[90] Nonetheless, it should be borne in mind that, for at least the next few years, both the comptroller general and the president of the Supreme Court are Pinochet appointees.[91] What is more, the fact remains that four of the council's members must be military officers, which effectively institutionalizes a tutelary role for the armed forces even after the retirement of its current members.

The constitution also established important limitations on the Congress and the executive in regard to constitutional matters and the legality of ordinary legislation. The 1980 constitution provided for the existence of a Constitutional Tribunal empowered with the ability to make absolute and

88. The original, prereform constitution had much stronger wording in regard to the role of the Council. Article 96 of the *Constitución Política de la República de Chile* stated that the council could "Representar, a cualquier autoridad establecida por la Constitución, su opinión frente a algún hecho, acto o materia que a su juicio atente gravemente en contra de las bases de la institucionalidad o pueda comprometer la seguridad nacional." Given the vagueness of "representar" in terms of whether it entails action, veto power, or simply an expression of opinion, negotiators succeeded in having the wording of the article changed to "hacer presente." For a discussion of the significance of this change, see Carlos Andrade Geywitz, *Reforma de la Constitución Política de la República de Chile de 1980* (Santiago: Editorial Jurídica de Chile, 1991), 233–34.

89. In Chile, the national police, or *Carabineros*, are under the umbrella of command of the armed forces.

90. The constitution says nothing concerning the resolution of questions in the case of a tie. Constitutional analysts have suggested that in such a case the council would simply adopt no accord.

91. The prevalence of Pinochet appointees at all levels in the justice system is further reinforced by the fact that the Eighth Transitory Provision of the 1980 constitution established that the required age for retirement of judicial officials (75) would not apply to senior judges serving at the time the constitution took effect. See *Constitución Política de la República de Chile*, Article 77 and the Eighth Transitory Provision.

binding decisions on questions of constitutionality at any phase of the legislative process.[92] The tribunal is made up of seven members appointed for
staggered eight-year terms. The president and the Senate select one each, the
National Security Council two, and the Supreme Court three. At any phase
of the legislative process, the tribunal has the power to determine the constitutional admissibility of all laws or legislation. It also has the power to
declare unconstitutional decrees issued by the president of the republic. For
these purposes the tribunal is the court of last resort and "no appeal whatso-
ever shall apply against [its] decisions."[93] The tribunal also has the responsibility to resolve conflicts between official representatives of the executive
and legislative branches. While in comparative cross-national terms the existence of such a court is not unusual, the fact that its composition is not
determined by popularly elected authorities is.

In an effort to provide a neutral, apolitical, and "mature" component
within the legislative branch, the 1980 constitution provided for the designation of nine appointed senators.[94] The president appoints two, one required
to be a former university president and one a former minister of state. The
Supreme Court names three. The National Security Council designates four
senators, each of whom must be a former commander of the army, national
police (Carabineros), navy, and air force, who has held that post for at least
two years. One senator must be chosen from each of the four services.

Reformers argued that because designated senators would be tied to no
constituency and would not have to face reelection, they would exercise
more judgment and act more genuinely in promoting the interests of the
nation as a whole rather than the goals of a particular political sector.[95]

92. The Constitutional Tribunal was not an innovation of the 1980 constitution. It was
originally created in 1970 as a final arbiter on constitutional matters. However, it was prevented from ever effectively functioning given its politicization during the Allende administration.

93. *Constitución Política de la República de Chile*, Article 83.

94. In the original text of the 1980 constitution, there were only to be twenty-six popularly
elected senators. However, according to Article 25 of Constitutional Reform Law No. 18.825
of 17 August 1989, the number of elected senators was increased to thirty-eight, providing
them more relative weight than was accorded in the original document.

95. For a discussion of the role of the designated senators, see Sergio Carrasco Delgado,
"Composición del Senado en Chile: Institución de los Senadores Designados," *Jornadas de
derecho público* 20 (1990): 117–30. While most legislators interviewed favored the elimination
of the designated senators, many also acknowledged that they had played a constructive role in
perfecting legislation, particularly in the areas in which they had special expertise. Of the
deputies interviewed, 100 percent of the Concertación deputies favored the elimination of the
designated senators, and 33 percent of the opposition supported this option. Several deputies
and senators pointed to the constructive role played by designated Senator Ronald McIntyre

Given that the first set of senators was appointed by Pinochet in an effort to ensure a majority for the Right in the Senate, their behavior has been anything but "apolitical." These senators have deprived the Concertación of the electoral majority it had garnered in the first three senatorial elections following the return of democracy, giving the Right a majority of seats in the upper house. While the "institutionals" certainly have not voted as a bloc with the Right in all situations, in general terms they have been a reliable ally for this sector.[96] Given the veto power for the Right that the designated senators provided, elected members of the legislature and the president were limited in the scope and types of legislation that could be proposed, given their recognition that it would need to be acceptable to the designated senators in order to pass. In the future, democratically elected presidents will play a larger role in the appointment of senators both in direct appointments and in promoting and naming the other officials responsible for designating senators. However, the requirement that several must be chosen from among the ranks of the armed forces or bodies influenced by them limits the latitude of presidents in the appointment process.

High Legislative Quorum Requirements

A final limit on popular sovereignty and the power of the legislature lies in the high quorum requirements established for the modification of the constitution. In order to reform the constitution, it is necessary to have the approval of the president and three-fifths of the membership of both houses of Congress (as opposed to those present and voting). For constitutional amendments concerning the powers of the president, constitutional rights and obligations, or the status of the armed forces, the Constitutional Tribunal, or the National Security Council, a two-thirds majority in both houses is

---

Mendoza in improving the complicated "Ley de Pesca" (fishing law), given the insights he could provide as a former naval official. Indeed, the two designated senators interviewed for this study, Olga Feliú and William Thayer, were among the most impressive in terms of their sophisticated and broad knowledge of legislative process and legal precepts. Their interviews were also two of the longest, given that neither senator had to face the time limitations produced by the necessity of dealing with constituents or traveling to a home district.

96. One of the biggest difficulties in undertaking legislative research in Chile is the reality that roll call votes and voice votes are not published as part of the public record, and until relatively recently were not made public at all. Therefore, it is difficult to determine how often appointed senators sided with the Right. The assertions made here were based on interviews with senators of both the government and the opposition who contended that the appointed senators were reliable allies for the Right.

required.[97] While these quorums may not seem particularly high in comparative perspective, one should again bear in mind the complete constellation of institutional variables inherited from the previous regime. The advantages accorded the parties of the Right by the electoral system and appointed senators make what seems like a moderate quorum quite a bit higher. Given the veto power provided to the Right by the designated senators, combined with the benefits it received as a result of the design of the electoral system, it was impossible for the Aylwin administration to be successful in undertaking any significant constitutional reform; in addition, reforms could not be undertaken during the Frei administration given the similar constellation of political forces. The significance of this quorum will change, of course, with a distinct partisan distribution of seats in the legislature. Nonetheless, given the reality of the continued existence of multipartism in Chile, it is doubtful that in any context a coalition can muster the "supermajority" necessary to engage in constitutional reform in the near future.

Conclusion

Military reformers were, thus, quite successful in creating powerful checks on civilian authorities and political parties, through an ingenious combination of presidential domination and electoral and institutional engineering.[98]

The scope of legislative prerogatives has been dramatically narrowed compared with earlier periods in modern constitutional history, and the president has become the dominant legislative actor. Congress is effectively barred from a significant role in the legislative process, and its oversight functions are toothless and have proven ineffective.

The parliamentary electoral system was designed in a clear attempt to limit the scope of parties represented in Congress and to give the Right disproportionate political influence. When the advantages reaped by the

97. There is a hierarchy of quorums established by the constitution depending on the type of legislation being passed. For regular or "normal" legislation, an absolute majority is required. For constitutional organic laws, a four-sevenths majority is required, while for "constitutional reforms" or "laws interpreting constitutional precepts" a three-fifths majority is necessary except in those areas discussed here. See Articles 63, 116, and 117 of *Constitución Política de la República de Chile*.

98. For a general discussion of constitutional engineering, the important variables that can be manipulated to undertake it, and what determines its effectiveness, see Giovanni Sartori, *Comparative Constitutional Engineering* (New York: New York University Press, 1994).

Right are combined with high quorums to amend the constitution, the controls on popular sovereignty discussed here clearly cannot be legislated away easily.

Finally, there are functional limits on the latitude of both the president and the Congress, given the existence of undemocratic mechanisms designed to check civilian power. It is the very institutions whose membership is influenced by the military that are primarily responsible for designating the officials who will serve in other state institutions that retain veto power over the actions of popularly elected leaders.

What significance does this institutional framework for limited democracy have in terms of long-term democratic governability in Chile? Preliminary evidence from the first four years of democratic government suggests that the military government succeeded in designing a framework for the smooth conduct of democratic politics. However, as the next chapter will argue, one should not be misled by the apparent success of the first administration, given the overwhelming influence of the positive economic and transitional political context that set the stage for governmental success. Chapter 2 turns to an analysis of the Aylwin administration, pointing to the contextual features of the transition process that helped to make it one of the most accomplished governments in Chilean history. This is followed by a preliminary evaluation of the Frei administration.

2

THE AYLWIN ADMINISTRATION AND THE POLITICS OF TRANSITION

A Preliminary Assessment of the Chilean Presidential System

To students of contemporary Chilean politics, the potentially dim picture of the future of executive/legislative relations in Chile suggested to this point may seem inconsistent.[1] Contrary to much of what has been presented here, the first four years of democratic government in Chile were characterized by excellent relations between the branches of government. What is more, Chile has been lauded as an exemplary case of stable democratic transition.[2] Are the arguments presented up until now invalid, given that empirical evidence from the Aylwin administration provides so little support for them? Contrary to what has been said so far, did the Chilean military succeed in devising an institutional framework for stable democratic governance?

1. I am grateful to Alejandro Foxley Tapia for his insights on several issues discussed in this chapter.
2. For discussions of the Chilean political transition, see Joseph Tulchin and Augusto Varas, eds., *From Dictatorship to Democracy: Rebuilding Political Consensus in Chile* (Boulder, Colo.: Lynne Rienner Publishers, 1991); Mark Falcoff, Arturo Valenzuela, and Susan Kaufman Purcell, *Chile: Prospects for Democracy* (New York: Council on Foreign Relations, 1988); Edgardo Boeninger, "Consolidation in Chile," *Journal of Democracy* 2, no. 3 (1991): 57–60; and Marcelo Cavarozzi, "Patterns of Elite Negotiation and Confrontation in Argentina and Chile," in *Elites and Democratic Consolidation in Latin America and Southern Europe*, ed. John Higley and Richard Gunther (New York: Cambridge University Press, 1992).

This chapter argues that the roots of the success of the Aylwin administration, and the smooth conduct of executive/legislative relations, are not the results of successful institutional engineering on the part of the military. Rather, the success of the first postauthoritarian government lies in the temporary party, social, and political contexts created by the process of democratic transition itself, which muted many underlying conflicts and divisions. The recognized necessity of maintaining the integrity of the democratic transition has helped to stem interbranch conflict and to override some of the potential problems of democratic governability created by the incongruence between society and institutions that this study posits.

This chapter goes on to argue that, once the contextual features of the Chilean transition fade in importance, or a future government faces a severe economic or other type of crisis, the incentives for the maintenance of this pattern of cooperation will diminish. A brief discussion of the Frei administration points to already emerging fissures in the postauthoritarian consensus. The chapter concludes that, with the gradual disappearance of the special context of the period of democratic transition, some of the consequences of the incongruence between society and institutions explored in following chapters will become more apparent.

The Aylwin Administration and the Politics of Democratic Transition

Unlike many of the presidential successions in recent Latin American history, President Aylwin transferred the presidential sash to his successor in 1994 with exceedingly high approval ratings. The Aylwin government was quite successful in confronting the myriad complex and controversial issues that invariably arise in an immediate postauthoritarian situation. The Ministry of Finance, headed by Alejandro Foxley, performed exceedingly well in maintaining macroeconomic stability and continuity in economic policy-making, reassuring the business community and successfully brokering negotiations with labor. Relations with the armed forces, though characterized by tense moments and sometimes acrimonious exchanges, were prudently managed. Though government authorities occasionally criticized the armed forces for meddling in civilian politics, the government never threatened the military's fundamental institutional interests, and there have been no serious threats of military incursions into politics. At the same time, the Commission for Truth and Reconciliation formed by President Aylwin systematically investigated most instances of human rights violations that occurred during the previous regime, though not to the extent hoped for by victims and their families, who have demanded an end to the government's policy of impunity for violators.

In terms of executive/assembly relations, during the first four years of democratic rule an impressive array of initiatives has been proposed, discussed, and promulgated. In the first four years of democratic government (1990–94), 440 bills were presented, discussed, and published as law.[3]

About 92 percent of these initiatives originated in the executive branch, demonstrating an impressive record of interbranch cooperation, especially considering that the government did not enjoy a majority in the Senate due to the bloc of institutional senators. Tables 2.1 and 2.2 present a breakdown of election results in terms of the percentage of popular vote received by each party and coalition. The party composition of both chambers during the Aylwin administration and the first four years of the Frei administration is also given.

There were approximately 250 working days per year during the first four legislative periods, meaning that it took the Congress and the president an average of only 2.3 days to dispatch a law (see Table 1.1 for a summary of promulgated laws). However, these figures take into account only the presidential messages and congressional motions that were converted into law. During this period, the Congress had to consider 1,166 proposals, an average of 1.2 proposals per day.[4] Throughout the Aylwin period, the president vetoed only 16 proposals. When he did, only one of these vetoes was overridden by Congress. What is more, only 6 of the president's proposals were voted down by Congress.[5]

However, simply passing and debating a high number of proposals is not the only significant indicator of interbranch cooperation and the legislative success of the government. The qualitative content of the laws passed is also important. During these years, the president and Congress simultaneously had to govern and face a number of legal voids left by the outgoing administration

3. Proyecto de Modernización, Congreso Nacional de Chile, *Proceso legislativo chileno: Un enfoque cuantitativo* (Valparaíso: Proyecto de Modernización, Congreso Nacional de Chile, 1995), 16.
4. Ibid., 16–17.
5. Ibid., 62 and 77. Of course, several were withdrawn by the president in order to avoid defeat.

Table 2.1. Election results and distribution of seats in the Chilean Chamber of Deputies by party and coalition, 1989, 1993, 1997 (N = 120)

Year		1989[a]			1993			1997		
Pact	Party	Percentage of Votes	Number of Seats	Percentage of Seats	Percentage of Votes	Number of Seats	Percentage of Seats	Percentage of Votes	Number of Seats	Percentage of Seats
Concertación		51.5	72	60.0	55.4	70	58.3	50.5	70	58.3
	PDC	26.0	39	32.5	27.1	37	30.8	22.9	39	32.5
	PR	3.9	6	5.0	3.0	2	1.7	3.1	4	3.3
	PS	0.0[b]	18	15.0	12.0	15	12.5	11.1	11	9.2
	PPD	11.5	7	5.8	11.8	15	12.5	12.6	16	13.3
	Other	10.1	2	1.6	1.5	1	.8	.8	0	0.0
Unión por Chile[c]		34.2	48	40.0	36.7	50	41.7	36.2	47	39.2
	RN	18.3	32	26.7	16.3	29	24.2	16.8	23	19.2
	UDI	9.8	14	11.7	12.1	15	12.5	14.4	17	14.2
	Other	6.1	2	1.7	8.3	6	5.0	5.0	7	5.8
Independent and others not on major lists		14.3	0	0	7.8	0	0	13.2	3	2.5

(Table 2.1 continued)

SOURCES: Distributions of Seats: Congreso de Chile. Electoral Data: 1989, Modified from Servicio Electoral de Chile; 1993, Participa; 1997, *El Mercurio*, 12 December 1997, D14.

ABBREVIATIONS: PDC = Christian Democratic Party (Partido Demócrata Cristiano), PR = Partido Radical, PPD = Party for Democracy (Partido por la Democracia), PS = Partido Socialista (Socialist Party), RN = National Renewal (Renovación Nacional), UDI = Independent Democratic Union (Unión Demócrata Independiente).

[a] There was a great deal of fluidity in party identification after the 1989 election, given limitations on the registration of parties imposed by the outgoing government, and problems with individual candidate registration. The breakdown of party identification listed here represents the parties that candidates eventually joined, not necessarily the label under which these candidates ran in the election.

[b] This figure is 0 for 1989 because of problems with party legality and registration and the question of whether the PPD should simply disband and join the Socialists (once legalized), given that the former was created as an instrumental party designed to unite sectors on the moderate left in their single-minded goal in eliciting a return to democracy in Chile. Thus, the movement of legislators between the two parties was fluid. Those candidates elected who eventually assumed the PS label really ran under the PPD label. This explains the lack of votes for the PS in the 1989 elections. Similarly, many candidates on the right characterized as "others" later joined one of the major parties of the right. While the statistics for votes reflect what parties polled in actual elections, the statistics for the makeup of both the Chamber and the Senate reflect the genuine party composition of the assembly for the majority of the Aylwin administration after party identification had been solidified.

[c] This pact in previous elections has also been known as Democracia y Progreso and Unión por el Progreso.

Table 2.2. Election results and distribution of seats in the Chilean Senate by party and coalition, 1989, 1993, 1997 (N = 48 [38 elected, 9 appointed] for 1989 and 1993; N = 47 [38 elected, 9 appointed, 1 former president] for 1997)

Pact	Party	1989			1993			1997		
		Percentage of Votes	Number of Seats	Percentage of Seats	Percentage of Votes	Number of Seats	Percentage of Seats	Percentage of Votes	Number of Seats	Percentage of Seats
Concertación		54.4	22	46.8	55.5	21	44.7	51.7	20	41.7
	PDC	31.9	13	27.7	20.3	14	29.8	29.4	14	29.2
	PR	2.2	3	6.4	6.3	1	2.1	1.8	0	0.0
	PS	0.0[a]	4	8.5	12.7	4	8.5	14.6	2	4.2
	PPD	12.1	1	2.1	14.7	2	4.2	4.3	4	8.3
	Other	8.2	1	2.1	1.5	0	0	1.6	0	0
Unión por Chile		34.9	25	53.2	39.5	26	55.3	36.6	28	58.3
	RN	10.8	13	27.7	14.9	11	23.4	14.8	7	14.6
	UDI	5.1	2	4.2	11.2	3	6.4	17.2	5	10.4
	Other	19.0	1	2.1	13.4	3	6.4	4.6	6	12.5
	Appointed[b]	0	9	19.1	0	9	19.1	0	10	20.8
Independent and others not on major lists		10.7	0	0	5.0	0	0	11.7	0	0

(Table 2.2 continued)

SOURCES: All sources are identical to Table 2.1. Only the 1997 Senate elections are from a distinct source (Servicio Electoral de Chile).

ABBREVIATIONS: See Table 2.1

NOTES: All elective Senate seats were up for election in the 1989 elections. However, according to the Constitution, only half of the Senate is elected every four years. Hence, the 1993 and 1997 elections reflect returns for elections determining the membership of half the Senate. Nonetheless, given that we are attempting to make some generalizations concerning the effects of partisan power, the turnout in terms of the final membership of the Senate is presented in the table.

General Pinochet stepped down as commander in chief of the armed forces in 1997 and assumed a lifelong Senate seat. He is included with the appointed senators after this date because his mandate, like those of the "institutionals," is not based on popular election. Pinochet is counted among the appointed Senators when calculating the percentage of total seats after 1997.

[a] There was a great deal of fluidity in party identification during and immediately after the 1989 elections due to problems with party legality and registration and the question of whether the PPD should simply disband and join the Socialists (once legalized), given that the former was created as an instrumental party designed to unite sectors on the moderate left in their single-minded goal in eliciting a return to democracy in Chile. Thus, the movement of legislators between the two parties was fluid. Those candidates elected who eventually assumed the PS label really ran under the PPD label. This explains the lack of votes for the PS in the 1989 elections. Similarly, many candidates on the right characterized as "others" later joined one of the major parties of the right. While the statistics for votes reflect what parties polled in actual elections, the statistics for the makeup of both the Chamber and the Senate reflect the genuine party composition of the assembly for the majority of the Aylwin administration after party identification had been solidified.

[b] Appointed senators have no obligation to support the right, but they are listed along with this sector because voting records suggest that they usually do, and that they provide effective veto power for the right on especially controversial legislation. One of the appointed senators during the Aylwin administration died in office and was not replaced, so only eight appointed senators served during his term.

in a short time. During the first four congressional periods, the Congress and president passed a number of major, complex, and often controversial measures into law, including:

• Modifications of the Fishing Law (Ley de Pesca—numerous laws)
• Establishment of democratic local governments (Law 19.130 and others)
• Laws on regional administration and government (Laws 19.097 and 19.175)
• Creation of a National Women's Service (SERNAM—Servicio Nacional de la Mujer) and National Youth Institute (Instituto Nacional de la Juventud) (Laws 19.023 and 19.042, respectively)
• Reforms in the Administration of Justice, including modification of the criminal code on terrorism and issues involving political prisoners (Law 19.027)
• Tax Reform Law (Reforma Tributaria) (Law 18.985)
• Creation of the National Return Office, to ease the reintegration of returning political exiles; and the National Reparation and Reconciliation Commission, to deal with restitution for victims of human rights abuses (Laws 18.994 and 19.123, respectively)
• Creation of the Ministry of the General Secretary of the Presidency (SEG-PRES) (Law 18.993)
• Establishment of customs benefits for political exiles (Law 19.128)

Interviews with members of the Chamber and the Senate confirm these impressive indicators of cooperation. During interviews, members of Congress from all parties, even the opposition, underscored the favorable state of relations between the branches of government. Ninety percent of all deputies and 83.4 percent of opposition deputies interviewed agreed with the characterization of the first four years of interbranch relations as "fluid and cooperative." In addition, when rating the quality of legislation originating in the executive branch, 86.7 percent of all deputies and 75 percent of opposition deputies sampled rated proposals originating in the executive branch as "good or average."

Thus, both statistical and interview data point to a favorable state of relations between the branches of government during the first four years of democracy in Chile. These results are paradoxical, given the conclusions of much recent theoretical work on presidentialism suggesting that political systems characterized by extremely powerful presidents tend to be more prone to interbranch conflict and less stable.[6] What are the roots of the success of this government, and more particularly the impressive record of executive/assembly relations?

Contextual Variables and the Legislative Successes of the Aylwin Presidency

Perhaps the most important contextual feature that allowed the Chilean presidential system to function so well in the face of all of the challenges posed to the new government was the unique circumstances of the democratic transition itself. Undoubtedly, the first democratic government benefited enormously from the fiscal health and economic policies inherited from the previous regime. However, from a political perspective, and unlike other Latin American democratic transitions, in Chile no set of actors involved was able to impose its will completely upon another. General Augusto Pinochet failed to achieve victory in the plebiscite of 1988 and stay on as president, but at the same time the leaders of the opposition were unable to defeat the constitutional straitjacket imposed by the outgoing regime, despite the constitutional reforms of 1989 and 1991. In addition, though the parties of the Concertación achieved an impressive victory in the first democratic election, they were denied a majority in the Senate because of the institution of appointed senators and had to deal with an opposition overrepresented in both chambers of Congress due to the characteristics of the electoral system designed by the previous government.[7]

These exigencies forced the government into a position in which it had to seek majorities through negotiation and compromise in order to introduce change and reform in a gradual manner. These dynamics set the stage for the *"democracia consensual"* (consensual democracy) that would be the defining principle of the first democratic government.

6. See Shugart and Carey, *Presidents and Assemblies*, and Mainwaring and Shugart, eds., *Presidentialism and Democracy in Latin America*. Later chapters of this study, and especially Chapter 5, discuss this reality in more detail.
    7. For a discussion of how the electoral system was designed to overrepresent the Right, and succeeded in doing so, as well as of the long-term significance of the electoral system in terms of democratic governability, see Arturo Valenzuela and Peter Siavelis, "Ley electoral y estabilidad democrática," 27–87.

Political elites recognized the precariousness of the political situation produced by the incomplete victory of civilian authorities. Throughout the
research for this study, only a handful of interviewees failed to refer to the
"special time" or "special context" of the transition as both an important
element shaping immediate postauthoritarian politics and an important
variable affecting their behavior.

However, it was not simply the general environment of the postauthoritarian political landscape that affected elite behavior; the transition itself
also produced some concrete and important political phenomena. In particular, the context of the democratic transition helped to produce two features that were key to the success of the Aylwin government, first in terms
of the party system, and second in terms of the structure and conduct of
executive/assembly relations.

The Transitional Party System and Governmental Success

One of the most important moderating features of the Chilean democratic
transition was how its contextual and legal framework encouraged competition between a center-left (the Concertación) and center-right (Unión por
Chile[8]) coalition. This dynamic of bipolar party competition, which characterized the political system during the first two postauthoritarian governments, was an important departure from the traditional three-bloc pattern
of competition that had been the distinguishing feature of the Chilean party
system since mid-century.[9] There is some controversy concerning the significance, and indeed the existence, of this pattern, which was known as the
"three-thirds" party system. It is undeniable that the size of these thirds has
varied a great deal and that it is not easy to fit all historically significant
party sectors into one of them, especially the populist Ibáñismo movement
of the 1950s. Nonetheless, in general terms, shifting alliances among these
three sectors constituted the predominant pattern of coalition formation
and interaction from 1925 until the advent of the authoritarian regime.

However, departing from this general pattern, a bipolar competitive
dynamic grew out of the natural correlation of forces produced by the 1988
plebiscite and contributed to the success of the transition by structuring

---

8. This alliance has changed its name before each election. It has been known as
Democracia y Progreso, Unión por el Progreso, and Unión por Chile.
9. The significance of the three-bloc pattern of competition known as the Chilean tres tercios has been described well by Arturo Valenzuela. See his "Party Politics and the Crisis of
Presidentialism in Chile."

competition between the government and a loyal opposition. In the period leading up to the plebiscite, the deep divisions that characterized the Chilean democratic opposition parties throughout the authoritarian regime were eclipsed by their effort to achieve one goal: an end to the authoritarian regime.[10] In addition, the democratic opposition recognized the political exigencies of the new electoral law, which made it clear that the only way to ensure a decent showing for its parties was to form joint congressional lists. The unified front that formed out of this collective effort led to an alliance in the presidential and legislative elections of 1989. The success of the first government, combined with similar electoral incentives, encouraged the maintenance of the Concertación alliance for the second presidential election in December 1993 and for the legislative elections of 1993 and 1997.

This pattern of party competition has had two major consequences. First, for the first two presidential elections, the traditional problem of Chilean presidents elected with a *"doble minoría"* (receiving less than 50 percent of the popular vote and lacking a legislative majority) has been avoided. Though the constitution of 1980 provides for a presidential second-round election if the highest-polling candidate does not receive a majority of the popular vote, for the first two elections both Patricio Aylwin Azocar and Eduardo Frei Ruiz-Tagle were elected with a level of support of more than 50 percent (55.17 percent and 58.01 percent, respectively).[11] This gave both clearer mandates than most Chilean presidents have had, and Frei the most significant majority of any president since 1931.[12] The ability of the major parties of the center-left and center-right to coalesce, and of each to choose a single standard-bearer in both elections, produced a dynamic of competition

10. For discussions of the political opposition to the military regime, see J. Samuel Valenzuela and Arturo Valenzuela, eds., *Military Rule in Chile: Dictatorship and Opposition* (Baltimore: Johns Hopkins University Press, 1986), and Manuel Antonio Garretón, "The Political Opposition and the Party System Under the Authoritarian Regime," in *The Struggle for Democracy in Chile*, ed. Drake and Jaksic.

11. According to the 1925 constitution, presidential races in which no candidate won a majority of the vote were decided in the Chamber of Deputies. Election results for Eduardo Frei are from Ministerio del Interior de Chile, "Informativo Elecciones 1993," Cómputo no. 4 (99.06 percent of the total vote computed), and for Patricio Aylwin from *El Mercurio*, 12 December 1993, A12. On the significance of second-round presidential elections for democratic governability, see Mark Jones, *Electoral Laws and the Survival of Presidential Democracy* (South Bend, Ind.: University of Notre Dame Press, 1995).

12. Four of the last five preauthoritarian presidents were elected without a majority of the popular vote: Gabriel González Videla, Carlos Ibáñez del Campo, Jorge Alessandri Rodríguez, and Salvador Allende Gossens. The only president who could claim as strong a popular mandate since the 1930s was the current president's father, Eduardo Frei Montalva, who received 55.67 percent of the vote in 1964.

between two major candidates (despite the participation of presidential aspirants from smaller, less popular parties).

But, more important, the two-candidate presidential race combined with the influence of the parliamentary electoral system led to the formation of joint lists for congressional elections. This dynamic of competition has consistently provided the Concertación government a majority in the Chamber of Deputies and a near majority in the Senate. Through negotiation with opposition and institutional senators, the government has been able to ensure the passage of the most significant legislation and to avoid executive/assembly deadlock. Had these two legislative and presidential alliances not existed, and the president not had the benefit of a multiparty governing coalition, the government would have faced a far more arduous task in terms of its legislative agenda.

There are additional characteristics of the party system that also helped to ensure the government's success in its legislative agenda. However, these features are a product both of the democratic transition and of the traditional behavior and norms of interaction of Chilean parties.

Historically, party elites in Chile maintained a great deal of control over political recruitment. For congressional elections before 1958, party leaders determined the order in which candidates would appear on electoral lists. Candidate order, in turn, determined which members of a list would be elected, irrespective of the number or percentage of the vote received by individual candidates. This gave party leaders the leverage necessary to ensure loyalty and party discipline. Reforms in 1958 provided that the highest-polling candidates on particular lists would be elected, undercutting the influence of party leaders. Nonetheless, party elites still kept a tight rein on parliamentary candidatures, providing for continuing influence in the legislative and electoral arena, by sanctioning members who consistently violated the rules of party discipline.

While a system of primaries was recently introduced within the Concertación coalition for congressional elections, the tradition of party control and discipline is still deeply ingrained. Even with primaries, voting is restricted to party members, who must face a comparatively difficult test of loyalty in order to vote in party elections. Rank-and-file members, though free to choose any candidate, are in practice influenced by party elites. This control and influence extend into the Congress itself, where party loyalty can mean the difference between receiving a party-backed candidature in the next election or not. This dynamic of elite party control has been reinforced by the new parliamentary electoral system. Given that there are a limited number of seats per district, and that it is party elites who engage in negotiations ultimately to determine which candidates they will officially back, parties have been able to continue to ensure discipline. The tradition of party cohesion and discipline was reinforced by the recognized delicacy of the transition process and by the precariousness of the Concertación's majority in Congress. Party cohesion has served the Concertación well in terms of the coherence of policy and coalition maintenance.

Government Structure, Elite Behavior, and the Success of Executive/Assembly Relations

While the dynamic of party competition described above helped to encourage cooperation, the impressive record of executive/assembly relations during the Aylwin government was also rooted in the structure of the executive branch and the behavior of executive and legislative actors. Many of these arguments also help to explain the success of the Frei administration, though, as will be noted later, the politics of *democracia consensual* do appear to be under much greater stress as of late.

In structural terms, each of the ministries during the Aylwin administration was staffed with an undersecretary that belonged to a different party of the Concertación alliance than that of the minister. In this way, the influence and interests of the various parties of the coalition were balanced through participation in ministerial decisions. This integration of the members of the coalition precluded the dominance of the main Christian Democratic Party and was key in maintaining the loyal collaboration of coalition members, both in the assembly and in the executive branch. A more vertical Christian Democratic–centered organizational framework would have been open to charges of attempting to dominate the governing process and would have been more likely to produce partisan infighting, weakening the coalition's strength and the legislative capacities of the executive branch.[13]

13. For a discussion of this point and other aspects of the organization of the presidency that helped to encourage cooperation, see Alfredo Rehren, "Organizing the Presidency for the Consolidation of Democracy in the Southern Cone" (paper presented at the Seventeenth International Congress of the Latin American Studies Association, Los Angeles, 24–27 September 1992). Rehren suggests that the discussion in the literature concerning the desirability of parliamentary systems may be missing the point. He contends that presidential leadership styles and the organization of the presidency may be more important contributing factors to the success of presidential governments. While his analysis concerning how these variables helped to make the Aylwin presidency a success are certainly not contradicted by evidence presented here, he perhaps overstates their importance. Leadership and organizational variables

Much of the coordination within the executive branch and between it and Congress is centered within the Ministry of the General Secretary of the Presidency (SEGPRES).[14] Elevated to the ministerial level early in the Aylwin administration, this body is composed of several divisions, each with a different area of responsibility. The Division of Interministerial Coordination is responsible for ensuring the coherence of government policy and for coordinating work and brokering negotiations between each of the ministerial commissions. It also plays a pivotal advisory role in the elaboration of all of the initiatives that the president sends to Congress. In maintaining functional and harmonious relationships between each of the ministries made up of individuals from the diverse parties of the Concertación, SEGPRES has been key.

All proposals for legislation from each of the ministries pass through the SEGPRES, which acts as both a clearinghouse and a "filter" for legislation.[15] The Judicial/Legislative Division then consults each of the other ministries with potential involvement in a given issue and elaborates proposed legislation, taking into consideration input from the ministries, the goals of the president, and questions of constitutionality. The SEGPRES often forms commissions made up of representatives of other ministries to draft bills and to discuss the goals and technical aspects of legislation. Once a project has been elaborated, and before it is sent to Congress, SEGPRES returns it to the appropriate minister for his or her signature, after which it is sent to the president for final approval. This process has ensured the coherence of proposed legislation within the government's program, and eased the potential for conflict between ministries (and between parties), given the extensive interministerial (and thus interparty) consultation to which each initiative is subject.

Equally important, the Division of Political Relations of the SEGPRES maintains open and fluid communications between it and other social and

---

only help to overcome the tensions a presidential system may create; they do not eliminate them. With different executives having distinct management and personal styles, the problems associated with exaggerated presidentialism can easily reemerge, as will be stressed in detail in the following chapters.

14. For a discussion of the foundation, structure, and key role of the Ministry of the General Secretary of the Presidency, see Blanca Arthur, "La otra cara de la Moneda," *El Mercurio*, 1 April 1990, D1–D2; Lucy Davila, "Los fundamentos de ese proyecto de ley que crea un Ministerio que ya existe," *La Epoca*, 22 April 1990, 9; and Emilio Rojo, "El trabajo silencioso de una división," *La Epoca*, 7 December 1992, 13.

15. Interview with César Ladrón de Guevara Pardo, advisor, Judicial/Legislative Division of the Ministry of the General Secretary of the Presidency, Santiago, 28 April 1993.

political organizations, including political parties, unions, the Catholic Church and, most important, the parliamentary *jefes de bancada* (leaders of the legislative parties). To maintain constant government contacts with members, SEGPRES also has a permanent staff within Congress.

During the Aylwin administration, there was also a high degree of interaction among executive and assembly representatives throughout the legislative process. Interbranch relations were conducted through a series of informal meetings between members of congressional committees and the representatives of the executive working in the same policy areas. In addition, all of the Concertación *jefes de bancada* met each Monday with ministers to determine the legislative agenda for the week. Representatives of the executive branch lobbied for fast consideration of the proposals that they deemed most important, while legislators updated the government on the status of pending proposals and on whether or not they needed more time to fully consider and vote on legislation. By mutual accord and negotiation, they decided which projects would have priority.[16] The president often based his declarations of urgency, or their withdrawal, on the outcome of these meetings.

This pattern of cooperation has not been limited to relations between parties of the governing coalition. The parties of the center-right also played a vital role as members of the loyal opposition willing to broker negotiations between the military and the Concertación, both in regard to the reforms of the 1980 constitution and later through participation in the *democracia consensual*, which characterized the first government. Indeed, President Aylwin and representatives of the executive branch often entered into negotiations directly with the center-right in order to reach solutions to controversial legislative issues, some would say going over the heads of Concertación members of Congress. This occurred most notably during negotiations on the proposal for Aylwin's Reforma Tributaria. Aylwin negotiated directly with business leaders and legislators on the Right to reach an agreement on the most controversial aspects of tax reform. Despite occasional criticisms by members of the governing coalition, this type of executive behavior moderated many of the Concertación's proposals, making them more acceptable to a broader range of political parties and more likely to pass in Congress.

Managing relations between the chambers of Congress has also been a crucial component of cooperation, given that the Concertación lacked a majority in the Senate. The constant contact between the president and

16. Interview with César Ladrón de Guevara Pardo, 28 April 1993.

members of Congress and opposition party leaders helped the government to navigate legislation through the Senate. The constitution provides that if the Chamber and the Senate cannot come to an agreement on a particular piece of legislation, a *comisión mixta* (mixed committee of members of both the Chamber and the Senate) is to be formed in order to resolve controversial aspects of legislation.[17] Nonetheless, the two chambers were able to agree on a vast majority of legislation during the Aylwin administration, with only 43 of the 440 bills passed being forced into a *comisión mixta*.[18]

This is not to suggest that the Senate and the Chamber have not clashed. During the 1993 legislative session, the Chamber of Deputies had begun to tire of what many of its membership saw as unnecessary modifications to legislation made by the Senate. Many members of the Chamber perceived these changes as "make-work," a waste of time, and simply an effort by the Senate to establish its predominance in the legislative process. Deputies of the governing parties agreed to send a message to the Senate. When the controversial bill restructuring the state television station was returned to the Chamber with extensive changes, a Concertación deputy was charged with determining which of the paragraphs the Senate had modified. When it came time for a paragraph-by-paragraph vote on the bill, the deputy indicated with a thumbs-up or thumbs-down whether the paragraph had been subject to Senate modifications. If it had, all members of the governing parties voted to defeat it, while if it had not, they voted to maintain it. Thus, the bill was forced into a mixed commission, and the deputies sent a strong message to the Senate that it should be more parsimonious and careful in undertaking modifications to pending legislation.[19] Despite periodic clashes, the Chamber and the Senate have been able to avoid prolonged conflict and deadlock. This is largely attributable to the crucial brokering role played by the government and the component parties of the Concertación.

Finally, interbranch relations have been helped by the unexpected role played by the designated senators. Despite initial expectations that they would always side with the opposition for key votes, the designated senators have been willing to reach agreements with the government to pass vital legislation. Certainly on legislation that was crucial to the Right, and

17. On *comisiones mixtas*, see Iván Mauricio Obando Camino, "El papel de las comisiones mixtas en el procedimiento legislativo," *Revista de derecho de la Universidad Católica de Valparaíso* 14 (1991–92): 343–68.
18. Proyecto de Modernización, Congreso Nacional de Chile, *Proceso legislativo chileno*, 74.
19. Off-the-record interview with a Concertación legislative aide, Valparaíso, 2 April 1993.

on that dealing with the legacy of the authoritarian regime, these senators provided important support and veto power.

However, structural features were not the only bases of the legislative success of the first government. The decisions and behavior of members of each of the branches of government have also been crucial. First, the executive branch avoided proposing legislation that challenged the fundamental interests of the right and of the military, including the status of the commanders in chief of the armed forces, prosecution for human rights abuses, and major constitutional reforms. The government was forced to take such a position because it lacked a majority in the Senate. At the same time, however, it also understood the need to maintain the *democracia consensual* fundamental to easing the tensions posed by the return of democratic politics.

Second, the president was willing to rescind urgencies, or to withdraw and redeclare them, in order to grant Congress extra time to consider proposals when necessary. Aylwin avoided unilateral executive decisions in regard to urgencies, consulting with members of Congress and respecting requests to withdraw urgencies when he was provided with valid evidence of the Chamber's need for more time to consider proposals.[20] What is more, during extraordinary legislative sessions, the executive was willing to allow the debate and study of bills presented by members of the Chamber and the Senate.

Third, though Congress is limited in the actions it can take in relation to the finances and the budget, the Ministry of Finance and President Aylwin engaged in voluntary and informal discussions and consultation with members of Congress in elaborating this type of legislation, giving legislators an effective voice in an area in which, in statutory terms, they should not have had any voice.[21] Both presidents certainly had incentives to provide members of Congress this input. Aylwin and Frei could conceivably have simply waited for the sixty-day limit on budgetary negotiations to expire, in which case their version of the budget would have taken effect.[22] However, budget negotiations have taken place each year between 1989 and 1998, and Congress has been able to extract concessions (albeit limited ones) from the president. Again, given the distribution of party forces, presidents have had limited incentives to attempt to impose their versions of the budget, given

20. Interview with César Ladrón de Guevara Pardo, Santiago, 28 April 1993.
21. Interview with Marta Tonda Mitri, Jefe de Gabinete, Ministerio de Hacienda, Santiago, 22 June 1993.
22. *Constitución Política de la República de Chile*, Article 57.

that they would be forced to deal with members of Congress later in reaching negotiated settlements on legislation unrelated to the budget.

On the assembly side, elite behavior and decisions also helped to stem conflict. Instead of attempting to block the urgencies designated by the president, the Congress was exceedingly cooperative in respecting the legislative agenda as determined by the executive branch, even though there were neither constitutional nor statutory penalties for ignoring the flood of presidential urgencies.

The picture of cooperation shown here, and the willingness of the president to negotiate the legislative agenda, is not to suggest that the president was sheepish in the employment of his powers, or that declared urgencies were ineffective or unnecessary. The Aylwin administration aggressively promoted its legislative agenda, extensively employing its power of exclusive initiative and declared executive urgencies. The use of executive urgencies was extremely important in ensuring the passage of the president's legislation. Fifty-six percent of the initiatives that were designated *"simple urgencia"* were converted into law, while 73 percent of those designated *"suma urgencia"* were passed. For the designation *"discusión inmediata,"* this percentage increased to a remarkable 92 percent.[23]

Aylwin was also quite successful in the use of his other faculties. Table 1.1 presented statistics on the origins of legislation that was converted into law. Nonetheless, it is also important to analyze how successful each branch of government was in having its bills considered at all, in order to get a complete picture of the likelihood of passage for congressional initiatives. Despite their cooperation during the first four years of democratic government, members of Congress rarely had their own initiatives even considered, let alone converted into law. Table 2.3 presents the total number of initiatives presented by both branches of government during the Aylwin administration, and whether they underwent the complete cycle of legislative consideration (irrespective of whether they were approved). Of all initiatives, the executive succeeded in navigating 70 percent of his proposals through Congress, while the legislature had only 13 percent of its own considered. A full 87 percent of Congress's proposals were left pending for the next government. Thus, two important determinants of the success of legislative initiatives were whether or not they originated in the executive branch, and the grade of urgency assigned to them.

23. Proyecto de Modernización, Congreso Nacional de Chile, *Proceso legislativo chileno,* 41. These data mask some important realities concerning the effects of urgency declarations. For a discussion, see Siavelis, "Exaggerated Presidentialism and Moderate Presidents."

Table 2.3. End Results of Presidential and Legislative Initiatives: Comparative Measures
of Success 1990-1993

| Status | Presidential Initiatives | | | | | |
	1990	1991	1992	1993	Total Number	Percentage
Presented	161	157	175	144	637	100
Considered	150	128	112	57	447	70
Pending	11	29	63	87	190	30

| Status | Congressional Initiatives | | | | | |
	1990	1991	1992	1993	Total Number	Percentage
Presented	137	156	148	88	529	100
Considered	35	22	10	2	69	13
Pending	102	134	138	86	460	87

SOURCE: Congreso Nacional de Chile.

Finally, in evaluating cooperation during the first postauthoritarian administration, it is important to acknowledge the influence of particular personalities and management styles in helping the government to succeed. The
capacity and personal characteristics of Patricio Aylwin helped to smooth
the way for cooperation. Though initially welcoming military intervention
in 1973, he quickly emerged as an early leader of the democratic opposition. In one of the first concrete expressions of resistance to the military
regime, Aylwin participated in drafting a proposed constitution distinct
from Pinochet's. He served as the official spokesman for the "No" campaign in the 1988 plebiscite and, despite his initial opposition to the constitution, was one of the first leaders to call for fighting the military regime
within its own legal framework. In the course of carrying out these roles, he
displayed remarkable conciliatory skills and gradually won the confidence
and support of leaders on the Left, whose suspicion of Aylwin for his initial
support of the coup eventually faded.

As president, Aylwin exhibited firm and decisive leadership. His skills as
a communicator, broker, and negotiator, combined with his respected
stature as a leader who played fair, helped to stem potential conflict between
the branches of government and to maintain coalition harmony. Aylwin's
successor, Eduardo Frei, is a much less distinguished public figure who,
many analysts believe, lacks the political skills of his predecessor. Chile was

fortunate to be able to rely on such skilled leadership at a crucial historical moment. However, as in any political system, Chile cannot count on a similar quality of leadership indefinitely.

In essence, Aylwin had enormous success in the legislative arena. He forcefully exerted his wide range of legislative powers without significantly alienating or losing the support of Congress. However, many of the roots of this success cannot be found in legal structures or institutional and constitutional arrangements. Nor are they generalizable to future governments. Rather, they are time- and actor-dependent. With a change in contextual variables in the future and the fading of the economic, social, and political factors that had a positive effect on transition politics in Chile, there is no guarantee that executive/legislative relations will be conducted as smoothly or effectively in the future. While in the beginning of the Frei administration, relations between the branches of government resembled those during the Aylwin administration, both institutional and partisan tensions have begun to emerge.

The Future of Executive/Assembly Relations

Many of the incentives that existed for executive/assembly cooperation in the legislative process are likely to be less influential in the future. Throughout the Aylwin presidency, the legislative agenda was set on the basis of interbranch and interparty cooperation and negotiation. If future presidents are elected without the support of a coalition of parties, or lose that support in midterm elections, the number of parties represented within the executive branch will decrease. With fewer parties represented, the mechanics of the legislative process will change. Without the guarantees provided by the representation of an array of parties within the executive branch, there is no insurance that a president will have the goodwill, good judgment, or opportunity, given the correlation of forces in the Congress, to organize the type of informal cross-branch and cross-party legislative consultations that were the defining features of the Aylwin government. Indeed, there is no incentive for a president to make such arrangements, because the party in power will want to reap the benefits of governmental achievements and will understandably be less willing to share the credit for success with other parties.

When a president lacks a legislative majority, the incentive structure created also influences the behavior of the legislative branch and increases the probability for both interparty and interbranch conflict. First, without a stake in government, members of other parties do not have as much invested in the success of the legislative process. Because the locus of the legislative process is the executive branch, the executive benefits more than individual legislators from the successful passage of legislation.

But more important, because of the winner-take-all nature of the Chilean presidency (especially in a context in which multiparty coalitions are not formed), the Congress is one of the only arenas for the articulation of opposition demands. Therefore, the marginalization of Congress also serves to exclude the opposition. Even members of the president's own coalition may begin to feel that the interests of their own party are being undermined by their subordinate role as actors within the political process. This is an especially acute problem in a multiparty system in which there are major differences in both the constituencies and platforms of parties. As the shadow of the military fades and the overriding regime cleavage that led to the creation of *democracia consensual* becomes less important, parties may have less and less to gain from *democracia consensual* and more to gain from *democracia confrontacional* (confrontational democracy).

There is potential not only for interbranch conflict but also for partisan conflict. The actions of the assembly during the Aylwin administration were a product of the goodwill of legislators and subject to the incentives acting on them at the time. However, given a return to a more partisan pattern of political competition, the costs of cooperation may exceed the benefits. The legislature may become increasingly hostile toward presidential domination of the legislative process, especially if the president lacks a majority. What is more, this chapter has shown that presidential urgencies are an important factor in determining whether or not legislation gets passed. A frustrated and obstructionist Congress can do a great deal to undermine political efficacy and create problems of democratic governability by refusing to respect declared presidential urgencies. While a future president can continue to declare legislation urgent at the same rate that Presidents Aylwin and Frei did, if some of the incentives outlined above begin to operate, there is no assurance that the assembly will respect those urgencies. It can either ignore them, or simply vote down all presidential initiatives in favor of consideration of proposals that originate in the legislative branch, from which individual legislators may have more to gain.

All of the scenarios described above are, of course, purely hypothetical, and presuppose distinct policy preferences between the branches of government. However, the point of this discussion is that constitutionally strong presidents can become *functionally* weak, given a change in contextual and party-system variables.[24] Presidents may indeed have the right of exclusive initiative in certain areas, the ability to declare legislation urgent, and strong veto powers. However, a simple change in the political context may leave a president with little power and influence. Presidential strength is situational and subject to majorities in Congress, social- and party-system contextual features, as well as the timing and sequencing of legislative and parliamentary elections (an issue discussed in depth in Chapter 6).

Contextual Change and the Emergence of Latent Conflict

There are some preliminary indications that frustration with presidential domination is growing, as the "special context" of the transition fades. It is important to recognize that within any political system there are compound rivalries based on administrative, institutional, and partisan divisions. While political and administrative support for Aylwin has consistently been strong, during his tenure there were already important indications of an underlying institutional rivalry between the branches of government. For example, despite the overall positive elite evaluation of the government and of inter-branch relations, when asked about the responses of the executive branch to *oficios*, only 46 percent of deputies interviewed felt that the government responded to them in a "responsible and efficient manner." A certain amount of this dissatisfaction can be explained by partisan divisions (only 25 percent of opposition deputies agreed with the statement). However, among deputies of Aylwin's own coalition, a significant 39 percent also felt that the government was unresponsive to its requests for information.

More seriously, 44 percent of government deputies and 50 percent of opposition deputies interviewed for this study felt that even the cooperative and extremely popular Aylwin had a tendency to "*obviar*" (pass over) Congress in relation to the most important legislative initiatives. Echoing a contention often expressed in the course of interviews with legislators, a Radical Party deputy contended that much legislation "*nos llega cocida*" (arrives precooked) for simple, and expected, passage by the Congress.[25] These types of activities undertaken by the executive prompted one deputy

24. Here the author expands on the idea of the "functional" weakness of presidential systems discussed by Waldino Suárez. Suárez contends that it is important not only to analyze the constitutional powers of Latin American presidents but also to consider the considerable variance in the actual ability of executives to employ them. See "El poder ejecutivo en América Latina: Su capacidad operativa bajo regímenes presidencialistas de gobierno," *Revista de estudios políticos* 29 (September–October 1982): 109–44.

25. Interview with Radical Party deputy Jaime Rocha, Valparaíso, 14 April 1993.

(and a member of the president's own coalition) to contend that now that the president has "moved into the house of authoritarianism, he feels quite comfortable there," employing all of the faculties granted to him.[26] A Ministry of Justice official came to the defense of Aylwin, contending that rather than abusing powers the president was simply acting in a way that would normally be expected, given the nature of the constitution and the weakness of Congress.[27]

Nonetheless, it is undeniable that the president has in many ways bypassed Congress to negotiate directly with opposition parties and certain sectoral interests, including big business and labor, in order to reach agreements outside of formal institutions. This reality is problematic for a number of reasons. First, it is uncertain whether future presidents will have the ability and the skills to engage in interparty and cross-sectional negotiations. Second, in a more politically charged atmosphere, it is doubtful whether a president will be able to expect the almost automatic approval of Congress if the latter is consistently excluded from the legislative process. Finally, disregarding Congress has important costs for the representative capacity of the democratic system.

On the other side of the equation, within the ministries there is a latent but increasingly apparent frustration with and suspicion of the capabilities of Congress as well. Most members of the executive branch interviewed for this study agreed that Congress has not done much to improve legislation originating in the executive branch. Despite varying responses, depending on the ministry and issue area, the general consensus within the most important ministries was that Congress did little to improve bills elaborated by the executive branch, and often obstructed the government through the interminable submission of *oficios*.[28]

In terms of partisan rivalries, there are signs that the retreat of a military threat is already beginning to loosen the Concertación's coalitional glue, complicating the future of interbranch relations. There is growing animosity between the parties of the Concertación, particularly in regard to candidacies and ministerial appointments.

26. Off-the-record interview with Socialist deputy, Santiago, 28 April 1993.
27. Off-the-record interview, Santiago, 23 June 1993.
28. This is partly a function of constitutional proscriptions on legislative action. Marta Tonda Mitri, for example, contended that, given the level of expertise of officials within the Ministry of Finance, and the limited voice of legislators on economic issues, the Congress really lacks the ability to improve much on executive initiatives. Interview with Marta Tonda Mitri, chief of staff, Ministerio de Hacienda, Santiago, 22 June 1993. Nonetheless, in general, members of the executive branch often contended that Congress did little to improve legislation.

In the first two presidential elections, the bloc of the Left, made up of the Partido Socialista (PS, Socialist Party) and the Partido Por la Democracia (PPD, Party for Democracy), has been denied the presidential candidacy of the Concertación, despite having a strong and tenable candidate in Ricardo Lagos. Lagos served successfully as Minister of Education in the Aylwin government and is one of the most important figures on the Left. After launching an unsuccessful primary bid to become the Concertación's presidential candidate in 1993, Lagos was offered the less than glamorous position of Minister of Public Works by the new Frei administration, apparently to decrease his stature as a national political leader. The principle of alternation characteristic of consociational arrangements would seem to suggest that a candidate of the Left should have been chosen for the 1993 presidential election. But because the presidential term of eight years was initially established,[29] and President Aylwin only served for four years under the transitional framework, the Christian Democrats contended that they as the majority party should present the "*candidato único*" of the Concertación. Though Lagos was eventually selected as the Concertación's standard-bearer for the 1999 elections, this was a difficult pill for the Christian Democrats to swallow, and it led one faction of the party to move to present its own candidate.

The importance of leadership style is also apparent in the distinct elite evaluation of the first two postauthoritarian presidents. Eduardo Frei has been criticized for his management style, which sharply contrasts with the conciliatory and personal nature of Aylwin's leadership.[30] Aylwin characterized his cabinet as a "homogeneous, pluralist team representing the whole rainbow of the Concertación," which he described as "a collective entity that is well coordinated and governs seriously, coherently and with energy."[31] In a country notorious for cabinet instability in the preauthoritarian period, Aylwin resisted making any significant changes in his cabinet, which helped to avoid interparty conflict and maintain goodwill and trust among ministers. Aylwin repeatedly underscored the idea that the Concertación government could remain "above" petty partisan politics, by discovering and promoting the common programmatic elements of the Concertación's component parties.

Frei, on the other hand, has increasingly come under fire for abandoning the principles of loyalty, trust, and, most important, party balance that have

---

29. The term was shortened to six years by constitutional reform in 1994.

30. For a general discussion of the management style of the Frei administration, see "Dr. Frei y Mr. Hyde," *Hoy* 906, 4 December 1994, 11.

31. Cited by Rehren, "Organizing the Presidency for the Consolidation of Democracy in the Southern Cone," 7.

helped to hold the Concertación together. First, though he respected the party agreements concerning the composition of the cabinet, he annoyed even leaders in his own party by appointing an inner circle largely made up of friends and supporters to cabinet positions, creating what a Santiago cartoonist dubbed a "*gabinete de Su Excelencia*" (cabinet of His Excellency), rather than a "*gabinete de excelencia*" (cabinet of excellence).[32] Alejandro Foxley, former finance minister, former president of the Christian Democratic Party, and presidential aspirant, was intentionally bypassed in the initial ministerial appointment process. He was eventually asked to head a series of ministries, including the Ministry of Education, that were not consonant with his status as an important national leader. As in the case of Lagos, this was seen as an effort by Frei to "*desperfilar*" (or undermine the position of) Foxley.

Second, a few months into his term Frei shocked his coalition partners with a cabinet reshuffle, with neither interparty consultation nor approval. While the party balance within the ministries was retained, the important Ministry of the Interior changed party hands with the firing of Socialist Germán Correa and his replacement by Christian Democrat Carlos Figueroa. Frei's decision caused furor on the Left and led to calls that the sector withdraw from the coalition. Frei's cabinet eventually came to be called derisively the "Círculo de Hierro" (the Iron Circle), an image that is at odds with Aylwin's "rainbow" cabinet.

Additional conflicts have erupted within and between parties over the appointment of the director of the state-run National Television station. While Aylwin insisted on complete autonomy for state television, Frei considered inappropriate (and some say treasonous) the growing number of antigovernment stories that appeared on the channel. The station's director, Christian Democrat Jorge Navarrete, was allegedly pressured by Frei to change certain policies of the station. In response, Navarrete tendered his resignation in an effort to force a vote of confidence of the Committee for State Television and to reinforce the independence of the station. Much to the surprise of Navarrete and the parties of the Left, two members of the Christian Democratic Party thought to support Navarrete voted to accept his resignation, apparently under pressure from Frei. This deprived Navarrete of a majority of the votes of the multiparty committee.

After pressuring the members of the committee to vote with him, Frei then failed to consult with coalition partners, and even members of his own party, in naming a replacement. He passed over both the candidate preferred by

32. Cited in Latin American Weekly Report, 20 January 1994, 20.

Foxley (then president of the Christian Democrats and as of this writing a senator) and the one put forward by the Socialists as a potential replacement. Frei's actions so angered members of the coalition that the parties of the Left were willing to back the candidate proposed by the Right in order to send a message that Frei's actions were unacceptable. The Right's candidate was ultimately victorious and was eventually appointed director.

Finally, the Frei government's defense of General Pinochet (detained in London on 16 October 1998 for extradition to Spain for his role in myriad human rights abuses during the 1970s and 1980s) has driven a deep rift between the Center and the Left (many of the Left favor extradition and trial).

All of these events have led to a general feeling among many within the Concertación that Frei is directing the coalition from above, while party elites have maintained that the alliance should form the guiding basis of government policies. A prominent leader of the Left responded to Frei's actions by declaring, "These negative events are all part of the bigger picture in which the Concertación has gone from being an alliance to simply being a collection of parties."[33]

Not all blame for the deterioration of unity within the Concertación should be attributed to the actions and decisions of Frei. The movement away from the delicacy of the transition has led to the removal of kid gloves and an environment in which political anger and political disagreements can be expressed more openly and virulently. Thus, relations between the parties of the Concertación alliance have been transformed since Frei took office as the special context of the transition has ended. The politics of *democracia consensual* have been supplanted by a "politics as usual" attitude. It is uncertain whether the heretofore dominant Christian Democrats will tolerate the dominance of the Left following the probable election of a Socialist president in 1999, amid a growing crisis of confidence in the Concertación.

Conclusion

As has been suggested, and as later chapters will argue more forcefully, the 1980 constitution provides a blueprint for presidential domination, and serious potential for executive and legislative conflict and deadlock. Nonetheless, the actions of members of the executive and legislative branches during the

33. Quoted in "Dr. Frei y Mr. Hyde," 11.

Aylwin administration, driven by the exigencies of maintaining the precarious balance that characterized the transition process, were able to overcome some of the inherent obstacles to interbranch cooperation created by the constitution. A series of formal, informal, and institutional arrangements helped to stem the potential for interbranch conflict, making for efficacious government and a great deal of stability.

A spirit of reconciliation, combined with the threat of armed incursion, produced a dynamic of cooperation that elites had strong incentives to maintain throughout the Aylwin government. The fortuitous interaction of Aylwin's personality and management style, a well-structured executive branch, and a great deal of interbranch trust produced a unique formula for governmental success.

Nonetheless, this formula for cooperation involved burying latent conflict and leaving the resolution of the most controversial issues for later governments. Favorable economic performance also meant that the Aylwin government encountered less daunting challenges than some of its counterparts on the continent. Future governments must face the unresolved issues and conflicts obscured by the transition process. However, they will not be able to rely on the favorable context created by the interaction of economic success and a spirit of political accommodation.

This unique historical context has already undergone significant transformation and is likely to change relatively quickly in the coming years. There are clear indications that the euphoria produced by the transition process is fading and that a more traditional pattern of political interaction may soon supplant the transitional one. An opposition deputy of Renovación Nacional, after an hour-long interview in Spanish, abruptly switched to English when addressing this issue. He said, "We are all on a honeymoon right now, and I don't know when the honeymoon will be over, but it will be. When it is, things won't be the same."[34]

Thus, the framers of the 1980 constitution may indeed have set down an effective institutional framework for democratic transition. Whether it is a framework for successful democratic consolidation and long-term governability, however, is a separate and more complex question that involves more than institutions alone. It is crucial to explore the socioeconomic and political context on which the institutions of government are superimposed to get to the root of the potential workability and efficacy of democratic institutions in the country.

34. Off-the-record interview, Valparaíso, 5 May 1993.

3

SOCIOECONOMIC AND POLITICAL CHANGE AND CONTINUITY

Chile in the 1990s

The conclusions of the first two chapters of this study may seem contradictory. While the first suggested that there are important impediments to democratic consolidation in Chile, given exaggerated presidentialism and a potentially exclusionary electoral system, the second underscored the exceptional performance of postauthoritarian governments, and particularly the Aylwin administration, within the institutional framework inherited from the previous regime.

Despite this seeming contradiction, one of this study's major themes is that distinct socioeconomic and political contexts can affect the performance of democratic institutions. Thus, a change in these variables can make the same set of institutions workable in certain context- and time-dependent situations but dysfunctional in others. While exaggerated presidentialism, and the institutional and legal configurations that support it, may be workable given the context of the democratic transition and the forced consensus it produced, the question at hand is whether it is functional given the evolution of long-term and more permanent trends in Chile's socioeconomic and political landscape. Chapters 3 and 4 seek to explore these contexts and to point to their significance for the future performance of democratic institutions.

The "Chilean model" of economic development and political transition has been heralded and admired around the world.[1] The extent to which either the political or economic reforms were concerted or coherent enough to be considered a "model" is questionable. Rather than constituting an entire package of coherent reforms introduced to produce certain ends, the process of economic reform was often reactive and characterized by different phases, some of which had contradictory policy ends. Nonetheless, the "Chilean model" is a term used often in the press and by economic policy-makers in Chile and elsewhere, and is thus used here to refer to the overall package of reforms instituted by the military government. What is more, this two-pronged model of neoliberal economics and strong presidentialism built by the military regime is often credited with the nation's spectacular success in avoiding many of the political and economic pitfalls of democratic transitions in other countries in the region.

Chapter 1 underscored how the military's negative view of society and politics guided the design of the political institutions inherited by democratic authorities. Thus, in evaluating the potential workability of the political model imposed by the authoritarian regime, it is important to ask whether the polarization and conflict that provided the intellectual backdrop for its design are still relevant in contemporary Chile. To what extent has the socioeconomic context of Chile been transformed? Are polarization and class conflict a thing of the past? What issues still divide Chilean society? Are the constitutional remedies for conflict designed by military authorities appropriate, given the socioeconomic and political changes that have occurred in the country? Will they do more harm than good?

To answer these questions, Chapters 3 and 4 analyze continuity and change in Chile's socioeconomic and political landscape, asking to what extent it has been transformed since the 1970s. This chapter deals with the socioeconomic and political context broadly considered, while the next focuses specifically on the party system. Both chapters conclude that, despite significant changes, there are continuities and new challenges that mean the transformation of Chilean society and politics has been less complete than it may appear superficially.

---

1. For an excellent discussion of the various stages in the military government's implementation of its economic program, see Pilar Vergara, *Auge y caída del neoliberalismo en Chile* (Santiago: FLACSO, 1985). See also Eduardo Silva, "The Political Economy of Chile's Regime Transition: From Radical to Pragmatic Neo-Liberal Policies," in *The Struggle for Democracy in Chile*, ed. Drake and Jaksic, 98–127, and Alejandro Foxley, *Experimentos neoliberales en América Latina* (Santiago: CIEPLAN, 1982).

Chilean society is today certainly less prone to class and ideological conflict, and there is consensus on the basic political and economic model that
should guide the country's future. However, despite transformations within
society and the party system, this chapter argues that the positive macroeconomic and political context that characterized the process of democratic
transition has obscured less severe though still significant economic problems, socioeconomic divisions, and political conflicts. While consensus exists,
this chapter will suggest that it may indeed be a "thin" consensus.

First, while many indicators point to macroeconomic health, an improving
economic situation for Chileans, and changes within the socioeconomic
structure of the country, there are some profound and nagging qualitative
and quantitative inequalities and underlying class conflicts. Second, the
potential for political and social conflict has not disappeared. Third, despite
increasing consensus within Chilean society regarding fundamental issues
facing the nation, there are indications of profound underlying disagreements and divisions that may more strongly assert themselves during the
process of democratic consolidation. There is also mounting evidence that
these socioeconomic and political divisions are beginning to manifest themselves politically. It is uncertain whether the current institutional framework
provides sufficient arenas for the negotiation and settlement of these conflicts. Thus, this chapter concludes that the transformations that have
occurred within Chilean society and politics make the controls imposed on
civilian authorities not only unwarranted but also counterproductive.

Socioeconomic and Political Change:
The Transformation of Chilean Society

Discussing socioeconomic transformation in Chile is a controversial enter-
prise. First, while in the 1990s the "Chilean model" has been heralded as a
potentially positive prototype for both the South American continent and
nations outside the hemisphere, superficial analyses of the country's economic transformations often overlook the profound social, cultural, and
economic costs paid by Chilean society for the favorable economic situation
that exists in the country today. Proponents of the Chilean model, who laud
the favorable macroeconomic statistics of the 1990s, often overlook the
periods of negative growth, high unemployment, and decreasing standards

of living that were the immediate costs of Chile's process of liberalization.[2] Many of these indicators have returned to their pre-1970 levels only in recent years. Also often forgotten are the profound human costs exacted by the military's policies. However, given the focus of this study, these controversial questions, and credit or blame for the authoritarian regime, will be set aside in an attempt to get to the root of how the country's socioeconomic structure has been affected by Chile's process of economic liberalization and social transformation.

Second, when analyzing social, economic, and political change in Chile, there has often been a tendency to speak in black-and-white terms. For what are often ideological and political reasons, analysts tend to portray the policies of the Pinochet regime as either a complete success or an unqualified failure.[3] In one view, Chilean society and the economic system have been fundamentally transformed and the civic habits of Chileans have improved. Other perspectives underscore the failure of the military's transformational project and point to the many underlying continuities and divisions within Chilean society, as well as to the persisting economic and political problems. However, it is important to recognize that the results of the military regime are really mixed in economic, social, and political terms. Despite fundamental transformations, there is still socioeconomic and political continuity, derived in large part from the historical unfolding of long-term economic trends, geography, and the perseverance of a well-defined and entrenched political culture that is resistant to change.

Finally, it is essential to underscore the multivariate nature of the process of social transformation that has occurred in Chile. This chapter in no way asserts a causal argument based on economic determinism. It is not simply economic liberalization that has led to social change. Rather, a series of

2. These realities are discussed in Vergara, *Auge y caída*, and Silva, "The Political Economy of Chile's Regime Transition."

3. A good example of this dichotomy, and its ideological bases, is Joaquín Lavín, *Chile: Revolución silenciosa* (Santiago: Zig-Zag, 1988), and Eugenio Tironi, *Los silencios de la revolución* (Santiago: Editorial Puerta Abierta, 1988). Lavín champions the economic growth and social progress that were products of the Chilean military regime, basing his argument on the absurd notion that the increased numbers of children watching television and using disposable diapers are indicators of important economic advances during the Pinochet government. Tironi, on the other hand, underscores the profound social and economic costs of Pinochet's "revolution" and ignores the many advances in social policy and in the overall prosperity of Chilean society. While clearly written with an eye to affecting the outcome of the 1989 elections, these works are characteristic of the form the debate between regime proponents and its critics has often taken.

complex domestic and international transformations have occurred along with Chile's process of economic liberalization, which, taken together, have made Chilean society different from that which existed in the mid-1960s and 1970s. This is the case despite the continuities that will be emphasized later in the chapter.

Socioeconomic Transformation

In terms of the contemporary socioeconomic conditions of Chileans, the evolution of economic indicators points to a more prosperous society, with increased purchasing power and an enhanced willingness and ability to save. Table 3.1 shows that between 1988 and 1996 the Chilean economy registered impressive rates of growth, averaging 8.1 percent. Private consumption also markedly increased for the years under consideration. After years of failed attempts, it appears that inflation is under control, with rates in the single digits.

This economic growth and stability, spectacular in Latin American terms, have been accompanied by an increase in real salaries and a high investment and savings rate. Between 1988 and 1992, real salaries increased by 13.8 percent.[4] In 1994, national savings totaled 25.4 as a percentage of GDP, of which 20.5 percent was private, a much higher rate than any of the OECD (Organization for Economic Cooperation and Development) countries.[5] National savings as percentage of GDP increased to 27.7 percent by 1996. Much of the success in increasing the private savings rate has been due to the growth of newly instituted private pension funds known as AFPs (Pension Administration Funds). Pension fund deposits in 1995 totaled US$25 billion.[6]

The often chronic unemployment that plagued Chile and much of Latin America in the last two decades may be a thing of the past, given the diversification of employment patterns and the profound restructuring of the Chilean economy (discussed in detail below). In Latin American terms unemployment has been quite low, averaging 9.4 percent for the 1985–89 period. As Table 3.1 shows, unemployment has also steadily declined for

4. Oscar Muñoz and Carmen Celedón, "Chile en transición: Estrategia económica y política," in *La política económica en la transición a la democracia*, ed. Juan Antonio Morales and Gary McMahon (Santiago: CIEPLAN, 1993), 133.

5. Official documents released to the World Bank by the Ministry of Finance of the Republic of Chile.

6. "The Financial Times Survey: Chile," *Financial Times*, 7 July 1995, 13.

Table 3.1. Selected Chilean economic indicators by year, 1988–1996 (Percentages)

	1988	1989	1990	1991	1992	1993	1994	1995	1996
Total GDP growth	7.3	10.6	3.7	8.0	12.3	7.0	5.7	10.6	7.4
Increase in private consumption	4.3	6.0	1.0	5.2	6.6	5.2	1.3	6.8	NA
Unemployment	8.1	6.2	6.0	6.5	4.9	4.7	6.0	5.4	7.0
Inflation (consumer prices)	15.0	16.2	26.6	22.0	15.6	12.1	12.0	7.9	7.3

SOURCES: Inter-American Development Bank (GDP, Unemployment, Inflation); United Nations (Consumption).

most of the 1990s, averaging 6.1 percent for the period between 1988 and 1996. While unemployment climbed to 7.0 percent in 1996, it is still comparatively low by historical and regional standards.

While economic policy-makers in the first two postauthoritarian governments are often portrayed as neoliberal converts bent on maintaining the entire package of economic policies inherited from the authoritarian regime, it is important to note that both President Patricio Aylwin (1990–94) and President Eduardo Frei (1994–2000) have taken concrete measures to improve the social and economic situation of the poorest Chileans. Between 1990 and 1993, government spending on social programs rose by 30 percent in real terms, with increases in government expenditures in the areas of housing, health, and vocational training.[7] The percentage of GDP dedicated to social spending increased from 14 percent in 1989 to 15.3 percent in 1993.[8]

Taken together, these impressive economic advances have led to a decrease in the percentage of the population living in poverty. In 1987, 38 percent of households were categorized as poor. By 1996, this rate had decreased to 20 percent, and the number of indigent households dropped from 13.5 percent to 4 percent in the same years.[9]

The Chilean labor market and employment patterns have also been transformed. Diversification of products, a widening domestic economy, and spectacular growth in noncopper exports have transformed Chile's single-product dependence. These changes have produced a more dynamic and diversified economy that is less prone to shocks produced by international commodity price fluctuations, and a labor market that has fewer of the structural characteristics that produced a great deal of union activism in the past.

Chile's dramatic growth has to a large extent been based on a model of export-led growth,[10] with exports as percentage of GDP climbing from 12.6

7. Cited by Timothy Scully, "The Political Underpinnings of Economic Liberalization in Chile" (unpublished manuscript, Kellogg Institute of the University of Notre Dame, 1994), 5.

8. República de Chile, official documents released by the Dirección de Presupuesto (National Budget Office), 1993.

9. Comisión Económica para América Latina, Statistical Yearbook for Latin America and the Caribbean: 1994 Edition (Santiago: CEPAL, 1995), 46, and Comisión Económica para América Latina, Panorama social de América Latina (Santiago: CEPAL, 1997). These measures of poverty were computed using CEPAL's "income method" of measurement, based on the level of income necessary to provide the basic needs of a household for all members of a family. For an explanatory note on the measurement of poverty, see page xxxiii of the Statistical Yearbook. For a complete breakdown of the evolution of poverty rates in Chile, see Table 3.5 in this book.

10. While there is some dispute on this issue, given that one could argue that growth has driven exports, it is undeniable that the importance of exports to the Chilean economy has dramatically increased.

percent in 1970 to 37 percent in 1993.[11] This growth was not a result of increasing production of Chile's export mainstay, copper, which in 1970 constituted 78.8 percent of exports but which in 1992 had decreased to only 36.7 percent.[12] While copper exports remained at about US$4 billion per year between 1989 and 1994, the value of noncopper exports increased from $4.06 billion to $7.40 billion.[13] Dramatic growth in the export of fruits, wines, fresh fish, fish meal, wood pulp, forestry products, and light manufactured goods explains the decline in copper's share of overall exports and much of the country's success in export markets.

However, growth was not limited to the export sector. There has been increased demand and production within the Chilean domestic market. In addition to light manufacturing, the development of a dynamic financial services sector and the privatization, and subsequent growth, in the insurance, health, and agribusiness industries have also resulted in increased domestic production and consumption.

This diversification of production has changed the occupations of Chileans.[14] In 1970, 48.1 percent of the economically active population was employed in the service sector, whereas by 1980 this figure had increased to 58.3 percent. This percentage decreased slightly to 57.7 percent in 1994—though it is still the highest rate of any Spanish-speaking republic in the region.[15] The percentage of the population working in the traditionally very organized and politicized mining sector has decreased.

The Chilean state has undoubtedly shed its role as one of the country's primary employers and business entities. The resulting decrease in public-sector employment has transformed the labor market. State employment rapidly expanded between 1940 and 1973, growing an average of 3.48 percent per year. Growth was even more dramatic in the years preceding the coup, averaging 6.6 percent per year between 1964 and 1973.[16] Between

11. CEPAL, *Statistical Yearbook* 1994, 78.

12. This transformation was not a result of declining price or production. Rather, copper prices remained relatively constant, and the dollar value of the metal's export more than doubled between 1985 and 1989, with modest increases since 1990. Ibid., 127.

13. "The Financial Times Survey: Chile," 14.

14. For a discussion of class and occupational structures in Chile, see Javier Martínez and Arturo León, *Clases y clasificaciones sociales: Investigaciones sobre la estructura social chilena, 1970–1983* (Santiago: Centro de Estudios del Desarrollo, 1987), and Javier Martínez and Eugenio Tironi, *Las clases sociales en Chile: Cambio y estratificación: 1970–1980* (Santiago: Ediciones Sur, 1985).

15. CEPAL, *Statistical Yearbook 1994*, 42, 722, and the Inter-American Development Bank.

16. Martínez and Tironi, *Las clases sociales en Chile*, 68.

1974 and 1989, 550 state-owned enterprises were privatized.[17] In 1970, public-sector spending totaled 40.6 percent of GNP, decreasing to 29.5 percent in 1985 and to 21.6 percent by 1992.[18] Beginning in 1973, mass firings and privatization produced a dramatic reduction in the number of state employees. Between 1976 and 1990, ninety-two thousand employees were pushed off state payrolls, representing a decrease of approximately 35 percent (Table 3.2).[19] Though union membership and the relative activism of state employees varied depending on the particular sector of employment, the reduction in the number of state employees has contributed to the overall decrease in the percentage of unionized workers.

Table 3.2 shows that the number of state-sector employees decreased dramatically, while the size of the overall labor force registered a large increase. What is more, the table shows that the percentage of service workers in employ of the state has dramatically decreased. There has been a shift of skilled service employees into the financial services sector, the growth of which has roughly corresponded to the decrease in skilled state employees. Between 1976 and 1990, the number of people employed in the financial services industry more than tripled, growing from 63,000 to 203,000—representing an increase from 2.0 percent to 4.3 percent of the total labor force.[20] Workers in this sector have been less prone to union organization and activism.

However, analysts of socioeconomic change in Chile have tended to overemphasize the simple withdrawal of the state without paying enough attention to transformations within firms and the labor market itself.[21] The combination of the enhanced dynamism of Chilean firms and relaxed labor laws has produced a business sector that has relied increasingly on temporary employment and subcontractors. Activities previously carried out by companies themselves, particularly within the large-scale industrial and mining sectors, have increasingly been farmed out to small and medium-size

17. Rolf Luders, "Massive Divestiture and Privatization: Lessons from Chile," *Contemporary Policy Issues* 9 (October 1991): 1–19.
18. Figures for 1970 are from Pilar Vergara, "Changes in the Economic Structure of the Chilean State Under the Military Regime," in *Military Rule in Chile*, ed. J. Samuel Valenzuela and Arturo Valenzuela, 89. Data for 1985 and 1992 appear in Salomon Brothers, "Chile: Receiving the Benefits of Structural Reform," *Emerging Markets Research: Latin America* (September 1992): 6.
19. Martínez and Tironi, *Las clases sociales en Chile*, 68.
20. Javier Martínez and Alvaro Díaz, *Chile: The Great Transformation* (Geneva: UNRISD, 1996), 122.
21. The one important exception is Martínez and Díaz's *Chile: The Great Transformation*.

Table 3.2. Employment in the nonfinancial public administrative sector, selected years, 1976–1990

Type of Employment	1976	1980	1983	1986	1990
Public employees (thousands)	267	231	215	201	175
Labor force (thousands)	3,128	3,636	3,768	4,270	4,729
Services employment (thousands)	1,597	1,948	2,122	2,267	2,474
Public employees/labor force (percentage)	8.4	6.4	5.7	4.7	3.7
Public employees/services employment(percentage)	16.7	11.9	10.1	8.9	7.1

SOURCE: Javier Martínez and Alvaro Díaz, *Chile: The Great Transformation* (Geneva: UNRISD, 1996), 121.

specialized subcontracting firms. Large employers profit by avoiding the benefit costs usually associated with full-time employees. Subcontracting firms, in turn, rely on temporary contracts or part-time workers to avoid these responsibilities.[22] When combined with the stagnation in the minimum wage discussed below, the cost of employing workers has dramatically decreased, providing for an economic environment that mitigates against labor organization, unionization, and activism.

Due to these structural economic transformations and changing occupations, the nature of state-labor and employer-worker relations has also been transformed.[23] The repressive labor policies of the Pinochet government, combined with the process of economic restructuring outlined above, have produced a weakened and less ideological labor movement less prone to strike. In 1970, official figures placed union membership at 24 percent of the economically active population, a figure that grew to 35 percent in 1973. Manuel Barrera and Samuel Valenzuela argue that these figures underestimate the real extent of labor organization, given that what they term "alegal" organizations (apparently those whose legal status is unclear) are not included in most estimates. At any rate, the level of unionization in preauthoritarian Chile was certainly higher than in most of the industrialized Western economies at the time.[24] Chile had one of the most militant, successful, and active labor movements on the continent in the preauthoritarian period. Labor unions gained influence through their close ties to political parties and success in gaining concessions from the government and business, including sectoral bargaining power, automatic wage increases, and industrial arbitration boards.

22. Ibid., 128–29.

23. For an analysis of the fate of the labor movement during the Pinochet government, see Guillermo Campero, *El movimiento sindical en el régimen militar chileno: 1973–1981* (Santiago: Instituto Latinoamericano de Estudios Transnacionales, 1984). Samuel Valenzuela and Jeffrey Goodwin provide a more general treatment of labor in the context of authoritarian regimes in "Labor Movements Under Authoritarian Regimes," Monographs on Europe Series no. 5, Center for European Studies, Harvard University, Cambridge, Mass., 1983. For a discussion of the evolution of the Chilean labor movement during the 1980s, see Alan Angell, "Unions and Workers in Chile During the 1980s," in *The Struggle for Democracy in Chile*, ed. Drake and Jaksic. A general theoretical overview of the role of labor movements in the process of democratic transition is provided in Samuel Valenzuela, "Labor Movements in Transitions to Democracy: A Framework for Analysis," Working Paper no. 104, The Kellogg Institute for International Studies, Notre Dame, Ind., 1988.

24. See Manuel Barrera and Samuel Valenzuela, "The Development of Labor Movement Opposition to the Military Regime," in *Military Rule in Chile*, ed. J. Samuel Valenzuela and Arturo Valenzuela, 230–69.

82   Postauthoritarian Chile

Table 3.3. Union formation and membership in Chile, 1988–1992

Year	Number of Unions	Number of Members	Percentage of Workforce
1988	6,446	446,194	9.8
1989	7,118	507,612	10.8
1990	8,861	606,812	12.8
1991	9,858	701,355	14.5
1992	10,756	724,065	14.4

SOURCE: Eduardo Saffirio, "El sistema de partidos y la sociedad civil en la redemocratización chilena," *Estudios sociales* 82 (1994): 63-103.

With the advent of the Pinochet regime, harsh labor policies took their toll on workers' organizations.[25] At the outset of the new government, unions were banned and the right to strike and collective bargaining were eliminated. The first five years of the military government were characterized by the almost complete disarticulation of labor. By 1979, the rebirth of limited and clandestine labor activity forced the government to respond with new legislation, and a set of laws known as the "Labor Plan" was promulgated. The brainchild of the labor minister, José Piñera, the plan ensured only voluntary affiliation, limited collective negotiations, eliminated the minimum wage, and set a sixty-day time limit on strikes.[26] Arbitration boards were abolished and wages were de-indexed.

Union membership and formation continued to fall throughout the 1980s. However, as Table 3.3 summarizes, the rate of union formation and the number of affiliates rebounded with the return of democracy and the easing of restrictions, though the current percentage is far from the almost one-third of the economically active population that it was in the 1970s.

Despite increases in these numbers, there has not been a significant resurgence of strikes and labor activity. Table 3.4 summarizes the number of industrial disputes that occurred in the country between 1960 and 1993, and supplies data on the number of workers involved in these disputes and the working days lost as a result. There was a marked increase in the indicators of union activism in the mid-1960s that continued until the coup in 1973. Between 1966 and 1973, there were at least 1,000 labor disputes each year, with the number ranging from 1,073 in 1966 to 3,325 in 1972.

25. The 1979 labor code also made organization difficult in other ways. In order for a worker federation to exist legally, twenty-five workers, making up at least 50 percent of employees in a particular firm, had to agree to organize. Arbitrary firings without demonstration of just cause were also allowed under the code.
26. The minimum wage was reinstated in 1982.

Table 3.4. Industrial disputes in Chile, 1960–1993 (Number of disputes, number of workers involved, and working days lost)

Year	Number of Disputes	Number of Workers	Working Days Lost
1960	257	89,000	NA
1961	262	112,000	NA
1962	401	84,000	NA
1963	416	117,000	NA
1964	564	138,000	NA
1965	723	182,000	NA
1966	1,073	195,000	2,015,000
1967	1,114	225,000	1,990,000
1968	1,124	293,000	3,652,000
1969	1,277	362,000	1,179,000
1970	1,189	656,170	2,814,517
1971	2,696	299,000	1,388,000
1972	3,325	394,000	1,678,000
1973	2,050	711,000	2,503,000
1974–79	NA	NA	NA
1980	89	29,730	428,000
1981	NA	25,000	676,000
1982	NA	2,400	52,000
1983	41	4,373	58,492
1984	38	3,595	41,980
1985	42	8,532	131,630
1986	41	3,900	60,730
1987	81	9,900	104,200
1988	72	5,600	87,400
1989	101	17,900	298,600
1990	176	25,000	245,200
1991	219	45,900	730,900
1992	237	25,300	329,500
1993	224	25,100	312,000

Sources: Data adapted and extracted from: James Wilkie, ed., *Statistical Abstract of Latin America*, vols. 29 and 31 (Los Angeles: UCLA Latin American Center Publications, 1995), 29: 409, 31: 429; B. R. Mitchell, ed., *International Historical Statistics: The Americas, 1750–1988* (Stockton, Calif.: Stockton Press, 1993), 120; International Labour Office, *Yearbook of Labour Statistics* (Geneva: International Labour Office, 1996).

NA = Not available.

The number of workers involved for this period ranged from 195,000 in 1966 to 711,000 in 1973.

Since the return of democracy, labor activism and unrest have decreased significantly in comparison with the historical average. As Table 3.4 shows, in no single year between 1989 and 1993 did the number of labor disputes rise above 250, and during this time the number of workers involved in disputes never rose above 46,000. Part of this decrease was certainly a legacy of the disarticulation of the labor movement during the entire Pinochet era. However, the close working arrangement between the parties of the government coalition and the leadership of the most important unions also contributed to at least a temporary truce in labor-government and labor-employer relations.

The presence of the Socialist Party (with important historical ties to labor) within the governing coalition has been pivotal to the success of the government in managing its relations with labor. Following the 1989 election, the Unitary Central of Workers (CUT—the same acronym of the leftist labor coalition that was disbanded after the military coup) became the main interlocutor between workers and employers, meeting with business leaders and government officials to negotiate reforms to Chile's labor code and an increase in the minimum wage. Rather than establishing a pattern of rival labor federations tied to competing political parties, which characterized the preauthoritarian labor movement, the CUT has assumed a more independent role. It has increasingly focused on bread-and-butter concerns rather than ideological issues.[27]

What is more, the 1990 reform of the 1979 labor code, which eliminated many of the severe restrictions on organization and financing of unions, was supported across the political spectrum.[28] Despite pressure from big business, Renovación Nacional, the major party of the center-right, supported labor-code reform in Congress, thus recognizing the validity of labor's demands.

In this sense, the traditional role of the labor movement in Chile has been altered. In the preauthoritarian period, conflicts among unions, between unions and business, and between unions and the government often took the form of epic struggles between competing ideologies, given the intimate relationship between labor federations and political parties of the Left.[29]

---

27. It is necessary to differentiate here between union leadership and the rank and file. While union heads may reconstruct old-style relationships with party elites, the question is whether union membership will follow. On this point, and for a discussion of labor during the 1990s, see Angell, "Unions and Workers in Chile During the 1980s," 205–8.

28. The 1990 reforms eliminated the possibility of arbitrary firings, lowered the threshold for union organization, legally recognized smaller unions, reformed the process of union financing, and reintroduced collective bargaining. Time limits on the duration of strikes were also abolished.

29. Alan Angell provides a discussion of the pre-Pinochet labor movement and its important links to parties of the Left in *Politics and the Labor Movement in Chile* (London: Oxford

Strikes and protests were often based on ideological issues rather than wages and benefits. Aylwin, Frei, and a number of union leaders have specifically called for the elimination of "old-style" confrontational trade unionism based on issues other than concrete benefits for workers.

In all of these ways, the socioeconomic structure of the country has been transformed. Chilean society is wealthier and more frugal, and the economy is more diversified and less prone to external economic shocks that result from reliance on single-product exports. The percentage of the population employed in mining and by the state (certain sectors of which were traditionally strong bastions of union organization) has decreased, and organization within the growing agribusiness, subcontracting, and service sectors has proven difficult. Lingering labor restrictions, combined with the political dynamic of the democratic transition, have limited union activism in manufacturing, despite modest growth in that sector. What is more, there has been a dramatic decrease in the overall number of strikes compared with the historical activity of the Chilean labor movement.

The exact nature of the relationship between levels of socioeconomic development and democracy is still subject to a great deal of dispute. Some have suggested that a high income level is an important background condition for democracy and that there is a significant correlation between income level and the ability of a country to sustain democracy.[30] However, such a stark line of causation is not intended here. Rather, it is suggested that higher income levels, lower levels of labor activism, and diversification of production and employment markets may make society less vulnerable to the economic forces that in the past have precipitated social and class conflict in Chile.

Economic Transformation, Social Change, and Increased Political Consensus

The profound economic changes that have occurred in Chile were accompanied by international and domestic political changes that have transformed

University Press, 1972). For a general discussion of Chile's preauthoritarian labor movement, see Manuel Barrera, *Desarrollo económico y sindicalismo en Chile, 1938–1970* (Santiago: Centro de Estudios Económicos y Sociales, 1979).

30. See, for example, Seymour Martin Lipset, "Some Social Requisites of Democracy: Economic Development and Political Legitimacy," *American Political Science Review* 53 (March 1959): 69–105.

the ideological orientation, attitudes, and opinions of Chileans. These developments manifest themselves politically in the form of increased consensus.

It is difficult to measure a concept like "consensus," although certain of its indicators can be identified. Public-opinion survey data show that there was some consensus concerning the general acceptance of the first postauthoritarian government. Studies undertaken during Patricio Aylwin's tenure as president demonstrated a great deal of support relative to the administration's management of government. In 1990, only 8.8 percent of those surveyed declared themselves in opposition to the political trajectory of the administration, even if they did not explicitly support Aylwin or the Christian Democrats in the 1989 election.[31] These data suggest that though there might not have been specific support for particular policies of the Aylwin government, there was general satisfaction for democratic leaders within the framework of formal democracy. Chileans are more capable of rendering an objective, nonideological evaluation of the performance of government.

Chileans also agree that the country is progressing. Between March 1991 and June 1993, a series of ten public-opinion surveys showed that at no time did the percentage of Chileans agreeing with the statement "Chile is progressing" drop below 50 percent. Responses consistently ranged between 50 percent and 68 percent.[32] More recent surveys demonstrated a similar though slightly diminished consensus in terms of the country's progress, with responses ranging from 42 percent to 49 percent between 1995 and 1997.[33] What is more, between 1992 and 1998 approximately 60 percent of Chileans consistently agreed that they were satisfied with life.[34]

Another indicator of increasing consensus is agreement concerning the appropriate role of the state. When asked to choose from a list of nine categories the two most important factors contributing to individual economic success or failure, only 14.8 percent of those surveyed mentioned government economic policy as their first or second choice, and only 10.8 percent mentioned economic help from the state as one of these choices. Indeed, more people mentioned "luck" (19.8 percent) than any government policy.[35] Indeed, the categories most often identified as contributing to economic success had more to do with factors related to the individual

    31. Centro de Estudios Públicos, "Estudio social y de opinión pública," June 1990, 41–42.
    32. Ibid., July 1993, 49.
    33. Centro de Estudios Públicos, "Estudio nacional de opinión pública No. 7," December 1997–January 1998, 51.
    34. Ibid., 42.
    35. Ibid., 36.

respondent. "Personal initiative" was mentioned most often (44 percent), followed by "working responsibly" (42.5 percent) and "level of education" (35.6 percent).[36] In a similar study, conducted by the firm Participa, 70.9 percent of those surveyed contended that the best way to confront the social problems they faced as individuals was either to solve those problems themselves or to join with like-minded people in an attempt to change them. Only 14.1 percent of the population contended that the state should be asked to help.[37]

Currently, there is a low estimation on the part of the Chilean citizenry of what the state can do to help the economic situation of individuals, which most likely translates into lower demands and an acceptance that the interventionist state of the 1960s and 1970s is a thing of the past. This is a remarkable development in a country characterized by a historically interventionist state in the areas of industrial policy, infrastructure development, and economic redistribution. Because of the lack of data on these questions for the period before the military regime, it is impossible to contend that there is any trend in favor of a decreased role for the state. Nonetheless, these results do demonstrate that there is currently some degree of consensus concerning its socioeconomic role.

In terms of concrete policy, there is widespread agreement with the government's program of "growth with equity," which has eliminated the formerly divisive question of the appropriate economic model for the country. Across the political spectrum, all major parties accept market economics and political democracy as the best formulas to guide Chile's future, though, as will be shown below, complete satisfaction with the qualitative characteristics of the country's democracy is absent. This agreement has helped to stem conflict among previously irreconcilable ideological sectors by introducing a basic set of accepted assumptions and trust on which additional political agreements have been built. This, again, is a dramatic development in a country that was historically deeply divided on the question of the desired basic economic and political models.

In terms of issues that concern the population most, it seems that many of the most divisive, politicized, and controversial issues of the immediate post-transitional period have been left behind. There is increasing preoccupation with issues that are usually of concern in established democracies. While in March 1989 some 22.7 percent of Chileans identified human

36. Ibid.
37. Participa, "Estudio sobre la democracia y participación política," Informe segunda medición, 1993 (Santiago: Participa, 1993), 65.

rights as one of the three most important issues facing Chilean society, by June 1993 this had decreased to only 10.2 percent. During the same period, the percentage of those identifying crime as one of their three most important concerns rose from 21.5 percent to 56.4 percent. Health care and poverty followed at 49.2 percent and 39 percent, respectively. By 1998, the percentage of those citing human rights had dropped to 7 percent.[38]

Thus, in contemporary Chile the epic ideological struggles, prolonged strikes, land seizures, and revolutionary political movements of the 1970s are probably a thing of the past. Analysts of preauthoritarian Chilean politics pointed to extreme positions, class polarization, and the erosion of the Center as key elements leading to the demise of democracy in Chile. In contemporary Chile, this pattern has been replaced by a fundamental consensus on the elemental issues of politics and economics, and by a society characterized by decidedly moderate political positions. Chapter 4, which discusses the contemporary Chilean party system, provides additional support for this assertion and for others made throughout this chapter. This transformed social context certainly decreases the likelihood and potential severity of conflict and creates a more propitious environment for negotiation, compromise, and indeed democracy.

Socioeconomic and Political Change: Enduring Realities and New Challenges

Despite what has been said about convincing indicators of profound socioeconomic transformation, the first years of postauthoritarian democratic government in Chile have been unique and exceptional. Some important and enduring socioeconomic and political continuities have been overshadowed by the democratic transition process. What is more, the transformed socioeconomic and political context of Chile presents some new realities and challenges that have yet to be fully recognized. These new and unrecognized challenges may in the future counteract the conflict-diluting realities outlined above.

---

38. Centro de Estudios Públicos, "Estudio social y de opinión pública," June 1990, 30, and Centro de Estudios Públicos, "Estudio social y de opinión pública," June 1993, 39. Centro de Estudios Públicos, "Estudio nacional de opinión pública No. 7," 42.

Socioeconomic Continuity

In macroeconomic terms, despite impressive increases, per capita GDP in Chile in 1998 was still only US$4,032.00, far below even third-tier European countries.[39] Therefore, while Chile clearly has a rapidly developing economy, it still lacks many of the important structural and social characteristics of an advanced industrial democracy.

In addition, even with spectacular growth in exports, Chile still relies on its comparative advantages and its natural resources for its principal export income, and its domestic market and share of regional production are relatively small in Latin American terms.[40] Falling copper prices, combined with international protectionism or growing competition in the areas of fruit production and fishing, could eventually undermine Chile's model of export-led growth and reveal as yet unforeseen debilities in the Chilean economy. Macroeconomic crisis would be aggravated by the extensive holding of pensions, savings, and investments within the domestic financial services sector and stock market. Thus, despite decreased sensitivity to international economic shocks, Chile's dependent position in the international economic system has not been transformed, and the country is not immune to economic crises originating beyond its borders.

Perhaps more important, positive macroeconomic indicators and the increasing prosperity of Chileans mask enduring and deep socioeconomic divisions. The strategy of the military government to fight poverty and improve distribution of income was to increase overall economic growth in order to generate new jobs and boost salaries. The limited government social programs that did exist during the Pinochet government were designed to eliminate extreme poverty and improve the economic situations of only the poorest of the poor.[41] It has already been noted that the first democratic government also attempted to even the socioeconomic playing field through increased social spending. However, certain marginalized sectors of Chilean society remain cut off from the benefits of economic growth and government social spending.

39. The Inter-American Development Bank.
40. Chile's national production is dwarfed by Argentina's, Brazil's, and Mexico's. In 1993, Brazil's GDP was seven times that of Chile, while Mexico and Argentina produced five and four times as much, respectively. CEPAL, *Statistical Yearbook 1994*, 190–91.
41. Tarsicio Castañeda discusses the military's strategy of targeting the very poorest Chileans and the actual mechanics and implementation of policy to combat extreme poverty. See *Para combatir la pobreza. Política social y descentralización en Chile durante los '80s* (Santiago: Centro de Estudios Públicos, 1990).

First, even though the percentage of the population living in poverty is at its lowest point in twenty years, it is still above the 17 percent rate of 1970, although the percentage of indigent households is slightly lower. Table 3.5 summarizes the evolution of poverty and the percentage of indigent households in Chile, demonstrating that, despite advances, about 20 percent of the Chilean population is still characterized as poor.

It was not until 1988 that Chilean per capita income reached its 1973 level in real terms. What is more, and despite remarkable growth, gaps in income distribution have increased. Between 1978 and 1988, the wealthiest 10 percent of Chileans saw their share of national income increase from 36.2 percent to 46.8 percent, while the income of the lowest 50 percent declined from 20.4 percent to 16.8 percent.[42] Though distribution of income became slightly less skewed during the Aylwin administration, largely as a result of the 1990 reform in the tax code, important disparities remain. In 1994, the wealthiest 10 percent of the population still earned 41.6 percent of domestic income.[43] What is more, wealthy and middle-class Chileans have garnered the bulk of the proceeds from the country's economic success. The average real minimum wage index in 1995 was only 91.2, compared with the index base of 100 in 1974.[44]

Second, the impressive employment statistics for Chile mask some important underlying structural transformations that make for a less attractive and less firm labor market than is apparent at first glance. Economic reformers in Chile point to the growing "flexibility" of the labor market, but this flexible market is composed in large part of contractual temporary workers and day laborers with low salaries and job insecurity. Employers have increasingly shifted to the use of part-time, subcontracted, seasonal, and temporary labor. In this sense, the transformation of the Chilean labor market has given new meaning to the term "informal sector." The use of the term usually conjures up the large number of untaxed domestic servants, street vendors, self-appointed parking attendants, watchmen, seamstresses, and box and glass collectors that are ubiquitous in large Latin American cites. As in other capitals, the streets and buses of Santiago are still full of roving vendors hawking everything from chewing gum to ice cream to bathroom fixtures and furniture. Thus, in terms of the superficial and most obvious use of the term informal sector, a large but difficult-to-measure informal sector still exists, suggesting higher levels of unemployment and underemployment

42. Jorge Castañeda, *Utopia Unarmed* (New York: Knopf, 1993), 260.
43. Republic of Chile, Ministry of Planning, 1994.
44. Martínez and Díaz, *Chile: The Great Transformation*, 46.

Table 3.5. Evolution of poverty in Chile: Percentages of poor and indigent households

Year	Poor Households	Indigent Households
1970[a]	17.0	6.0
1979[b]	36.0	NA
1980[b]	40.3	NA
1982[b]	31.2	NA
1983[a]	NA	30.3
1984[b]	48.5	NA
1985[a]	45.0	25.0
1986[b]	50.9	NA
1987[a]	38.2	13.5
1990[a]	34.5	11.6
1992[c]	28.0	7.0
1994[c]	23.0	6.0
1996[c]	20.0	4.0

SOURCES: 1970–1990: Nora Lustig, ed., *Coping with Austerity: Poverty and Inequality in Latin America* (Washington, D.C.: Brookings Institution, 1995), 52, 289. 1992–1996: Economic Commission for Latin America and the Caribbean, *Panorama social de América Latina* (Santiago: CEPAL, 1997).

NA = Not available.

[a] Income includes monetary income of the family, including income transfers (monetary subsidies). In rural areas, an estimate of self-production and consumption is also included. *Indigent poor*: Household income equal to or less than the cost of one minimum food consumption basket (a basket that meets the caloric and protein requirements). *Poor*: Household income is equal to or less than the cost of two minimum food consumption baskets.

[b] Metropolitan areas; not adjusted for underreporting; proportion of households in poverty.

[c] Based on the CEPAL income method: the level of income necessary to provide the basic needs of a household for all members of a family.

than government statistics suggest. However, only about one-third of Chile's poor are so obviously "marginalized."[45] A more sophisticated understanding of the "informal sector" based on the structural transformation of firms suggests that there is a "new informality" in the Chilean economy and helps to explain how and why the remaining two-thirds of the poor are also, but to a lesser degree, marginalized.[46] The extensive use of subcontracted and temporary workers has increased the precariousness of waged employment. Javier Martínez and Alvaro Díaz have estimated that between 17 percent and 30 percent of Chilean workers

45. Ibid., 126.
46. Martínez and Díaz use the phrase "new informality" to describe the "change in the composition of the urban informal sector" and the "informalization of an important segment of capital-labor relations, as well as relations within capital" (ibid., 114).

have no formal contract. While employers enjoy the "flexibility" of this type of labor market, employees are often hemmed into rigid employment situations with little job security, high barriers to collective negotiations, substandard working conditions, and little room for advancement.[47]

Finally, accompanying the deterioration in the distribution of income has been the creation of a "dual society" in terms of access to health care, education, retirement benefits, and social services.[48] The widespread process of privatization undertaken by the military regime has created a two-tier private/state system in each of these areas, often leaving behind those who lack sufficient resources for access to upper-tier private firms and forcing many Chileans to rely on the inefficient services provided by a shrinking state.[49]

For example, the reformed pension system (AFPs, mentioned above) provides for private, member-funded investment accounts for retirees. Employees can select from a series of for-profit financial entities that administer pension funds, but the AFPs cover only the future retirement of persons currently contributing to their AFP account. Those covered by the old state-run social security system have been forced to rely on underfunded state allotments with very low benefit levels. Granted, this is a temporary problem that will be resolved as older Chileans work their way through the system, but a more pervasive problem is that the very poor and much of the marginalized informal sector do not understand the intricacies of the AFP system and do not have the resources to invest in it.

Military reforms also institutionalized dualism in health care. Decree Law 3626 issued in 1981 allowed for the creation of private hospitals and health insurance entities, which meant that Chileans now had the opportunity to choose more expensive private services (ISAPRES, Private Health

47. Ibid., 127.

48. The term "dual society" is used by Tironi. See Eugenio Tironi, *Autoritarismo, modernización y marginalidad: El caso de Chile 1973–1989* (Santiago: Ediciones Sur, 1990). For a discussion of educational reform in Chile, see José Joaquín Brunner and Cristián Cox, "Dinámicas de transformación en el sistema educacional de Chile," in *Educación, equidad y competitividad económica en las Américas*, ed. Jeffrey M. Puryear and José Joaquín Brunner (Washington: INTERAMER, 1995).

49. For separate discussions of the privatization of each of a series of activities previously carried out by the state in Chile, including those discussed below, see Cristián Larroulet, ed., *Private Solutions to Public Problems* (Santiago: Editorial Trineo, 1993). See also Tarsicio Castañeda, *Combating Poverty: Innovative Social Reforms in Chile During the 1980s* (San Francisco: ICS Press, 1992). For a more critical view of these transformations, see Martínez and Díaz, *Chile: The Great Transformation*. On the relationship between municipal government and social reform, see Joan Caivano, "Authoritarian Politics: The Dynamic Interplay Between A New Municipal Institutionality and Social Policies in Chile Under Pinochet" (Master's thesis, Georgetown University, 1991).

Preparedness Institutions) or to stay with the public national health system (FONASA, National Health Fund). Despite growth in the membership of privately funded ISAPRES, 68 percent of the Chilean public in 1993 still relied on state-run health care institutions,[50] which are plagued by problems, such as personnel shortages.[51] For example, in 1973, the nationalized health system relied on 110,000 employees to service a national population of 9,860,000, while in 1988 only 53,000 workers cared for the more than 11,000,000 Chileans not connected to the ISAPRE system.[52] In addition, shortages of supplies force patients to bring their own bandages, bedding, and medication if they come to state clinics. While private ambulance services with sophisticated equipment whisk patients with private medical insurance to modern clinics in a matter of minutes, patients relying on public ambulances often have to wait hours for slipshod, substandard, and often dangerous service, even in life-threatening situations. Levels of service are also much lower in state clinics, given that the best-trained health care professionals work for private medical establishments whose level of service and equipment is on a par with that in the United States and Western Europe.

Recently demand has been growing not only for increased social spending but also for a better quality of state-provided services, and for increased remuneration for state employees charged with providing the services. The 1993 strike of medical professionals working in the state sector demonstrated the growing discontent among higher-level state professionals. Thus, in the area of social services policy-makers have a long way to go in terms of improving distributional equality.[53]

Despite the transformations within the labor movement outlined above, and relative tranquillity on the labor front, there are also indications of growing discontent and a potential for increased activism among workers, both in traditional labor sectors and in new areas of the economy. However, the decrease in labor activity and the low number of strikes do not necessarily indicate contentment among Chilean workers, nor do they signal an end to the historically powerful labor movement. Rather, as noted above, the profile of labor has been transformed through a combination of the policies

50. Mercedes Cifuentes, "Health Care," in *Private Solutions,* ed. Larroulet, 53–93.

51. For a discussion, see Joseph Scarpaci, *Primary Medical Care in Chile: Accessibility Under Military Rule* (Pittsburgh: Pittsburgh University Press, 1988).

52. Manuel Delano and Hugo Traslaviña, *La herencia de los Chicago boys* (Santiago: Ediciones del Ornitorrinco, 1989), 149.

53. Though it is not analyzed here, a similar dualistic situation prevails in education.

of the Pinochet government, changing occupational patterns, and the exigencies of the democratic transition.

The complete suppression of the labor movement during the Pinochet regime produced a legacy of disarticulation. The military regime forced the country's most important labor federation, the Central Unica de Trabajadores, to disband and killed, exiled, and imprisoned many of its members. The atomization of the labor movement took its toll on workers. In 1989, workers earned 8 percent less in real terms than they did in 1970, and the minimum wage was 9 percent lower.[54]

The economic policies of the military regime, and the structural changes those policies produced, further undermined labor's position. The severity of the shocks experienced during the process of economic restructuring hurt labor, with unemployment rising to 30 percent at the height of the 1983 economic crisis. In addition, as a result of economic restructuring, areas in which labor was traditionally strong (principally mining, manufacturing, and the state sector) have become relatively less important. Many large, state-owned industries, which relied on state subsidies and tariff protection, collapsed, taking with them the relatively high salaries and benefits of the most sought after working-class jobs (mining, of course, being the great exception).

What is more, spectacular growth within the financial services and insurance and health sectors has created a large yet atomized pool of "white-" and "pink-" collar clerical workers, who for structural reasons organized labor has had trouble reaching. Similarly, workers in the export-oriented commercial agricultural sector, consisting of a growing percentage of temporary migrant workers, have been difficult to organize because of the often seasonal nature of the employment and the geographical dispersion of the workers. Women make up a large percentage of the labor force in the areas that are experiencing spectacular growth, and most are not union members, given the nature of this new occupational structure. The difficulty in organizing women is compounded by the fact that, during the 1980s, 40.2 percent of economically active women were employed in the informal sector (about half of those in domestic service).[55]

Labor's support for the Concertación government, and its willingness to help ensure the integrity of the democratic transition, meant that labor was willing to tone down its demands for the short term in exchange for

54. Ricardo Ffrench Davis, "Desarrollo económico y equidad en Chile: Herencias y desafíos en el retorno a la democracia," *Colección estudios CIEPLAN* 31 (March 1991): 31–52.

55. Angell, "Unions and Workers in Chile During the 1980s," 189.

promises of an eventual change in labor codes and in wage policy during future governments. Labor leaders explicitly recognized their role as an important element of the social and political pact necessary for a successful transition to democracy. Extreme positions and vocal demands were set aside in favor of consolidating democracy, which was recognized as the only viable political system in which labor could have a voice.

However, once the crucial period of the democratic transition passes, demands for more latitude in collective bargaining and for an increase in the minimum wage are likely to become increasingly vocal. The government estimates that only about 10 percent of the work force has the capacity to engage in collective bargaining, and it has explicitly recognized that the pro-business bias of the labor code inherited from the previous regime should be redressed, even beyond the 1990 reforms.[56] Despite government efforts to introduce legislation that would increase the de facto bargaining power of labor, businesses have exerted pressures to delay further changes in the labor code, resulting in the frustration of workers. As the structural reorganization of the economy proceeds, and labor organizations take full advantage of reforms in the labor code, it is likely that the number of labor unions and the scope of organization will increase both in traditional areas and in new areas.

Labor leaders have already expressed their unhappiness with the low priority the government has assigned their demands. In July and August 1991, strikes occurred at the Chuquicamata and El Teniente copper mines (Chile's largest). The unions believed that the government would intervene in their favor, but they became disillusioned when it refused to support strikers' demands. Some labor leaders believed that the governing coalition had reneged on the social pact by which labor and government abided to ease the transition to democracy. Labor's disillusionment is likely to grow if the government does not take concerted action to satisfy its demands.

As the urgency of the transition period lessens, and there is growing frustration with the perceived marginalized position of labor, it is likely that the demands of organized labor will increase and become more vocal in coming years. Indeed, though labor activism has significantly decreased compared with the historical average, Table 3.4 also shows a gradual, albeit moderate, increase in industrial disputes since 1989. What is perhaps a more serious threat to economic and political stability is the role that will be assumed by

56. "The Financial Times Survey: Chile," 13.

unorganized and marginalized workers. There are few formalized forums for articulating the demands of this large sector of the work force.

Other structural economic transformations that are usually considered positive may also have unanticipated results. The withdrawal and shrinking of the Chilean state, considered the most important aspect of the economy's restructuring, also have some negative consequences. Contrary to the predominant opinions of many economists in Latin America and elsewhere, a simple reduction in the size of the state and in the scope of its activities will not guarantee efficiency and clean government. These changes also have costs in terms of the representative capacity of the political system. For many Chileans, demand satisfaction involved appeals to members of Congress and/or local authorities who often lobbied ministries and state agencies to resolve problems related to everything from basic state services to social security and pensions. Privatization has transferred many of these functions to private firms, transforming and depoliticizing the traditional norms of demand satisfaction. On the one hand, depoliticization may seem to be a good thing. On the other hand, in a system historically characterized by interest representation and satisfaction through direct ties to the state, the reduction in its scope of activities may result in a politically and economically marginalized population, as some citizens' only formal ties to the state are severed. While one could argue that this view confuses representation with clientelism, at the very least it is clear that the question of the capacity of elected authorities to serve their constituents becomes more pressing when other avenues of representation are closed. It is also crucial that alternative avenues of demand satisfaction and interest representation are established as redemocratization proceeds. The state has also withdrawn or scaled back many of its regulatory activities, creating a ripe environment for the growth of incipient corruption.[57] In addition, the withdrawal of the Chilean state is not yet complete. The state continues to be involved in the still nationalized copper, port, and railroad industries. The economic role of the state remains an important and controversial political issue that future governments will need to resolve.

More serious perhaps is that state domination in most of the nonmining sectors of the economy has been replaced by domination of a few big firms

57. In numerous interviews, officials in the executive and legislative branches contended that the government has not been steadfast enough in stemming a swelling tide of corruption caused by the withdrawal of the state and the limited oversight capabilities of the Congress. Members of the government and opposition parties in equal numbers cited corruption as a growing problem.

associated with large economic groups. These conglomerates control more than 85 percent of exports, on which the country's economic recovery and growth in recent years have been based. Concentration of national resources in the state sector has been replaced by a similar concentration in a few large firms, for a number of reasons. The state's efforts to rescue the country's ailing financial entities during the crises of the early 1980s resulted in the transfer of state resources to the private sector. At the same time, the sale of many efficient and profitable state-owned businesses at bargain prices offered an opportunity both for acquisition of resources and for rapid capital accumulation among the country's largest firms. During much of the 1980s, the undervalued peso created incentives for a massive transfer of resources to the export sector, which was also dominated by large economic groups. While this concentration of capital and decision-making authority is not necessarily negative in terms of macroeconomic performance, it does concentrate power among a few whose loyalty lies with stockholders and the bottom line.[58] For better or for worse, for the country's largest industries, state or public interest no longer enters into economic decision-making.

Finally, some difficult-to-measure but significant phenomena have affected short-term policy-making, but they will have long-term consequences in terms of socioeconomic transformation. It is important not to ignore the political context in which socioeconomic changes have played out. The first government undertook economic policy-making fully aware of the potentially negative political consequences of a significant change in the economic model of the authoritarian regime. There was also an exaggerated optimism among Chilean political and economic elites. While the economic success of Chile caught the attention of Latin America and the world, the country's policy-makers basked in the adulation that came with economic success. Chilean policy-makers participated in workshops and seminars around the world detailing how the Chilean model could be duplicated and applied in other contexts. An almost arrogant optimism has developed concerning the long-term success of Chile's process of economic liberalization.

The political context of the transition period and the exaggerated optimism of Chilean elites are significant for the socioeconomic future of the country for two reasons. First, given an end to the special context of the transition period, and a return to what can be considered a more normal pattern of political interaction, demands for a share of the macroeconomic

58. These realities are discussed by Martínez and Díaz, *Chile: The Great Transformation*, 72–74.

success of the nation are bound to grow, both in terms of calls for increased income and in terms of better access to and provision of social services. Second, excessive optimism on the part of policy-makers may lead them to overlook or underrate the importance of the many structural difficulties still plaguing the Chilean economy.

Thus, in socioeconomic terms, despite much progress and significant changes, challenges still remain in terms of further economic diversification, distribution of income, articulation of labor demands, and access to social services. The restructuring of the Chilean state, labor market, and private firms provides a more complex context for meeting these challenges, given that the traditional form of interest representation through direct ties to the state has been displaced, and the reality that formal institutions of representation like Congress have been weakened.

Disagreement and the Continued Salience of Politics

Despite what has been said about widespread agreement on certain issues and about Chilean society being less conflictual and less ideological, there is certainly not complete consensus within Chilean society and political differences have not ceased to be relevant. This suggests that although some of the structural sources of conflict may have been attenuated, some others have been masked by the recent positive economic, political, and social context of the country.

Notwithstanding deep socioeconomic transformations, class conflict still plays a significant role in Chile. A study aimed at measuring the type and extent of tension between different groups and institutions in Chilean society found that "conflict between the rich and poor" was rated as most significant from a list of ten categories. In 1991, 55.9 percent of those surveyed rated it as a "*gran conflicto*" (a large or important conflict), and in 1992 the number had increased to 58.9 percent. This category polled higher than "conflict between the government and armed forces," which received 43.3 percent and 51.6 percent in these two years, respectively (years when tension between the government and the armed forces was quite prevalent and important).[59]

59. Participants were asked to respond to the following statement: "Algunas personas creen que en Chile existen diversos tipos de conflictos entre grupos; otros creen que estos conflictos son menores o no existen. En cada caso que le nombraré dígame si Ud. cree que, hoy en Chile, existe un gran conflicto, un conflicto menor, o que no hay conflicto." ("Some people believe that in Chile there exist diverse types of conflict between groups; other believe that these conflicts are less important or do not exist. For each case that I give you, tell me if you

Growing economic disparity between the rich and the poor is the most likely culprit for this growing class animosity. The respected director of a Santiago-based polling organization pointed out that the socioeconomic transformations that are taking place are increasingly undermining Chilean values and traditional middle-class modesty. She contended: "Chile is not an austere country; it is becoming a show-off country. This means the poor are more conscious than ever of missing out on the benefits of growth."[60]

In addition, even though it is generally accepted that democracy is the most workable and appropriate regime, in 1993 only 57 percent of Chileans agreed that they were satisfied or very satisfied with the way Chilean democracy functioned.[61] This percentage dropped to 27 percent in 1996,[62] quite low considering both Chile's long history with democracy and the reality that the level of satisfaction with democracy is about the same in countries that have much less propitious economic and political situations. Indeed, of the nine Latin American nations covered in a 1996 Latino-barómetro survey, Argentina, Peru, Ecuador, and Venezuela had rates of satisfaction that were slightly higher than Chile's, and the region-wide average rate of satisfaction was 31 percent.[63]

In terms of the strength of democracy, only 25.3 percent of those polled in a survey evaluating Chilean democracy characterized it as "*más bien sólida*" (more or less solid). From 1991 to 1992, the percentage of those characterizing Chilean democracy as "*más bien débil*" (more or less weak) increased from 56.8 percent to 61.9 percent. Furthermore, 70 percent of those surveyed agreed with the statement "Nuestra democracia tiene muchos problemas que hay que mejorar" (Our democracy is characterized by many problems that need to be improved). Though in certain respects these results

---

believe that today in Chile there exists a great conflict, a lesser conflict, or if no conflict exists.") Participa, "Estudio sobre la democracia y participación política," 36.

60. Marta Lagos, quoted in "The Financial Times Survey: Chile," 13.

61. Participa, "Estudio sobre la democracia y participación política," 17.

62. These data are used with permission from the 1996 Latinobarómetro survey and are cited in Marta Lagos, "The Latinobarómetro: Media and Political Attitudes in South America" (paper presented at the 1996 Meeting of the American Political Science Association, San Francisco, 29 August to 1 September 1996, fig. 4). The wording of the survey was slightly different from that cited above. The satisfaction score included those who answered "very satisfied" and "fairly satisfied." Other choices were "not very satisfied" and "not at all satisfied," which scored 54 percent and 15 percent, respectively.

63. The 1996 Latinobarómetro survey cited above also found that only 54 percent of Chileans considered democracy preferable to an authoritarian regime, while 19 percent agreed that in certain situations an authoritarian regime can be preferable and 23 percent contended that the two regimes are essentially the same (see fig. 5).

represent something of the type of consensus outlined above, it is a negative consensus with regard to the way democracy is functioning.[64] Further, though the public supports democracy as the desired political model, there continues to be dissatisfaction with the way it currently functions. To a certain extent, these results probably mirror a growing dissatisfaction with democratic institutions around the world. However, a continuing negative perception of the functioning of democracy could result in increased demands for change and in disillusionment with existing political parties and political institutions.

These data are not presented to suggest that there is a level of regime-threatening dissatisfaction with democracy within the country. Rather, they simply point to qualitative difficulties within Chilean democracy and to how difficult it is to improve the functioning of the system.

Unresolved political issues also continue to haunt democratic leaders. In May 1995, despite the absence of outright military incursions, Chile experienced its most severe political crisis since the return of democracy. The standoff between civilian leaders and military authorities over the convictions of General Manuel Contreras and Brigadier General Pedro Espinoza reminded Chileans that the authoritarian chapter in Chilean history was not yet completely closed. Following Contreras's conviction for his role as an intellectual author of the Washington, D.C., bombing assassination of former Foreign Minister Orlando Letelier in 1976, the general refused to submit to civilian authorities. General Pinochet lent his support to Contreras, aggressively reminding Chilean democratic authorities that "our people remain members of our institution forever" and that "the army never abandons one of its men who is in trouble."[65]

Though Contreras was eventually jailed after several months in a military hospital, the conflict served as ample reminder of the many unresolved political issues still facing the country. The most important is the problematic question of how far civilians should go in pursuing cases of crimes and human rights abuses that are not subject to the military-proclaimed amnesty, and how military leaders can be made to submit to civilian judicial proceedings. While public-opinion survey data consistently show that a majority of Chileans favor "turning the page" on the past, problems not addressed in the transition process may be more difficult to resolve, as the Espinoza and Contreras cases suggest.[66] The conflict and violent disturbances that emerged following Pinochet's arrest in London in October 1998 are further testa-

64. Participa, "Estudio sobre la democracia y participación política," 13–14.
65. Quoted in the *Chicago Tribune*, 18 June 1995, 18.

ment to continuing disagreement concerning the significance of the military regime to Chilean history, and for Chile's future.

Finally, though there has been an ideological narrowing of the electorate, this does not signify an end to ideology. Party attachments remain quite strong in Chile, a reality that is explored in detail in the next chapter. What is more, Timothy Scully and J. Samuel Valenzuela have shown that there is a high correlation between the electoral preferences of the Chilean population in the preauthoritarian and postauthoritarian periods.[67] The authors argue that the traditional pattern of *tres tercios* persists, a contention that evidence presented in the next chapter also supports.

In addition, Arturo Fontaine has convincingly argued that though the meaning of "Left" and "Right" in Chile has certainly changed, the terms remain valid in categorizing the continuing basic divisions within the Chilean electorate. Many of the traditional cleavages and ideological differences that gave birth to the Left, the Right, and the Center are less salient. However, Fontaine has argued that there are three basic axes along which these ideological sectors can still be differentiated: socioeconomic (development vs. equity), political (order vs. democracy and civil rights), and historic (Pinochet vs. Allende). He has found strong correlations between ideological self-placement and the side that Chileans come down on in expressing opinions relative to a number of controversial questions. For each question, those who identified themselves as supporters of parties on the Right expressed support for the first item in each of the above dichotomies. Those on the Left chose the latter, and most members of parties of the Center expressed an intermediate position.

For example, on the one hand, those who describe themselves as identifying with the Left expressed much more support for state efforts to promote equality and to ensure individual rights. They were much less concerned with public order, and more likely to have a favorable estimation of the Allende administration and a negative view of the Pinochet regime. On the

66. Though Chile is well known for its thorough and in-depth investigation of human rights abuses during the military regime, and particularly for its Commission for Truth and Reconciliation (the so-called Rettig Commission), investigations were not intended to result in the prosecution of those guilty of human rights abuses. For many victims' families, the simple investigation of abuses does not go far enough.

67. See J. Samuel Valenzuela and Timothy Scully, "Electoral Choices and the Party System in Chile: Continuities and Changes at the Recovery of Democracy," *Comparative Politics* 29 (July 1997): 511–27. For a longer version of the same article with more data, see Scully and Valenzuela, "De la democracia a la democracia: Continuidad y variaciones en las preferencias del electorado y en el sistema de partidos en Chile," *Estudios públicos* 51 (Winter 1993): 195–228.

other hand, those who placed themselves on the Right considered economic development more important than equality and were concerned more with public order than with individual rights. Those on the Right gave high marks to the Pinochet regime and low marks to the Allende administration. Finally, on each of these issues, those who placed themselves in the Center of the political spectrum expressed a level of concern somewhere between the concerns expressed on the Right and the Left, and a mixed evaluation of both the Pinochet and Allende governments. Thus, despite some basic consensus, Fontaine's data suggest that distinct political sectors remain, with programmatic and indeed ideological differences between them.[68]

Survey data measuring ideological self-identification of the Chilean public also underscore the existence of a society that continues to be divided politically. When speaking of ideology in Chile, it is important to bear in mind (as suggested above) that the nature of ideological attachments has indeed changed. As the following chapter on the party system argues, all parties have undergone processes of ideological reformulation, and the strength of partisan attachments appears to have ebbed. Nonetheless, programmatic issues associated with particular partisan options apparently continue to be significant. In essence, while the party spectrum is narrower in terms of "ideology" (as it is usually understood), partisan differences based on controversial issue areas are still significant and are subsumed within the traditional notions of the Left, the Right, and the Center in Chile, an argument consonant with that of Fontaine. What is more, the population continues to define itself in these terms.

How then has the ideological self-identification of Chileans evolved? Public-opinion data shown in Table 3.6 demonstrate a marked shift toward the Center in the ideological self-identification of the Chilean population in 1986 (three years before the democratic transition began). This reality led scholars and political analysts to conclude that the Chilean citizenry had made a decisive and permanent move toward the Center. However, data from 1991 suggest a return to a more typical pattern of competition in the country. If the "no response" category were not considered for 1991, there would appear to be a movement away from centrist identification.

In addition, more recent data provide strong confirmation of this trend. For the purposes of comparison, unfortunately, most public-opinion surveys since the transition group ideological categories differently than those dis-

---

68. Arturo Fontaine Talavera, "Significado del eje derecha-izquierda," *Estudios públicos* 58 (Fall 1995): 79–137.

Table 3.6. Ideological distribution of the Chilean electorate, 1958–1991: Right, Center, and Left

Question: Do you feel closer to the Right, Center, or Left?						
	1958 (%)	1961 (%)	1964 (%)	1970 (%)	1973 (%)	1986 (%)	1991 (%)
Right	31.4	23.8	17.4	26.6	21.9	16.6	13.4
Center	17.8	28.2	29.0	24.2	26.8	41.2	23.2
Left	24.5	26.5	32.0	26.0	42.9	14.2	24.2
Independent/No response*	26.3	21.5	21.6	23.2	8.4	28.0	39.1
Total	100	100	100	100	100	100	100

SOURCES: Adapted from Timothy Scully. *Los partidos del centro y la evolución política chilena* (Santiago: CIEPLAN, 1992); additional data added. 1991 data: Centro de Estudios Públicos, *Estudio de opinión pública*, July 1991.

*Note: As noted in the text, more recent data grouped in the same way is difficult to obtain, given that most public opinion research now subdivides the sectors into center-right, Center, center-left. It would appear that Scully's data may include independents in the no response category, as the percentages appear quite large to be only "no responses." For the 1991 data added to Scully's chart, interviewees could choose an independent position, and for better or worse this data was grouped together with those who were "non-respondents."

cussed above, breaking down categories into Right/center-right, Center, and Left/center-left. Thus, more recent data are not directly comparable to those presented in Table 3.6. Nonetheless, as Table 3.7 suggests, data grouped this way suggest a dramatic decline in centrist identification.

There has also been a trend away from the Center in the two parliamentary elections since 1989 (1993 and 1997).[69] The two most center-oriented parties, the Christian Democrats (PDC) and Renovación Nacional (RN), lost ground to parties to their right and left, particularly in the 1997 election. These results caused a shake-up in both parties. The leaders of the moderate group of RN's board of directors, Andrés Allamand and Alberto Espina, were forced to resign, representing a rejection by the party of two of the most important and visible leaders on the Right. There was also evidence of dissent in the Christian Democratic Party immediately following the election, given the party's dramatic decline in support from about 27 percent to 22 percent, and an increase in support to about the same level for the PS-PPD pact. Support for the Communist Party also increased.

Given ideological moderation in contemporary Chile, this phenomenon is certainly not as problematic as the erosion of the Center pointed to by

69. This was also undeniably a function of the fact that the most important governing party is a centrist party and would have borne the brunt of dissatisfaction with the government.

Table 3.7. Ideological self-placement of the Chilean electorate, June 1990–July 1997

Response to the question:
"With which political position do you identify or sympathize most?"

	Right/Center-Right	Center	Left/Center-Left	Independent/ Don't Know/Other[a]
June 1990	14.3%	25.3%	28.5%	32.0%
October 1990	15.2	29.5	28.2	27.1
December 1990	13.4	29.9	23.7	33.1
March 1991	17.7	28.8	21.0	32.5
July 1991	13.4	23.2	24.2	39.1
October 1991	19.7	33.0	23.2	24.1
December 1991	21.9	30.8	23.3	24.1
April 1992	19.0	24.9	24.1	32.1
August 1992	22.6	22.4	31.4	23.6
December 1992	26.9	22.4	36.7	13.9
March 1993	22.7	24.6	33.7	19.0
June 1993	22.5	20.4	36.2	21.0
October 1993	28.6	18.5	33.4	19.4
November 1993	26.1	19.8	33.7	20.4
December 1993	28.4	17.6	37.1	16.9
November–December 1994*	28.0	17.0	28.0	26.0
May–June 1995	25.0	16.0	24.0	35.0
November 1995	25.0	16.0	26.0	33.0
June–July 1996	26.0	16.0	24.0	34.0
November–December 1996	28.0	11.0	22.0	40.0
June–July 1997	22.0	10.0	21.0	47.0

SOURCES: Centro de Estudios Públicos, "Estudio social y de opinión pública," Santiago, December 1993, Centro de Estudios Públicos, "Estudio nacional de opinión pública," Santiago, December–January 1997–98.

[a] This category also includes those who did not answer or who answered "None." Unfortunately, these categories were not disaggregated by those conducting the survey. Knowledge of those who self-define as Independents would have been useful. Beginning in 1994, all data are based on surveys of urban population.

*Surveys began rounding to largest whole numbers in 1994.

Valenzuela as the overriding cause of the 1973 breakdown.[70] Nonetheless, it does suggest something of a polarization of attitudes on important political issues facing the country, and some less-than-smooth political waters for the future.

The Politicization of Divisions

While existing socioeconomic divisions, potential economic problems, and political conflicts are in themselves significant, for the purposes of this study what is more important is politicization of these issues by political leaders. Indicators of politicization are difficult to identify for a number of reasons. The positive context of the political and economic situation of the country repeatedly underscored throughout this study has helped to stem politicization. What is more, given that all major parties in Chile have statements in their platforms concerning the elimination of inequality and better access to social services, it is difficult to locate and operationalize conflict related to distributional issues. Finally, mounting evidence, including that presented in the next chapter, suggests that the connections between society and parties in Chile have weakened somewhat.[71] The shrinking of the state has reinforced this tendency, given that the ability of parties to control the distribution of state resources has dramatically decreased. Thus, party manifestations of conflict might be more muted than in the past, given the breakdown of the political connections between parties and society. Perhaps vertical political links have been cut, and elites are less aware of popular dissent than in the past.

Nonetheless, there are some limited and growing indications of the politicization of the issues discussed here. As discussed in Chapter 2, cracks are already appearing in the Concertación coalition, and indeed within individual parties, over policy differences related to the socioeconomic issues dealt with throughout this chapter. In addition, political debate in Congress

---

70. Arturo Valenzuela, *The Breakdown of Democratic Regimes: Chile* (Baltimore: Johns Hopkins University Press, 1978).

71. Felipe Aguero, Eugenio Tironi, Eduardo Valenzuela, and Guillermo Sunkel provide an interesting discussion of this issue. See "Voters, Parties, and Political Information: Fragile Political Intermediation in Post-authoritarian Chile" (paper presented at the Twentieth International Congress of the Latin American Studies Association, Guadalajara, Mexico, 17–19 April 1997).

and in the press has recently taken the form of more traditional ideological discourse.

In 1997, two of the Concertación's associated parties jumped ship to join the traditional ideological Left. The MAPU (Movimiento de Acción Popular Unitaria) and the Alianza Humanista-Verde abandoned the Concertación, rationalizing their departure as a response to the inability of the Concertación alliance to confront the agenda of Chile's traditional Left: alleviating poverty, stemming marginalization, and engaging in political reform to enhance popular representation.

In terms of the politicization of policy differences, despite what has been said about the acceptance of market capitalism, disagreement over the extent and terms of privatization has divided the Concertación along party lines. This was most visible in the almost two-year debate concerning the privatization of water treatment facilities in the country. The appropriateness of privatizing the industry (as part of the national "patrimony"), combined with concerns about the fate of sewage employees, drove a wedge between the Center and the Left. Though the bill was eventually approved, it revealed clear differences in political orientations of the ruling coalition in terms of the role of the state. What is more, the tenor of the debate in the press and in Congress took on a surprisingly ideological (in traditional terms) tone.

The politicization of divisions is also reflected in the resurrection of historical, ideologically based animosities and the fusion of concrete issues to these animosities. The efforts of the PPD-PS sector to bring the Communist Party (PC, Partido Comunista) into the governing coalition for the December 1997 parliamentary elections was vetoed by the Christian Democrats, despite clear evidence that the addition of the PC's 6 percent vote share would have helped Concertación candidates to pass thresholds established by the electoral system. In exchange for the alliance, PC Party Secretary Gladys Marín went so far as to offer to withdraw her Senate candidacy from one of Santiago's Senate districts in order to enhance the probability of a Concertación victory. The Christian Democrats rejected the alliance, citing the PC's antidemocratic orientation.[72] The dismissal of the Communists, combined with the (then) possible rejection of Socialist presidential candidate Ricardo Lagos for the 1999 presidential election, brought the Left closer to its traditional ideological partners and away from the Center. The Left has,

72. It is also arguable that the Christian Democrats believed that the alliance would alienate centrist supporters, and thus the party would stand to lose as many voters on one of its ideological extremes as it had the potential to gain on the other.

in turn, politicized divisions in Chile, drawing on traditional appeals and traditional programs despite its deeper ideological reformulation.

Most dramatically, the very issue that brought the Concertación together recently threatened to split the coalition and demonstrated that even the democratic/authoritarian cleavage that helped forge the alliance is less resilient than it once seemed. In April 1998, a number of Concertación deputies initiated a constitutional accusation against General Pinochet. Though protected by a general amnesty for acts committed between 1973 and 1978, Pinochet was charged with "undermining the national honor and security of the country"[ ] while commander in chief of the armed forces after the return to democracy. The sponsors of the accusation, among them six Christian Democrats, aimed to prevent Pinochet from assuming his constitutionally guaranteed lifetime Senate seat after he stepped down as commander in chief of the armed forces.[73] The issue divided not only the left-wing and centrist parties of the Concertación but also the Christian Democratic Party itself. The measure failed by a vote of 62 to 52, but it was the eleven Christian Democratic deputies who joined the opposition that resulted in its defeat. The debate in the Chamber of Deputies was particularly dramatic, involving frequent references to the military coup, human rights abuses, and insults traded between parties.[74] The fallout from the failure of the accusation underscored the increasing politicization of underlying issues yet to be completely resolved. The debate following Pinochet's 1998 London arrest had a similar tenor, with formal protests, catcalls, and fist-fights erupting during the president's traditionally somber State of the Union address on 21 March 1999.

Conclusion

This chapter has argued that the vision of society that guided the design of the institutions for control set down in the 1980 constitution is clearly at odds with the current socioeconomic and political conditions that exist in Chile. The image of a society plagued by extreme divisions, social conflict, and ideological polarization is clearly no longer applicable, given the international and domestic transformations that have affected the socioeconomic and political landscape of the country.

73. The seat was guaranteed him as a former president, not as a former commander in chief.
74. See Cámara de Diputados, Boletín de Sesiones, 9 April 1998.

However, this chapter also revealed that there are some profound economic and distributive difficulties that still need to be addressed in what remains a complex society, characterized by diverse groups with distinct interests and unmet demands. While Chile is often regarded as a unique case of positive socioeconomic transformation, it has a number of things in common with other Latin American countries in terms of the challenges it faces. Issues of distribution of income, social benefits, health, and education will be important items on the political agenda for the next few years. What is more, future leaders will be forced to address controversial issues like abortion, divorce, the role of the state in industry, and, more serious, the question of if, when, and how to deal with the crimes of the previous regime.

Positive macroeconomic performance, combined with the universally recognized need to sustain the transition process and maintain the governing coalition, have made it possible to delay action on these issues. However, with the lessening of the urgency that characterized the immediate postauthoritarian period, future governments will be forced to address those issues, perhaps in a much less propitious economic and political environment.

In addition, important political divisions within Chilean society have been masked by the process of democratic transition and the "forced consensus" it created. This consensus is perhaps much thinner than analysts of Chilean politics have suggested. Despite widespread agreement on the desirability of democracy and market economics, the Chilean public remains divided on policy options and priorities within the framework of market democracy.

Finally, it is also important to recognize that the social context for democracy is malleable and subject to rapid changes beyond those discussed. In the postauthoritarian era, the country has yet to face a significant economic or political crisis. With the emergence of such a crisis in a less consensus-forcing post-transitional context, many of these latent conflicts may become much more manifest and significant.

4

CONTINUITY AND CHANGE IN THE POSTAUTHORITARIAN CHILEAN PARTY SYSTEM

Analysts of Chilean politics often underscore the importance of party-system polarization in contributing to the breakdown of democracy in Chile. While the roots of democratic instability and breakdown in much of Latin America are often traced to the weakness of political institutions and political parties in the face of powerful social mobilization,[1] students of Chilean politics more often pointed to the *strength* of political parties in encouraging political mobilization as one of the determining causes of regime crisis.[2] Culminating a historical process that had begun much earlier, in the period leading

1. For this type of interpretation, see Samuel Huntington, *Political Order in Changing Societies* (New Haven: Yale University Press, 1968).
2. For an example of this type of analysis and for the best study on the events and circumstances leading to the collapse of democracy in Chile, see Arturo Valenzuela, *The Breakdown of Democratic Regimes: Chile*. Valenzuela, employing many of the tools of Giovanni Sartori's framework for understanding party systems, traces the dialectical interaction of the social, political, and structural variables that led to the breakdown of democracy in Chile, arguing that the erosion of the political Center coupled with the mobilizing and ideological nature of Chilean party politics helped to contribute to the breakdown of democracy in 1973. For a discussion of the mobilizing role of parties in the democratic breakdown, see H. Landsberger and T. McDaniel, "Hypermobilization in Chile, 1970–73," *World Politics* 28 (July 1976): 502–41. For a more negative view of the role of political parties, see Bernardino Bravo Lira, "Orígenes, apogeo y ocaso de los partidos políticos en Chile," *Política* 7 (July 1985): 9–42.

up to the breakdown of democracy, there was a dynamic interaction between the drives polarizing society and the centrifugation of the party system. This, in turn, given the strength of individual parties, led to inflexibility, to maximalist tendencies, and ultimately to polarization of the party system and a breakdown of the regime.

Since the return of democratic politics, party competition has been characterized by a moderate pattern of bipolar coalitional competition between an alliance of the center-left (the Concertación por la Democracia) and the center-right (Unión por Chile[3]). This model of competition has led certain analysts to suggest that there has been fundamental quantitative and qualitative change in the Chilean party system.[4] They contend that the polarization and division that characterized the party system in the past have been overshadowed, ushering in a new era of party-system integration and increased interparty cooperation. Others have suggested that socioeconomic transformations, coupled with the integrative drives of the majoritarian electoral formula devised by the military regime, have led, or will lead, to a reduction in the number of significant political parties from Chile's historic average.[5]

Given the crucial role that political parties have played in the development, maintenance, and breakdown of Chilean democracy,[6] and given the

3. For the 1989 elections, this alliance was known as Democracia y Progreso, and for the 1993 elections, Unión por el Progreso.

4. See Rhoda Rabkin, "Redemocratization, Electoral Engineering, and Party Strategies in Chile: 1989–1995," *Comparative Political Studies* 29 (1996): 335–56. Hernán Larraín also discusses this debate. See "Democracia, partidos políticos y transición: El caso chileno," *Estudios públicos* 15 (Winter 1984): 111–15. Hernán Gutiérrez argues that the impact of the authoritarian regime has led to a profound transformation of the Chilean party system, contending that the pattern of *"tres-tercios"* that historically characterized the Chilean party system may be a thing of the past. Hernán Gutiérrez, "Chile 1989: Elecciones fundacionales?" *Documento de trabajo, Serie estudios públicos*, no. 3, FLACSO, Santiago (October 1990). On the postauthoritarian party system in general, see Eduardo Barros, "El nuevo orden de partidos: Algunas hipótesis," *Estudios públicos* 38 (Fall 1990): 129–39.

5. See, for example, Eugenio Guzmán, "Reflexiones sobre el sistema binominal," *Estudios públicos* 51 (Winter 1993): 303–25.

6. While political parties in much of Latin America have been weak and underinstitutionalized, Manuel Antonio Garretón accurately describes the Chilean party system as the "backbone" of society permeating all aspects of social and political life. See his *The Chilean Political Process*, 11–13. On the preauthoritarian party system, see Arturo Valenzuela, "The Scope of the Chilean Party System," *Comparative Politics* 4 (January 1972): 179–99. For additional discussions of Chilean parties, see Norbert Lechner, ed., *Partidos y democracia* (Santiago: FLACSO, 1985), and Marcelo Cavarozzi and Manuel Antonio Garretón, eds., *Muerte y resurrección: Los partidos políticos en el autoritarismo y las transiciones del cono sur* (Santiago: FLACSO, 1989).

recognized importance of party-system configuration in the performance of democratic institutions,[7] it is important to arrive at an understanding of the probable physiognomy and interactive dynamic of the Chilean party system. The nature and competitive format of the party system have a profound effect on the functioning and workability of democratic institutions. Distinct institutional arrangements create different incentives for cooperation and negotiation, depending on the party system and the nature of individual parties.

The three most important questions for analyzing the relationship between the party system and the performance of democratic institutions in Chile are: (1) Have the domestic and international transformations outlined in Chapter 3 led to a narrowing in the ideological scope of the party system? (2) Have these variables, in conjunction with the two-member district electoral system, resulted in a reduction in the number of significant political parties in Chile? and (3) Has there been a transformation in the competitive dynamic of the party system? This chapter will contend that the respective answers to these questions are yes, no, and probably not. That is to say, this chapter will argue that the contemporary party system in Chile is characterized by elements of both continuity and change, as was similarly evident in the previous chapter's discussion of Chile's socioeconomic conditions.

Ideological Scope and the "De-Ideologicalization" of Chilean Political Parties

The starting point for a discussion of the breadth of ideological tendencies of Chilean parties must be a realization that the political and intellectual environment of Chile and Latin America in the 1990s is profoundly different from what it was in the years leading up to the 1973 breakdown of democracy. The radicalism that characterized the parties of the Left in Latin

---

7. On the significance of political parties in Latin America and for a useful framework for understanding them, see Scott Mainwaring and Timothy Scully, eds., *Building Democratic Institutions: Party Systems in Latin America* (Stanford, Calif.: Stanford University Press, 1995). See also several works by Scott Mainwaring, including "Presidentialism in Latin America: A Review Essay," *Latin American Research Review* 25, no. 1 (1990): 157–79; "Presidentialism, Multipartism, and Democracy: The Difficult Combination," *Comparative Political Studies* 26 (July 1993): 198–228; and his introduction, with Matthew Shugart, to *Presidentialism and Democracy in Latin America*, ed. Mainwaring and Shugart.

America during the late 1960s and early 1970s has been replaced by a commitment to democratic politics and, to varying degrees, to market economics. The fall of the Berlin Wall, and the growing acceptance of democracy as the only workable political option, have transformed the Latin American Left.[8]

But it is not only the parties of the Left that have changed in Chile. The party system as a whole and each of its component parties have also been transformed. The three most important ideological transformations have been the programmatic renovation of all relevant parties, the "de-ideologicalization" of parties across the political spectrum, and the process of political learning that resulted from the experience of authoritarian rule. Each of these realities has helped to narrow the ideological scope of the Chilean party system and to transform the system's competitive incentives.

Party Renovation

International and domestic transformations, coupled with what had been learned from the authoritarian experience, have encouraged a process of ideological renovation in Chile, with a decisive move toward the Center in the proposed policies and platforms of all significant political parties.[9]

Among relevant parties, there has been a universal abandonment of the notion that development can come by way of any type of "vía revolucionaria." No major party actor in Chile questions that the preferred type of political system for the country is democracy. Even more significant is that, with the exception of the electorally weak Communist Party, no party sector denies the legitimacy of the market as the major engine of the Chilean economy.[10]

Although programmatic transformation has been the norm for all Chilean parties, it is most apparent on the left of the political spectrum.[11] The con-

8. Castañeda provides an impressive and comprehensive discussion of the post–Cold War Latin American Left. See his *Utopia Unarmed*.

9. For a discussion of the platforms of individual parties, as well as a compilation of their leaders during the Aylwin administration, see Servicio Electoral de Chile, *Partidos políticos* (Santiago: Servicio Electoral de Chile, 1990).

10. For a general discussion of the ideological reformulation of parties in Chile, see Gustavo Cuevas Farren, ed., *Renovación ideológica en Chile* (Santiago: Universidad de Chile, 1993). For a discussion of party renovation on the Left, in particular, see Luis Maira and Guido Vicario, *Perspectivas de la izquierda latinoamericana: Seis diálogos* (Santiago: Fondo de Cultura Económica, 1991).

11. There is a great deal of literature on the preauthoritarian Chilean Left. See C. Feuci, *The Chilean Communist Party and the Road to Socialism* (London: Zed Books, 1984); Paul Drake, *Socialism and Populism in Chile* (Urbana: University of Illinois Press, 1978); Julio César Jobet, *El Partido Socialista de Chile*, 2d ed. (Santiago: Ediciones Prensa Latinoamericana, 1971);

temporary parties of the Left, the PS (Partido Socialista—Socialist Party) and the PPD (the Partido por la Democracia—Party for Democracy),[12] which both evolved from divisions between traditional socialist sectors in Chile, have abandoned not only ideologically based models for society but also the instrumental view of formal democracy that was characteristic of the traditional Chilean Socialist Party.[13] This renovation was due to a complex interaction of phenomena that included international transformations, the experiences of the Left with "real socialism" in exile, and the lessons provided by the events of 1973.

For example, the UP (Unidad Popular) government led by Salvador Allende included the following in its electoral program in the 1970s: "Chile is a capitalist country, dependent on the imperialist nations and dominated by bourgeois groups who are structurally related to foreign capital and cannot resolve the country's fundamental problems—problems which are clearly the result of class privilege which will never be given up voluntarily."[14]

Meanwhile, the official declaration of principles of the Socialist Party in 1997 argued for a state that "regulates markets" and that "should promote growth, savings, and investment, ensuring stability of prices and external equilibriums."[15] Similarly, the PPD's program included in its 1997 statement of principles the assertion "some object, contending that we are a party without an ideology. It is true, our party is one of ideas and not ideology. We reject encompassing and integral visions of life and society."[16]

These examples illustrate changing attitudes on the part of Chile's traditionally very ideological Left. Ideological and programmatic transformations permitted the parties of the moderate Left to assume easily a role as active participants in the Aylwin government, supporting the Concertación's program of gradual reform within a capitalist model of development. In

M. Dinamarca, *La república socialista chilena: Orígenes legítimos del Partido Socialista* (Santiago: Ediciones Documentas, n.d.); and Hernán Ramírez Necochea, *Origen y formación del Partido Comunista de Chile.*

12. The PPD originally developed as an "instrumental" party to unite socialist sectors in prompting a transition to democracy, given both disunity on the Left and the proscription of the Socialist Party in the first postauthoritarian elections. The PPD eventually took on a life of its own once leaders ended the policy of dual membership in it and the Socialist Party and forced members to opt for one or the other. The party is now seen as a more pragmatic and "modern" option on the Left, closer to the Christian Democrats than the traditional Socialist Party.

13. See Garretón, *The Chilean Political Process*, 243, and Ignacio Walker, *Socialismo y democracia en Chile: Chile y Europa en perspectiva comparada* (Santiago: CIEPLAN, 1990).

14. Cited in Brian Loveman, *Chile* (New York: Oxford University Press: 1979).

15. Translation by the author. Partido Socialista de Chile, *Declaración de principios.*

16. Translation by the author. Partido por la Democracia, *Declaración de principios.*

combination with the transformations that have occurred in the centrist Christian Democratic Party, the ideological regeneration of the Left has produced an unprecedented and positive context for cooperation between it and centrist parties.

While the Communist Party still exists and competes in most elections, it has not undergone as complete a process of ideological transformation and has become much less relevant.[17] The Chilean Communist Party (PCCh) was one of the strongest and best-organized Communist parties in the Americas. In the preauthoritarian period, the party was electorally oriented and supported the institutions of formal democracy.[18] However, the experience of authoritarian rule, and the repression unleashed against the party, led to its increased radicalization and to eventual acceptance that acts of violence should not be excluded from the tactics that might be used to undermine the authoritarian regime.

Throughout the democratic transition, the Communist Party was consistently left behind for refusing to play a constructive role in the return to democratic politics.[19] By recommending a boycott of the 1988 plebiscite and by refusing to engage in the collective process of negotiations between the government and opposition, the party was increasingly viewed as an impediment to the gradual process of democratization accepted by the opposition as the only way to end the Pinochet regime.

Nonetheless, recent developments within the party suggest that it is indeed modifying its previous extremist position. To a great extent this is a result of the moderating tendencies of the democratic transition. The party in many respects is attempting to "catch up" with the democratization process by agreeing to accept the new rules of the game and turning its back on an insurrectionary route to power.[20] The most vivid example of the willingness of the party to shed its ideologically driven past and enter the realm of responsible, prosystem parties was its demonstrated willingness to ally with the Concertación for the December 1997 congressional elections.

17. It is difficult to trace the contemporary evolution of the Communist Party given its frequent permutations, name changes, and shifting alliance strategies. In recent elections it has run under the banner of the PAIS, the MIDA, and El Pacto Comunista.

18. Ronald McDonald and J. Mark Ruhl, *Party Politics and Elections in Latin America* (Boulder, Colo.: Westview Press, 1989), 198.

19. For an elaboration of this point, see Timothy Scully, "Cleavages, Critical Junctures, and Party Evolution in Chile: Constituting and Reconstituting the Center" (Ph.D. diss., Graduate Division of Political Science, University of California at Berkeley, 1989), 443.

20. *Latin American Weekly Report*—WR-90-43 (London: Latin American Newsletters Ltd., 8 November 1990): 2.

Despite the partial renovation of the Communist Party, public-opinion survey data suggest a marked decline in support for the party, perhaps because of its unwillingness to participate constructively in the democratic transition or, more seriously for the party, because of fundamental transformations in the Chilean sociopolitical landscape. In 1973, the party had more than two hundred thousand members and garnered 17 percent of the vote in the elections of that year, while in 1989 none of its dozen or so candidates was elected to national office.[21] The decline of the Communists is further confirmed by public-opinion research that shows that only 2.4 percent of those surveyed in 1990 chose the PCCh as the party with which they most identified or sympathized. Two percent did so in 1993, and only 3 percent opted for the Communists when answering the question in 1998.[22] Public-opinion survey data also suggested generalized enmity for the party among the public. In a 1997 survey, 29 percent of the Chileans canvassed chose the Communists as the party with which they *least* identified or sympathized. The next-least-preferred party was the rightist Unión Demócrata Independiente (UDI), which 13 percent of those surveyed identified as the party with which they least identified or sympathized.[23]

But the Communist Party's public-opinion ratings belie its performance in elections, where it has polled as high as 6.5 percent in the municipal election of 1992 and 6.9 percent in the parliamentary election of 1997. Nonetheless, in terms of the electoral future of the party, some qualifications concerning its electoral performance are in order. Though the party garnered almost 7 percent in the municipal elections of 1992, its support was concentrated in the northern provinces—particularly in the city of Iquique, where a particularly popular and charismatic Communist candidate helped to pull up the party's national vote total. And though the party received almost 7 percent in the December 1997 parliamentary elections, many analysts interpreted this support as protest voting. In this election, no Communist won national office, and the number of Communist officials now serving at all levels of government is quite low.

Given the profound redrawing of the ideological map of Chilean politics, only through a renovation similar to that undergone by socialist sectors will

21. Ibid.
22. Centro de Estudios Públicos, Santiago, "Estudio de opinión pública," Documento de Trabajo No. 136 (Santiago: Centro de Estudios Públicos, August 1990), 52, and, by the same authors, "Estudio de opinión pública," Documento de Trabajo No. 208 (Santiago: Centro de Estudios Públicos, August 1993), 44, and "Estudio nacional de opinión pública No. 7" (Santiago: Centro de Estudios Públicos December 1997–January 1998), 61.
23. "Estudio nacional de opinión pública No. 7" (Santiago: Centro de Estudios Públicos December 1997–January 1998), 28.

the Communists be likely to reassume a significant role in the country's politics. What is more, even if the party undergoes a profound transformation, it will be difficult for it to move into mainstream politics, because the political market on the Left is already saturated with two relatively popular parties, whose support appears to be growing.

On the political Right, a process of ideological regeneration has also occurred.[24] Toward the end of the military regime, parties of the Right had a great deal of difficulty coalescing into coherent organizations with solid institutional bases. This was partly a reflection of the sector's personalistic dedication to Augusto Pinochet and faith in his ability to win the 1988 plebiscite. Even those on the Right who had contempt for Pinochet realized that he was the only national political leader who could unify conservatives and underwrite their fundamental interests. Thus, they supported him, though they may have preferred the formation of a more coherent party organization that was not as tied to the personality of Pinochet.

More important, disorganization on the Right reflected a long tradition of the sector's profound misgivings concerning the utility and desirability of political parties as agents of representation. Echoing military leaders, the Right openly disparaged partisan politics and supported Pinochet's eventual decision not to encourage the development of a political party tied to the military government. What is more, certain sectors on the Right actually feared the long-term destabilizing consequences of the formation of a populist Pinochetista party and resisted coherent forms of party organization.

The most important characteristic of the renovation of the parties of the Right (RN, Renovación Nacional; and UDI, Unión Demócrata Independiente) has been the abandonment of the notion that political representation can be organized in a way other than what is commonly and procedurally understood as democracy.[25] The contemporary Chilean Right has been able to absorb successfully elements that in the past envisioned an organic and corporative organization of society, and to accept finally that political parties should exist and are effective mechanisms of interest representation.

In addition, Andrés Allamand is correct in noting that the Right, and principally the RN, has also been transformed in three additional and fun-

24. Some of the best studies of the parties of the Right are Marcial Sanfuentes Carrión, *El Partido Conservador: Doctrina y convenciones* (Santiago: Editorial Universitaria, 1957); José Miguel Prado Valdés, *Reseña histórica del Partido Liberal* (Santiago: Imprenta Andina, 1963); and Enrique Tagle Rodrígues, *Liberales y Conservadores* (Santiago, 1917).

25. Although the UCC (Unión del Centro Centro) formed a part of the coalition of the Right in the 1993 elections, it is really incorrect to categorize the UCC definitively as a party of

damental ways that make it a more responsible player within the party system. First, the Right is characterized by a much more politically and technically sophisticated cadre of leaders; second, the Right has for the first time systematically elaborated its own strategies, plans, and platforms, rather than simply reacting negatively to its opponents' programs of transformation; and third, the above two processes have strengthened the intellectual bases of the parties of the Right and resulted in improved organization and leadership, and the elaboration of plans with a real content and effective enough leadership to carry them out.[26]

A process of renovation, but a much more complex one, is also apparent within the UDI. Unlike the RN, whose intellectual roots can be found in the traditional Liberal and Conservative parties of the Right, the UDI grew out of the *"gremialista"* movement of the 1960s, which challenged the organizational basis of Chilean society. With a corporativist view of social organization based on Thomistic foundations, the *gremial* movement, and its principal ideological progenitor, Jaime Guzmán, pointed to the bankruptcy of traditional Chilean political parties. With the advent of military rule, many of this movement's leaders assumed important and influential positions in the Pinochet government.

With the return of democracy, Pinochet allies joined with leaders of the traditional parties of the Right to form the RN. However, the fundamentally different roots of these two sectors, and their distinct visions of society, led to a split in 1988 and to the reestablishment of the UDI as a separate entity. Though personality conflicts played a role in the breakup, the principal lines of division had more to do with the parties' distinct orientations in terms of their constituencies and policies. The UDI attempted to distance itself from the "traditional" parties of the Right by stressing the need to abandon the "classist" attitudes of the established Right. The UDI sought to actively incorporate lower classes by underscoring values and the Catholic tradition of the country and by championing social and economic liberty as the central tenets governing the party's policies and outlook.[27] Leaders of the party pointed to the statist orientation of the traditional parties of both the Left and the Right in Chile, and sought to establish the party as a new political force in the country.

---

the Right, given the tumultuous nature of its relationship with this sector, and the party's uncertain ideological orientation. Thus it is not discussed here.

26. Andrés Allamand, "Partido Renovación Nacional," in *Renovación ideológica en Chile,* ed. Gustavo Cuevas Farren, 30.

27. For a statement of these principles, see Servicio Electoral de Chile, Partidos políticos, 101.

Though characterized by some as an extremist party in the immediate postauthoritarian period, the UDI now clearly has taken its place among those democratic parties in Chile committed to the maintenance of democracy. Since the return of formal democracy, the party's messianic message and corporatist outlook have been tempered by active participation within the institutional structure it helped to build. In terms of concrete political activities, its formerly sometimes extremist position has been moderated by postauthoritarian political stability and participation in Congress and in the institutions of local government. Indicative of this new orientation was the party's willingness to reach an agreement with the Concertación to determine Chamber and Senate leadership by engaging in active negotiations and leaving behind RN. In addition, despite the assassination of its leading intellectual force, Jaime Guzmán, by a left-wing terrorist group in March 1991, the party has a core of sophisticated leadership and clearly delineated policies and platforms.

Renovation and the "De-ideologicalization" of Political Parties

A comprehensive discussion of the importance of ideology for parties in Chile must go beyond simple measures of ideological scope. The traditional ideological *nature* of individual parties must also be taken into account. During the late 1960s and early 1970s, parties across the political spectrum came to be dominated by separate, exclusionary, and "ideological" visions of the preferred model for the political, economic, and social development of the country.

In the late 1960s, the Socialists explicitly declared the instrumental and transitory nature of political democracy. Both the Socialists and the Communists underscored the need for revolution to transform all aspects of Chilean economic, political, and social life. Only through a process of profound revolution, albeit a peaceful and democratic one, could the Chilean masses and working class inherit what they had been denied by the rich and the owners of land and capital. The policies of Allende's Popular Unity (UP) government reflected these revolutionary goals. The UP proposed the formation of a people's assembly to oversee and direct the complete transformation of Chile.

In response to the threats of the Left, the Right increasingly built on certain of its latent traditional intellectual trends to advocate "organic" and corporative notions of democracy, based on a fundamental suspicion of parties and politics. *Gremialista* factions increasingly gained more power, and their ideas more influence. The Right contended that it was best able to govern the country because it had not been contaminated by the type of party politics characteristic of the Center and the Left. The Left's project of transformation, and suspicions concerning the reformist position of the Christian Democrats, further encouraged the development of a messianic vision of politics on the Right, which was also aimed at transforming society. Leaders on the Right disparaged party organizations and underscored the need to institutionalize limits on popular sovereignty through constitutional reform. This tendency was clear in the rhetoric surrounding the candidacy of Jorge Alessandri in 1970. Alessandri, calling himself the only candidate capable of "rising above" partisan politics, contended during his campaign: "Es cada vez más urgente ir a una renovación drástica de nuestra Carta Fundamental que vigorice la autoridad y la acción del Poder Ejecutivo y ponga fin de una vez por todas a los desbordes del Congreso. . . . Quien vote por mí, se está pronunciando por un cambio drástico de nuestro sistema institucional que permita desterrar definitivamente nuestros pésimos hábitos, para hacer un gobierno realmente nacional y eficiente."[28]

However, it was not only the parties of the Right and the Left in Chile that were driven by an ideological view of society and politics. Even the centrist Christian Democratic Party could be considered ideological.[29] The party professed its mission to be a "third option" between capitalism and socialism. It was driven by a communitarian view of society in which reform could be undertaken while elements of conservative, Christian social doctrine were retained. As Chapter 1 stressed, this ideological orientation was new among parties of the Center and ultimately helped to lead to regime crisis. Given the Christian Democrats' location at the Center of the ideological spectrum, it

28. "Every day it becomes more urgent and necessary to engage in fundamental reform of our Constitution aimed at strengthening executive authority and definitively putting to an end the excesses of Congress. . . . Those who vote for me are voicing their desire for a drastic change in our political institutions that will definitively eliminate our poor civic habits and create a genuinely national and efficient government." Translation by the author of extracts of Alessandri's speech appearing in Richard Friedmann, *La política chilena de la A a la Z: 1964–1988* (Santiago: Editorial Melquíades, 1988), 103.

29. On Chilean Christian Democracy, see J. Castillo Velasco, *Las fuentes de la Democracia Cristiana* (Santiago: Editorial del Pacífico, 1955), and *Teoría y práctica de la Democracia Cristiana chilena* (Santiago: Editorial del Pacífico, 1972); M. Fleet, *The Rise and Fall of Chilean Christian Democracy* (Princeton: Princeton University Press, 1985); G. Grayson, *El Partido Demócrata Cristiano chileno* (Buenos Aires: Francisco de Aguirre, 1968); and A. Lovarría, *Chile bajo la Democracia Cristiana* (Santiago: Editorial Nascimiento, 1966).

was the only party capable of building bridges to stem the tide of polarization that eventually overwhelmed the Chilean political system. Its failure to do so for ideological and political reasons helped to further encourage this dynamic of polarization.[30]

Thus, this process of the "ideologicalization" of parties across the spectrum became increasingly more significant in the decades preceding the coup, making coalition formation much more difficult, and compromise much more costly in ideological terms.

In contemporary Chile, parties are no longer characterized by the messianic, all-encompassing, and exclusionary ideological notions that led to the polarization of politics and the disappearance of compromise in the 1970s. Chilean politics can now be better understood as an open, pluralist playing field where there is room for almost every partisan option and where most accept the others as legitimate players. Instead of an instrument to engage in battle for competing ideologies, political interaction is now seen as the necessary, albeit difficult, process of negotiating recognized and important differences of opinions.

As a result, the tendency for Chilean parties to view their ideological message as the only desirable and workable option for the country has been attenuated, helping to grease the wheels of interparty cooperation by making the ideological stance of parties less important in the process of coalition formation. Parties are more willing to consider coalitions, taking the ideological credentials of possible party allies into account less and less.

For example, the Christian Democrats resisted the temptation to go it alone in the first postauthoritarian elections, despite their position as the preeminent Chilean political party. Similarly, the parties of the Left were willing to make common cause with the Christian Democrats despite a great deal of historical baggage and animosity. This is the case for all of the parties of the Left—except for the most extreme, which have been left behind in the transition process as a result. Certainly both the Christian Democrats and the Left knew that neither could have won alone. Nonetheless, the coherence of policy and widespread agreement between the parties of the Concertación demonstrate clearly that the coalition was more than just a marriage of convenience. At the same time, the parties of the Right, and particularly the RN, have not ruled out the possibility of an alliance with the Christian Democrats

---

30. For a discussion of the significance of the Christian Democratic failure to bridge this ideological gap, see Arturo Valenzuela, *The Breakdown of Democratic Regimes: Chile*, 3–48.

in the near future, and neither has the latter discounted such a coalition. If the fissure between the Center and the Left widens, a more fluid pattern of coalition formation is probably on the horizon.

The Authoritarian Regime, Political Learning, and the Moderation of Parties

In addition to the effect that renovation of individual parties has had, the ideological scope of the party system has been affected in another fundamental way. Sixteen years of authoritarian rule have helped to override the social cleavages that led to an ideological party system in the first place. The traditional religious and class cleavages that typified the development of the Chilean party system have been crosscut by another: a democratic/antidemocratic regime cleavage. As Seymour Lipset and Stein Rokkan show, party-system manifestations of critical cleavages often persist much longer than their empirical significance.[31] However, "critical junctures" in party-system development can force a realignment that reflects the prevailing social cleavage at the time. The experience of the authoritarian regime may have been such a critical juncture.[32] In Chile, solidarity among the parties that find themselves on the same side of this regime cleavage may override earlier class-based cleavages, resulting in a decrease in class-based party competition and ideological patterning.

The consequences of these developments bode well for the emergence of a moderate, though competitive, party system in Chile. The reduced intransigence of both the Christian Democrats and the Socialists suggests a future of interparty cooperation and, when necessary, constructive confrontation. The regime cleavage can serve as a powerful basis for cooperation among the parties that have a fundamental commitment to a democratic regime. In addition, with the increased institutionalization of democracy and its complete acceptance by the Right, shifting coalitions and moderate pluralism are likely to be the models for the Chilean party system for the near future.[33]

---

31. Seymour Martin Lipset and Stein Rokkan, "Cleavage Structures, Party Systems, and Voter Alignments: An Introduction," in *Party Systems and Voter Alignments*, ed. Lipset and Rokkan (New York: The Free Press, 1967).
32. Scully has argued that the authoritarian regime constitutes such a critical juncture. See Scully, "Cleavages, Critical Junctures, and Party Evolution in Chile."
33. "Moderate pluralism," as understood by Giovanni Sartori, *Parties and Party Systems: A Framework for Analysis* (Cambridge: Cambridge University Press, 1976).

The Number of Relevant Political Parties

Certain analysts of Chilean politics have suggested that the ideological transformations outlined above, combined with the reductive effect of the majoritarian parliamentary electoral system imposed by the military regime, have led, or will lead, to a decrease in the number of relevant parties in the country.[34] Nonetheless, despite the ideological reformulation of Chilean parties, and a narrowing of the ideological scope of the party system, the electoral system has not contributed to a decrease in the actual number of relevant parties in Chile compared with the preauthoritarian average, nor is it likely to do so in the near future.

The question of the reductive effect of majority/plurality electoral formulas was addressed in its most classic form by Maurice Duverger in what have come to be known generally as "Duverger's laws." His thesis that the "simple majority, single ballot system favors the two-party system" has been debated in the literature on electoral systems for decades, as has his contention that this relationship approaches the status of "a true socio-logical law."[35] Duverger's argument has been extended to suggest that small-magnitude systems (those with a small number of legislative seats per district) will have a similar reductive effect on the number of political parties.

How many relevant political parties are there likely to be for the long-term in Chile? It is difficult to answer this question definitively, especially

34. Portions of the remainder of this chapter appeared previously as "Continuity and Change in the Chilean Party System: On the Transformational Effects of Electoral Reform," *Comparative Political Studies* 30 (December 1997): 651–74.

35. See Duverger, *Political Parties: Their Organization and Activity*, 217. Because the Chilean system is characterized by district magnitudes of two, one could argue, correctly, that it is not a pure plurality system. Nonetheless, the functional dynamic of the Chilean electoral system is certainly much closer to that of a plurality system than a proportional one, given its extremely small district magnitudes. The distinction between plurality and proportional representation systems is often a false one, in that many variables affect the proportionality of PR systems, including district magnitude, minimum thresholds, and the counting system. In this sense, plurality and proportional systems are really the two theoretical end points on a continuum of electoral systems. Thus, there is significant theoretical support for the supposition that the functional dynamic of small-magnitude systems is similar to that of single-member district systems. I am grateful to Arend Lijphart for his insights on the importance of the operational characteristics of electoral systems. For an elaboration of these themes, see Douglas Rae, *The Political Consequences of Electoral Laws* (New Haven: Yale University Press, 1971), chap. 7, and Arend Lijphart and Bernard Grofman, introduction to *Choosing an Electoral System*, ed. Arend Lijphart and Bernard Grofman (New York: Praeger, 1984). Here, the Chilean system will be referred to as a plurality system and the designations proportional and plurality used to identify those systems that fall nearer to one end of the continuum than the other.

because there have been only three legislative elections since the return of democracy to Chile. Nonetheless, one can arrive at a preliminary measure of the number of relevant parties that exist in Chile today in comparison to the historical average.

Simply counting the number of parties represented in Congress is not sufficient. Given the permissiveness of the preauthoritarian Chilean proportional representation (PR) system, many of the parties with small contingents in parliament in the past were neither relevant nor in possession of a significant level of national support. Also, given the exclusionary characteristics of the current binomial system, it is possible for parties to have relevance and receive a significant share of the national vote without winning much representation in Congress. Simply counting the number of parties in Congress does not reveal much, but how relevant is a party if it does not have even one representative in Congress?

The format of Table 4.1 attempts to take these considerations into account in order to devise a comprehensive set of measures of the number of relevant political parties throughout Chilean history. First, the table summarizes the number of parties that received at least one parliamentary representative in each election between 1925 and 1997. However, in an attempt to assess the relevance of these parties, the table also supplies data on the number of parties that won parliamentary representation but also received at least 5 percent of the national vote, or what the author calls a measure of "simple relevance." The percentage of the total vote earned by parties with "simple relevance" is also supplied. "Simple relevance" is included because, despite the development of more sophisticated measures of party relevance that are also presented in Table 4.1, it is important that elementary and intuitive measures of the number of significant parties not be ignored. While they are not definitive, these measures do provide valuable additional information about the dynamic of the party system when considered along with other indices.

Two widely accepted measures of party relevance are also presented: Markuu Laakso and Rein Taagepera's "effective number of parties" (N) and Juan Molinar's "number of parties" (NP). The Laakso and Taagepera index is a measure of the effective number of parties based on Douglas Rae's "index of party fractionalization" (F), but it provides the additional benefit of a more tangible depiction of fractionalization in terms that closely approximate the actual number of parties.[36] The Molinar index (NP) is also a measure

36. Rae's index measures the probability that any two randomly selected voters will have chosen a different party for each election. See Rae, *The Political Consequences of Electoral*

of the number of parties, but it seeks to depict the actual importance of parties more realistically by controlling for the tendency of other indices to give
too much numerical weight to large parties while being excessively sensitive
to small ones.[37] While (NP) can be calculated using either the percentage of
votes or the percentage of seats in parliament, it is here calculated using the
percentage of votes, given the importance of exploring whether parties do
indeed continue to participate in parliamentary elections despite the potential reductive effect of the electoral system. One could argue that it makes
less sense to use votes because the constituent parties of the Concertación
cannot present candidates in all districts as a result of negotiations. Nonetheless, the number of districts in which parties run is in a sense a function
of their electoral weight.[38]

Table 4.1 supplies all of these measures for Chilean Chamber of Deputies
elections between 1925 and 1973, the mean indices from all elections during this period, and the indices for the 1989, 1993, and 1997 Chamber of
Deputy elections. Table 4.1 shows that there has been little discernible
decrease in the number of significant political parties. While between 1925

Laws, 47–64. The following is his formula for computing fractionalization: (F_e) where T_i = any
party's decimal share of the vote:

$$F_e = 1 - \{\Sigma\ T_i^2\}$$

The Laakso and Taagepera index of the effective number of parties is really a variation of Rae's
index: N equals the number of relevant parties, where P_i equals the share of votes garnered by
the "ith" party:

$$N = 1/(\Sigma\ P_i^2)$$

Markuu Laakso and Rein Taagepera, "Effective Number of Parties. A Measure with Application to Western Europe," *Comparative Political Studies* 12 (1979): 3–27.

37. An explanation of the logic behind the Molinar index and tests of its effectiveness as a
comparative measure of the effective number of parties appear in Juan Molinar, "Counting the
Number of Parties: An Alternative Index," *American Political Science Review* 85 (December
1991): 1383–91. To control for difficulties with other indices, Molinar contends that it is necessary simply to count the winning party as one, regardless of its size (because, as the winning
party, it surely counts as one relevant party), and then go on to determine the effect of minority
parties. Molinar's index (NP), directly drawn from his work is as follows:

$$NP = 1 + N\ \frac{(\Sigma\ P_i^2) - P_1^2}{\Sigma\ P_i^2}$$

where

$$N = 1/\Sigma\ P_i^2$$

and P_1^2 is the proportion of votes of the winning party, squared.

38. I am grateful to Mark Jones for this insight. Another reason for using this version of
the index is the importance of employing the effective number of electoral parties in light of
arguments (presented here) suggesting that municipal elections may provide the electoral
lifeblood necessary to encourage participation in national elections even among those parties
not represented in every district.

Table 4.1. Measures of relevant parties in Chilean Chamber of Deputies elections, 1925–1997

Year	Number of Parties with Representatives in Chamber	Number of Parties of "Simple Relevance"[a]	Percentage of Vote Received by Parties of "Simple Relevance"[a]	Laakso & Taagepera Index (N) "Effective Parties"	Molinar Index (NP) "Number of Parties"
1925	4	4	95.9	4.17	3.34
1932	17	6	72.5	9.31	7.44
1937	11	4	71.9	6.93	5.75
1941	12	5	85.5	6.50	5.55
1945	12	6	84.6	6.66	5.19
1949	14	5	74.1	7.08	5.72
1953	18	7	68.7	11.89	9.63
1957	13	7	79.0	8.62	6.19
1961	7	7	99.5	6.44	5.40
1965	7	6	93.4	4.07	1.92
1969	5	5	94.9	4.92	3.58
1973	8	4	84.2	5.19	3.91
Mean	10.7	5.5	83.7	6.82	5.30
Median	11.5	5.5			
1989	10	4	75.4	7.83	4.69
1993	7	5	82.5	6.29	4.38
1997	8	5	77.9	7.32	5.49

SOURCES: Computed by the author from data from the following sources for the indicated time period: 1925–1969, Dieter Nohlen, *Enciclopedia electoral latinoamericana y del Caribe* (San José: Instituto Interamericano de Derechos Humanos, 1993); 1973, Arturo Valenzuela, *The Breakdown of Democratic Regimes: Chile* (Baltimore: Johns Hopkins University Press, 1978); 1993, Servicio Electoral de Chile, *Resultados Electorales*, 1993; 1997, *El Mercurio* 12 December 1997, A1, A23.

[a] Parties with at least one representative in the Chamber of Deputies and that polled at least 5 percent nationally.

and 1973 Chile's permissive PR system certainly allowed the representation in parliament of a greater number of small parties, there has not been a substantial reduction in the number of *significant* political parties. In the 1989, 1993, and 1997 elections, the number of parties that were successful in garnering more than 5 percent of the vote and achieving congressional representation was about the same as in the preauthoritarian period, as was the percentage of the total vote received by these parties. Indeed, it is interesting that for the 1993 and 1997 elections the number of parties that fit the criteria of "simple relevance" actually increased from the 1989 election. More important, the more sophisticated measures of party relevance also demonstrate remarkable continuity. The evolution of the Taagepera and Laakso indices demonstrates a number of "effective parties" close to the historical average. While the Molinar measure of the "number of parties" shows slightly less fractionalization than the historical average for 1989 and 1993, it is not really a statistically significant difference.

In addition, Table 4.1 demonstrates that there was actually a downward trend in the fractionalization and number of relevant parties from a historic high in 1953, despite the fact that the same PR electoral system was used throughout the 1953–73 period.[39] The mean indices for fractionalization, and the number of relevant parties, then, have actually been above the historical norm for the last twenty years of Chilean democracy. If only the mean indices for the period between 1961 and 1973 are considered, the indices of the "number of parties" (NP) and "effective number of parties" (N) in 1989, 1993, and 1997 are found actually to have been higher.

Despite important transformations within the party system and the adoption of an electoral system characterized by small district magnitudes, all of the measures of party fractionalization and the number of relevant parties demonstrate a pattern that is strikingly consistent with that found when the PR electoral system was in force. Rather than the electoral system exercising a reductive effect on the number of parties, what seems to have happened is that parties have simply adjusted to the exigencies of the electoral system, acting to ensure their continued existence.

In fact, certain features of the binomial system may have even permitted the participation of parties that would not have won seats in Congress, or as many seats, had elections been held employing a moderate proportional

---

39. María Teresa Miranda has analyzed this process of "de-fractionalization" in the Chilean party system during the 1960s. See "El sistema electoral y multipartidismo en Chile 1949–1969," *Revista de ciencia política* 4 (1982): 59–69.

system. Certainly under the PR system employed in Chile in the preauthoritarian period, just as many parties would have received representation in Congress in the last three elections. However, if a moderate proportional system with small district magnitudes (between three and five) had been in place, many of the minor parties that garnered parliamentary seats under the rules of the binomial system would not have done so with a moderate PR system, unless, of course, they formed preelection alliances.[40]

Small parties have adapted to the electoral system and retained their ability to achieve congressional representation by negotiating with large parties for parliamentary candidacies. Because of the importance of the electoral thresholds established by the binomial system (discussed in detail in the next chapter), larger parties may feel a need to include in their coalitions a smaller, ideologically compatible party in order to attract a bit of extra support that will put them over the top. Because smaller parties can offer the promise of attracting additional votes to a preelectoral coalition, larger parties have shown a willingness to share in the allocation of a small number of electoral slates in exchange for the additional votes that a smaller party's participation in a coalition can attract. For example, despite the relatively weak showing of the Radical Party in surveys leading up to postauthoritarian congressional elections, the larger parties of the Concertación were willing to provide the party with a number of candidacies disproportionate to its national level of support. The Concertación believed that the few additional percentage points of support that the Radical Party could attract nationally would be useful in helping the alliance reach the required electoral thresholds in individual districts throughout the country.

Smaller parties also were aware that the only way to win legislative seats was to negotiate to join a larger coalition. Despite the desire of the Unión del Centro Centro[41] (UCC) to portray itself as a party "above politics," it

40. This contention is based on the results of a complete set of electoral simulations undertaken by this author that compare the performance of the binomial system with a moderate PR system having distinct combinations of vote returns and party coalitions. These simulations demonstrate that, had a moderate PR system with district magnitudes of between three and five been in effect, the small parties that received parliamentary representation in the elections of 1989 and 1993 would not have done so. Even parties that received as much as 8 percent of the national vote in the simulated elections were unsuccessful in garnering even one parliamentary seat. The simulations were based on the PR electoral system outlined in the Aylwin government's proposal for electoral reform, announced in the presidential message of 5 June 1992. See Siavelis, "Nuevos argumentos y viejos supuestos."

41. Now the Unión del Centro Centro Progresista (UCCP).

was willing to join the coalition of the Right for the 1993 elections in order to ensure that at least some of its candidates would win office. The UCC (despite its uncertain programmatic position) was welcomed by the RN and UDI because of the Right's uncertainty that it could cross the established electoral thresholds. In this regard, the binomial system, contrary to its goals, has actually contributed to the continued existence of small parties by forcing a process of negotiation among all party sectors in order to form joint lists for parliamentary representation.

In empirical terms, there are additional variables that hamper the potential reductive capacity of the electoral system that have not been taken into account by students of Chilean electoral politics when discussing the integrative tendencies of the binomial system. Although the binomial formula is employed on the national level for election of members to the Chamber of Deputies and the Senate, a PR system is used for the election of local authorities. This helps guarantee the continued existence and differentiation of smaller parties, in that they can achieve representation on the local level with relatively smaller percentages of the votes than they need to win representation on the national level. Thus, even if the national electoral system were capable of producing something of a reductive effect, the local electoral system has the capacity to keep the multiparty system alive because smaller parties can compete effectively in at least one electoral arena. The existence of two levels of elections, each of which is based on a different principle of representation, reinforces the continued existence of small parties, and increases the leverage of smaller parties in the national negotiation process if they can demonstrate significant electoral appeal on the local level.

These results are also interesting from a theoretical perspective. Findings from the Chilean case contradict many of the theoretical arguments about the overriding importance of district magnitude. For example, the theoretical argument that plurality systems exercise a reductive effect on the party system does not hold in the case of Chile, or at the very least, the case demonstrates that Chile's experience shows that this effect can be counteracted and overcome by other factors. Given the strength of parties and their ability to adjust pragmatically to the electoral system, the number of significant political parties in Chile has not been reduced. In addition, despite the reputation of plurality electoral formulas for producing party-system integration, in the Chilean case the binomial system has actually permitted the continued existence of small parties. Parties both large and small have successfully adopted coalition strategies to counterbalance the exclusionary tendencies of the parliamentary electoral system. These findings are supported by the results of Michael Coppedge's cross-national study of the influence of district magnitude. His evidence suggests that underlying cleavages rather than district magnitude may be more important determinants of the number of relevant parties that exist in a country.[42]

Though these findings contradict theoretical assertions about the effect of electoral systems, they do not invalidate them. Rather, they send up a warning flag concerning the need for caution when making theoretical connections between electoral and party systems, as distinct sociopolitical contexts can counteract some of the effects of electoral and institutional engineering.

The Competitive Dynamic of the Party System

Even though neither ideological transformation nor the Chilean binomial system has succeeded in reducing the number of significant and relevant political parties, it is important to analyze the competitive dynamic of the party system as well. Party systems cannot be adequately described simply by counting the number of parties. The nature, direction, and pattern of competition must also be taken into account.

Some proponents of the binomial electoral system have emphasized that although the system has not reduced the effective number of parties, it has changed the competitive dynamic of the party system.[43] They contend that the three-way competition between the Center, the Right, and the Left, referred to by analysts as a pattern of *"tres-tercios"* (three-thirds), has been fundamentally transformed. Though the plurality law has not succeeded in creating a two-party system, they contend, it has created a bipolar pattern of party competition for the short-term that, when coupled with the ideological transformation of Chilean society, may eventually lead to a two-party system. How valid is this contention?

These analysts are correct in noting that for the last three congressional and two presidential elections something of a bipolar pattern of competition has existed between an alliance of the center-left set off against another of the moderate Right. In both presidential elections since the return of democracy,

42. Michael Coppedge, "District Magnitude, Economic Performance, and Party-System Fragmentation in Five Latin American Countries," *Comparative Political Studies* 30 (April 1997): 156–85.
43. For an argument of this type, see Guzmán, "Reflexiones sobre el sistema binominal," and Rabkin, "Redemocratization, Electoral Engineering, and Party Strategies in Chile, 1989–1995."

each coalition was successful in choosing a single presidential candidate for what amounted to an essentially two-candidate race. In addition, each of the coalitions presented joint parliamentary lists following negotiations between their various component parties, making for a pattern of competition between two major coalitions for both presidential and parliamentary elections.

The binomial system has undoubtedly enhanced the incentives for coalition formation, and contemporary coalitions are more robust than past alliances forged during Chile's experience with proportional representation. Nonetheless, these phenomena do not necessarily signal a fundamental transformation of the dynamic of party competition from the preauthoritarian period, as some observers have suggested.

First, the simple existence of two major presidential candidates and two parliamentary lists does not necessarily make for a bipolar pattern of competition. The three-bloc configuration of party competition in Chile has historically elicited certain kinds of coalition behavior that are generalizable for most of the preauthoritarian period. Most Chilean presidents have been elected running as center-party candidates relying on the support of either the Left or the Right. Despite what may appear to have been an incipient bipolar dynamic for the first two postauthoritarian presidential elections, the current dynamic of competition, rather than exhibiting a fundamental change in the pattern of competition in the system, may simply be a recurrence of a similar historical phenomenon. That is, what really occurred in 1989 and in 1993 was the election of centrist presidential candidates with the support of the moderate Left and not bipolar competition between the center-left and Right. In essence this debate boils down to the question of whether competition is centering around one (bipolar competition) or two (tripolar competition) poles. Evidence presented throughout this chapter suggests that the argument for bipolar competition is at best superficial and at worst downright wrong.

In terms of parliamentary elections, coalition formation has also been a necessity. Only once (in 1965) did a party garner a majority in a national parliamentary election. Given this pattern of competition, and despite the existence of three major ideological blocs, parliamentary membership often coalesced into two groups—one supporting the government and one acting as an opposition. So, just as in the case of presidential elections, the current coalescence of parliamentary membership into two major groups does not necessarily signal a pattern of bipolar competition. Genaro Arriagada underscores this point when he suggests some of the difficulties created by the binomial electoral system: "Contra toda lógica, contra nuestra historia

y tradición, la ley [electoral] obliga a un 'bipartidismo de facto' y entonces
en cada elección es necesario que 'negociadores' construyan, a través de
interminables acuerdos, un bipartidismo electoral que es falso, que no tiene
asidero en la vida del país."[44]

Second, as Table 4.2 shows, if returns from the three parliamentary elections held since the return of democracy are disaggregated into forces representing the Right, the Center, and the Left, the support for each of the
historical blocs displays remarkable continuity with the preauthoritarian
period.[45] Certainly it is important not to overestimate the significance of the
"three-thirds" pattern, given that the size of each of the thirds has varied a
great deal, and certain important political movements do not fit easily into
this pattern (especially the populist Ibáñismo phenomenon of the 1940s and
1950s).[46] However, in terms of the future of party competition, it is important to bear in mind that the parties of the Center have often been the fulcrum
of the party system, given their willingness to alternate between alliances with
the Right and the Left. Thus, these data suggest a degree of historical continuity in the party system, and the potential for a more traditional pattern of
competition in the future.

Third, despite a so-far conciliatory pattern of interaction between the
parties of the Center and the Left, profound differences between parties of
the Concertación remain in terms of platforms, political interests, and party
subcultures. Once more controversial issues such as crime, poverty, social
benefits, divorce, and abortion overshadow the conflicts of the transition
that put the parties of the Concertación on the same side of the democracy/
authoritarianism cleavage, there is likely to be a reemergence of a more traditional pattern of party competition.

In the future, as partisan differences become more pronounced with the
fading of the urgency that characterized the immediate postauthoritarian

44. El Mercurio, 9 May 1993, D1: "Against all logic, and against our history and tradition, the [electoral] law forces a 'de-facto two-party system,' that, for every election, necessi-
tates the construction, through interminable negotiations, of agreements resulting in an electoral 'two-party system' that is false and without precedent in the political life of the country."
Translation by the author.

45. This analysis of continuity in the ideological orientation of the Chilean electorate is
supported in J. Samuel Valenzuela and Timothy Scully, "Electoral Choices and the Party
System in Chile," and J. Samuel Valenzuela, "Orígenes y transformaciones del sistema de partidos en Chile," *Estudios públicos* 58 (Fall 1995): 5–78. For an early and prescient argument
concerning continuity in the party system, see Arturo Valenzuela, "Orígenes y características
del sistema de partidos en Chile: Proposición para un gobierno parlamentario," *Estudios públicos* 18 (Fall 1985): 88–154.

46. I am indebted to Michael Coppedge for this observation.

Table 4.2. Vote received by parties of the Right, Center, and Left in Chilean Chamber of Deputies elections, 1937–1997 (Percentage of total vote)

	Party Sector			
Year	Right (a)	Center (b)	Left (c)	Other
1937	42.0	28.1	15.4	14.5
1941	31.2	32.1	33.9	2.8
1945	43.7	27.9	23.1	5.3
1949	42.0	46.7	9.4	1.9
1953	25.3	43.0	14.2	17.5
1957	33.0	44.3	10.7	12.0
1961	30.4	43.7	22.1	3.8
1965	12.5	55.6	22.7	9.2
1969	20.0	42.8	28.1	9.1
1973	21.3	32.8	34.9	11.0
Mean	**30.1**	**39.7**	**21.5**	**8.7**
1989	34.1	33.1	24.3	8.5
1993	33.5	30.9	31.6	4.1
1997	36.3	26.1	34.1	3.6

For 1937–73:
SOURCE: Arturo Valenzuela, *The Breakdown of Democratic Regimes: Chile* (Baltimore: Johns Hopkins University Press, 1978), 6.
(a) Right: Conservative, Liberal, National after 1965.
(b) Center: Radical, Falangist, Christian Democrats, Agrarian, Laborist.
(c) Left: Socialist, Communist.

For 1989–93:
SOURCES: 1989 Elections, Programa de Asesoría Legislativa, "Análisis de Actualidad," no. 43 (June 1992): 54–57; 1993 and 1997 data, *El Mercurio*, 12 December 1997, A1.
(a) Right: National Renovation, Independent Democratic Union, National, Independents on Congressional Lists of the Right. For 1989 this also includes the Union of the Center Center. For later elections the UCC, subsequently known as the UCCP (Progressive Union of the Center Center), was listed as "Other" given its uncertain programmatic stance.
(b) Center: Radical, Christian Democrats, Social Democrats, Center Alliance Party, Radical Social Democratic Party.
(c) Left: Party for Democracy, Socialist Party, Almeyda Socialist Party, National Democratic Party, Christian Left, Humanists, Greens, Independents of Congressional Lists of the Left, Communist Party of Chile.

period, a pattern of alliance formation revolving around coalitions of the Center and either the Right or the Left may reemerge. As mentioned above, the ideological distance between the Christian Democrats and the major moderate party of the Right is not so wide as to preclude formation of a center-right coalition.

Therefore, though parties may be closer together on the ideological spectrum, the number of relevant parties and ideological sectors has not necessarily been reduced, nor will the dynamic of competition between them necessarily change. Whereas the traditional class and religious cleavages that differentiated parties in the past have narrowed, issues of social and environmental policy, questions of political representation, and quality-of-life concerns serve to substantially differentiate party platforms.

Finally, purely political issues and struggles for power may also produce divisions within the Concertación coalition, making for a more traditional pattern of competition between the Center and the Left. There are indications that the parties of the Left are beginning to tire of their junior party status within the Concertación. This is in part a result of some of the divisive decisions made by the Frei administration (see Chapter 2) and a fallout from the struggle to nominate a single Concertación candidate for the 1999 presidential elections. However, leaders on the Left have also contended that their parties' national stature and importance have been overshadowed by the dominance of the Christian Democrats during the first ten years of democracy. In order to reassume their due role on the national political stage and to clarify their separate programmatic commitments, certain leaders on the left have contended that they must present the Left as an independent option not tied to the Christian Democrats. This may be particularly attractive if the Frei administration fails to perform well in its final years.

In terms of the competitive dynamic of the party system, it is also important to ask whether the direction of competition between parties in the future is likely to be centripetal or centrifugal. Supporters of the binomial electoral system have employed Downsian[47] logic to suggest that parties will seek to compete for centrist positions.[48] Nonetheless, game theoretical and empirical analyses suggest that the binomial system may actually encourage centrifugal competition because it establishes dual electoral equilibria.[49] Analysts employing Downsian logic overlook the fact that double-member districts create a distinct dynamic of competition compared with the single-member district systems on which Downs's analysis was based.

Although there are many indicators of continuity within the party system, it has also been transformed in some fundamental ways. The two-alliance pattern of competition that has characterized Chilean politics for the first ten

47. Downs, *An Economic Theory of Democracy.*
48. Rabkin, "Redemocratization, Electoral Engineering, and Party Strategies in Chile, 1989–1995," and Guzmán, "Reflexiones sobre el sistema binominal."
49. See Eric Magar, Marc Rosenblum, and David Samuels, "On the Absence of Centripetal Incentives in Double Member Districts: The Case of Chile," *Comparative Political Studies* 31 (December 1998): 714–39, and Jay Dow, "A Spatial Analysis of Candidate Competition in Dual Member Districts: The 1989 Chilean Senatorial Elections," *Public Choice* 97 (1998): 451–74.

years of postauthoritarian democracy is unprecedented. Though historically multiparty coalitions were crucial to governing, the coalitions were more transitory and less solid than those that exist in contemporary Chile. This does not mean that Chile is a two-party system. It means that incentives for coalition formation and maintenance among diverse parties with differing ideologies, platforms, and organizational structures are much stronger than they were in the past. The question for the future is whether the incentives for coalition formation will overcome some of the divisive elements of continuity within the party system.

Conclusion

Contrary to the argument that the transformational intentions of the military regime, coupled with the small-magnitude binomial system, have succeeded in producing fundamental party-system transformation in Chile, there is significant evidence that neither the number of parties nor the pattern of preauthoritarian partisan competition has been substantially altered. Chile remains a country characterized by consolidated multipartism, and there are some convincing indications that the three-way ideological division that has historically characterized the party-system remains. What has changed is the ideological orientation of individual parties and the incentives for coalition formation.

The radicalization and ideologicalization of the party system that sowed the seeds for instability and for the polarization of Chilean politics in the 1970s have disappeared, along with the need for "control" as understood by the military regime. All significant parties have undergone renovation, and the party system is less ideological both in terms of its scope and in terms of the distance between parties, making ideological considerations less important in coalitional deliberations and decision-making. The improved environment for interparty cooperation and the increased incentives for coalition formation have helped to ensure the integrity and durability of both the governing and the opposition coalitions.

However, while the significance of transformations within the party system should not be underestimated, neither should the elements of continuity. The continued existence of a multiparty system, combined with the socioeconomic continuities and challenges outlined in the previous chapter, has profound consequences for interbranch relations and the potential workability and efficacy of the institutional framework set out in the constitution.

First, just when exclusive and messianic visions of politics have disappeared, Chile's institutional framework in many ways fosters single-sector domination of the political system. The concentration of power in the presidency, and the potential exclusion of significant political parties from Congress may limit the strong incentives for cooperation described here. Second, given the complete renovation of the most important parties across the political spectrum and the strong incentives for the moderation of platforms through coalition formation, the rationale for limiting the influence of prosystem parties has disappeared. However, the military's attempt to restrict party influence through political and electoral engineering has an additional and perhaps unanticipated cost: a dramatic decrease in both the representative capacity of the political system and the incentives for the institutional resolution of conflict. These realities are explored in the next two chapters.

5

MULITPARTISM, EXAGGERATED PRESIDENTIALISM, AND CONGRESSIONAL WEAKNESS

Constraints to Interbranch Cooperation and Democratic Governability

Chapters 3 and 4 of this study painted a moderate yet still divided picture of Chilean society and party politics. Postauthoritarian political elites and parties have built upon socioeconomic and political transformations to create a new, moderate pattern of party competition in Chile. The military's dire predictions of the chaos and instability that would result with a return to democracy proved unfounded, and the Aylwin government—one of the most successful and stable in Chilean history—demonstrated the ability of civilian authorities to effectively govern Chile and consolidate the positive economic legacy of the military regime.

However, the preceding chapters also argued that, despite profound economic transformation and emerging consensus, Chile is characterized by narrowing yet still extreme socioeconomic divisions, moderate political divisions, and a well-consolidated multiparty system. The process of democratic transition has also created a somewhat artificial political situation in which many potential conflicts have been set aside to be solved sometime in the future. This is accompanied by excessive optimism and a propitious economic environment, which mask many of the structural infirmities of both the Chilean economic miracle and the political model imposed by the authoritarian regime. The workability of political institutions has not really been tested by crisis or significant conflict.

The next two chapters seek to link and synthesize previous chapters by analyzing the relationship and interaction between the institutional framework for democracy (Chapters 1 and 2) and socioeconomic and political variables (Chapters 3 and 4). This chapter will analyze the implications of congressional weakness and presidential strength for interbranch relations, political efficacy, and democratic governability in the context of the socioeconomic, political and party system of the country. It will begin by underscoring the central and multifunctional role of the Congress in contributing to the workability of a complex multiparty system in the past. It will emphasize how executive/legislative negotiations, and the mediation of disputes within the legislature, formed the core of wider social and political conflict resolution and contributed to preauthoritarian democratic governability.

It will then analyze the consequences of executive strength and legislative weakness in contemporary Chile, as well as their potential implications for the future. The chapter contends that legislative weakness undermines the ability of the Congress to play the positive and multifunctional roles it played in the past, principally in the areas of lawmaking, interest representation, conflict resolution, and enhancing the global legitimacy of the democratic system. It argues that given Chile's socioeconomic context and multiparty system, the current institutional framework fails to provide the political currency, arenas, and incentives for negotiation that allowed Congress to perform these roles in the past and that would permit it to do so in the future.

The Preauthoritarian Party System and the Congress as a Vehicle for Accommodation

In analyzing the consequences of legislative weakness in Chile, it is important to understand the pivotal role played by the legislature within the complex interaction of parties, presidents, and the Congress, which helped sustain democracy in Chile for much of its modern history.

Though the constitution of 1925 restricted legislative strength, compared with the period of the preceding so-called Parliamentary Republic, the Congress quickly developed a key position as an arena for accommodation within a complex multiparty system.[1]

1. For a discussion of the genesis of the 1925 Constitution, see Jaime Eyzaguirre, *Historia de las instituciones políticas y sociales de Chile* (Santiago: Editorial Universitaria, 1967),

By the mid-1930s the Chilean party system had developed the basic functional dynamic that would characterize it until the crisis of 1973. During this period, the Chilean electorate was characterized by a three-way fragmentation of the party system between forces representing the Left, the Right, and the Center. While the existence of these three ideological blocs is something of a caricature and has been exaggerated, the structuring of coalitions among broad sectors, even when not easily pigeonholed (i.e., Ibáñismo), was a reality of the party system. What is more, though characterized by distinct and sometimes numerous parties, each ideological sector for much of Chilean history consistently garnered between one-quarter and one-third of the vote in legislative elections (with the important exception of the Christian Democrats in 1965). Thus, for most of contemporary Chilean history no one party was consistently capable of garnering a majority of the vote.[2] Between 1932 and 1969 the average number of parties with representatives in the Chamber of Deputies was 11.6, ranging between five and eighteen during each of the ten congressional sessions.[3] Though varying in relative weight and importance, each party had a distinct vision of society and the preferred economic role of the state. This meant that the party system had an extremely wide ideological range.

Along with ideological breadth, the party system also was characterized by parties that were national in scope, penetrating every level of Chilean social organization. Parties served as the basic organizational units for labor unions, professional associations, student government, municipal organizations, and sports and social clubs. Party affiliation constituted an important component of social interaction and of Chilean self-identity.[4] Chileans of the same ideological stripe even vacationed together in the same beach resort towns.

191–213, and Bernardino Bravo Lira, *De Portales a Pinochet* (Santiago: Editorial Jurídica de Chile, 1985), 150–72.

2. For two excellent analyses of Chilean elections from the promulgation of the 1925 Constitution until 1973, see Ricardo Cruz-Coke, *Historia electoral de Chile* (Santiago: Editorial Jurídica de Chile, 1984) and Germán Urzúa Valenzuela, *Historia política electoral de Chile* (Santiago: Editorial Jurídica de Chile, 1986).

3. For measures of the relevance and relative weight of these parties, see Chapter 4. The figures cited were computed from data appearing in Arturo Valenzuela, "Partidos políticos y crisis presidencial en Chile: Proposición para un gobierno parlamentario," in *Hacia una democracia moderna: La opción parlamentaria*, ed. Oscar Godoy (Santiago: Ediciones Universidad Católica de Chile, 1990), 145.

4. Arturo Valenzuela convincingly makes this point. See his *Breakdown of Democratic Regimes: Chile*, 3–11. On Chilean political parties in general, see Adolfo Aldulante, Angel Flisfisch, and Tomás Moulián, *Estudios sobre sistemas de partidos en Chile* (Santiago: FLACSO,

The reality that the party system was highly institutionalized, but at the same time fragmented and competitive, forced reliance on a pattern of shifting coalitions for both presidential and parliamentary elections. Given that presidents were unable to rely on legislative majorities of their own parties, the need to negotiate to achieve goals extended beyond intraparty and interparty relations to also include relations between the president and Congress. One distinguishing feature of the Chilean party system was its ability to reconcile this fierce competition with the need to form coalitions. Though interbranch conflict was an enduring reality of Chilean history, what is perhaps most amazing is that in the modern era it did not reach crisis proportions until 1973.[5] Why was this the case?

The ability of the political system to reconcile the seemingly contradictory drives of competition and compromise lies in the complex interactive dynamic between the president, the Congress, the party and electoral systems, and the norms of elite political interaction.

The nature of the party system demanded and contributed to a dynamic of cooperation both within the Congress and in interbranch relations. Because no party or party sector could muster a majority, coalition-building in the Congress was necessary for presidents to carry out policy initiatives. Before the powerful emergence of the Christian Democrats in the mid-1960s, the political Center, and principally the Radical Party, played a crucial role as the linchpin of the party system. The Radical Party consistently and pragmatically built bridges between itself and its ideological neighbors on both sides. In this sense the Radical Party was in many ways the fulcrum upon which political balance was maintained.[6] Since 1932, with only two exceptions, every president elected has been a centrist party candidate relying on

---

1985); R. L. Echaiz, *Evolución histórica de los partidos políticos chilenos* (Santiago: Editorial Francisco de Aguirre, 1971); Alberto Edwards and Eduardo Frei, *Historia de los partidos políticos chilenos* (Santiago: Editorial del Pacífico, 1949); Germán Urzúa Valenzuela, *Los partidos políticos chilenos* (Santiago: Editorial Jurídica, 1968); Federico Gil, *Los partidos políticos chilenos: Génesis y evolución* (Buenos Aires: Ediciones Palma, 1962).

    5. It did of course in the 1890s.

    6. See Arturo Valenzuela, *The Breakdown of Democratic Regimes: Chile*, 3–21. See also Tomás Moulián, who describes the "mobile and pendular" characteristics of the Radical Party in "Violencia, gradualismo y reformas en el desarrollo político chileno," in *Estudios sobre el sistema de partidos en Chile*, ed. Adolfo Aldunate et al., 60–66. For general discussions of the Radical Party, see Francisco Barria Soto, *El Partido Radical, su historia, su obra* (Santiago: Editorial Universitaria, 1957); Alfredo Guillermo Braun, *El Partido Radical y el Frente Popular* (Santiago: Editorial República, 1936); Florencio Durán Bernales, *El Partido Radical* (Santiago: Nascimiento, 1958); and Luis Palma Zúñiga, *Historia del Partido Radical* (Santiago: Editorial Andrés Bello, 1967).

the support of either the Left or the Right. A centrist candidate was elected with support of the Left on three occasions (1938, 1942, and 1946), once with the support of the Right (1964) and twice with the support of both the Right and the Left (1932 and 1952).[7]

Though these coalitions often fell apart following elections, they helped prevent presidents from having to assume office with minority support at the outset of their terms. What is more, the pattern of informal bargaining and the building of temporary working coalitions within the Congress and between Congress and the executive branch helped to prevent the immobilism of governments.

Given the structure of the party system, a moderately powerful Congress was a key and necessary element to preauthoritarian democratic stability. It is of course problematic to speak definitively of congressional strength or weakness, given the important distinction between partisan and constitutional powers.[8] Thus, the strength of both the president and the Congress varied depending on whether majority coalitions existed and on whether presidents could rely on them for support. At the very least, it can be said that in most historical contexts individual legislators and parties had the capacity to engage in bargaining and to consistently extract concessions from the government while avoiding extended periods of executive/legislative deadlock, irrespective of the partisan distribution of Congress (the end of the Allende administration was the great exception, but this exception also shows how the Congress could be quite powerful in certain situations).[9]

Though particularism and clientelism usually have negative connotations, it is important to recognize that they can contribute to the institutionalization of party systems. In many ways, particularism became the political currency of negotiation in Chile, where patronage, pork-barrel politics, and clientelism combined in a fascinating way to help institutionalize the party system and stem ideological polarization. The ability of individual legislators to bargain within the Congress and make deals for the mutual support of particularistic and clientelistic legislation established a pattern and spirit

---

7. Arturo Valenzuela, "Party Politics and the Crisis of Presidentialism in Chile."

8. For a lucid discussion, see Matthew Shugart and Scott Mainwaring, "Presidentialism and Democracy in Latin America: Rethinking the Terms of the Debate," in *Presidentialism and Democracy in Latin America*, ed. Mainwaring and Shugart, 12. While their discussion applies mostly to presidents, a parallel argument applies to legislatures.

9. For an analysis of the functioning of the Chilean presidential system in the preauthoritarian period, and the importance of constant negotiation between presidents and the Congress, see Julio Faundez, "In Defense of Presidentialism: The Case of Chile 1932–1970," in *Presidentialism and Democracy in Latin America*, ed. Mainwaring and Shugart.

of negotiation and compromise that led to additional compromise on larger issues.[10] Arturo Valenzuela has convincingly shown how success in achieving clientelistic political goals on the local level helped to moderate the more ideological orientation of politics on the national level.[11] Success also strengthened parties and their connections to voters. The awarding of funding for a youth center in Copiapó or for a streetlight in Coyhaique could grease the legislative wheels for agreement on larger, more controversial issues, such as the national budget and social policy.

What is more, Arturo Valenzuela and Alexander Wilde argue convincingly that the role of Congress in satisfying particularistic demands was key to maintaining the institutional balance of powers that helped sustain Chilean democracy. They argue that Chilean politics was divided into a center arena (where ideology was of overriding importance) and a local arena (where extracting concrete resources from the national government was paramount). For Valenzuela and Wilde, success in satisfying demands in the local arena extended to the center arena and helped to diffuse bitter conflict between those with distinct visions of society. The structuring of agreements on small issues helped to establish a pattern that facilitated consensus on large issues, and moderated ideological conflict. The gradual disintegration of congressional prerogatives, most notably the provisions of the 1970 Constitutional Reforms that barred particularistic legislation, was instrumental in the decline of the Congress and contributed to the polarization that led to the eventual breakdown of democracy.[12]

Members of Congress were empowered to sponsor and ensure passage of this type of legislation, given the ability to both propose particularistic bills, and to attach them to presidential initiatives in the form of "miscellaneous laws." These laws (discussed in detail in Chapter 1) often had little or nothing to do with the larger bills to which they were attached, but were accepted by presidents to ensure passage of executive initiatives that were in doubt. Jobs, increases in pensions, or provision for financial benefits for widows and orphans often rode the coattails of presidential initiatives. Members of the Congress had the ability to trade votes for miscellaneous laws and amendments tacked on to executive initiatives, in exchange for their support of the presidents' legislative agenda.

10. See Arturo Valenzuela and Alexander Wilde, "Presidential Politics and the Decline of the Chilean Congress," 189–215.

11. This argument is drawn from Arturo Valenzuela, *Political Brokers in Chile: Local Government in a Centralized Polity* (Durham, N.C.: Duke University Press, 1977).

12. Valenzuela and Wilde, "Presidential Politics and the Decline of the Chilean Congress."

Though constitutionally limited, members of Congress were also more influential than it appears in the elaboration of the budget law. Though they could not propose new expenditures to be included in the national budget, they could exert pressure to have their pet projects designated in a particular budget line. Because presidents usually lacked majorities, they were willing to incorporate the legislators' requests into the national budget law, and not use their line veto to cut pork, in exchange for support from members.[13]

The electoral system also encouraged a political dynamic in which meeting particularistic demands was important for political success and at the same time provided an important legitimizing function. The multimember district system and the large number of candidates and parties from which voters had to choose, meant that congressional candidates had to differentiate themselves from others in order to win elections. This was particularly the case after 1958, when the percentage of votes received by individual candidates, not the position on the list (which was previously decided by party organizations), determined the winners. One of the best ways to stand out among the field of candidates was through personal contact with constituents, satisfying demands by using the clout that came with being a member of the Congress. Members were able to navigate the immense state bureaucracy and lobby state agencies to get what they wanted and to resolve constituents' problems. More important, constituents perceived that the route to resolving problems and getting what they wanted was through their member of Congress.[14]

However, personalism and clientelistic legislation were not the only elements that made the Chilean Congress a more important nucleus of the political system than studies that portray the Congress as merely a "rubber stamp" suggest. First, because presidents usually lacked majorities, the Congress became the forum for negotiating controversial legislation. The president could not simply impose his or his party's legislative agenda. The role of the Congress as an arena for negotiation is apparent in legislation dealing with a number of significant areas, including creation of a comprehensive social security system (1924) and the National Corporation for Development (CORFO, 1939), approval of a minimum wage (1943), implementation of an extensive program of agrarian reform (1967), and the constitutional reforms of 1943 and 1970.[15]

13. Ibid., 201.
14. Arturo Valenzuela, *Political Brokers in Chile*, 153–55.
15. Arturo Valenzuela, *The Breakdown of Democratic Regimes: Chile*, 17–21.

Second, the 1925 constitution provided that if no candidate received a majority in the presidential election, the Congress would elect a winner. This often forced presidents to begin their terms with a certain amount of dependence on those parties and members who did support their election. To retain this support and further advance their legislative programs, presidents often paid hefty programmatic costs. Jorge Tapia Videla argued that the "Statute of Constitutional Guarantees" extracted by the Christian Democratic Party as a prerequisite for the party's support in electing Salvador Allende is the most dramatic example of the influences exerted by parties and the Congress from the very beginning of presidential terms.[16]

Third, despite the common but inaccurate portrayal of the Congress as subservient, it often challenged presidential control to actively participate in the formulation of national policy and to act as an oversight on executive authority.[17] The constant necessity of negotiation for majorities made it impossible for the president to ignore Congress. What is more, particularly in the final years of pre-coup Chilean democracy, the Congress became progressively more aggressive in vetoing presidential initiatives and exercising its full array of oversight functions. Some go as far as to contend that these activities violated the spirit of the law, including attempts to exercise political control over the president's ministerial appointments through an endless stream of constitutional accusations.[18]

Fourth, Weston Agor's study of the preauthoritarian Chilean Senate analyzes the formal and informal mechanisms of decision-making within the Senate that allowed it to have real influence on legislation and public policy in Chile. Agor argues that the urgency powers of the president outlined in the constitution of 1925 led scholars to underestimate the empirical law-making capabilities of legislators. In reality, he contends, both houses of the Congress had the ability to influence executive proposals before their actual formulation, through informal consultation and bargaining. Agor points to Senate committees as particularly important mechanisms where interparty agreements were hammered out, off the public record.[19]

16. Jorge Tapia Videla, "The Chilean Presidency in a Developmental Perspective," *Journal of Interamerican Studies and World Affairs* 19 (November 1977): 451–81.

17. For a discussion of this point, see Federico Gil, *The Political System of Chile* (Boston: Houghton Mifflin, 1966), 117–22.

18. Jorge Tapia Videla, "The Chilean Presidency in a Developmental Perspective," 467–68.

19. Francisco Soffia, Secretary for Senate Committees, confirmed that these committees perform a similar function in postauthoritarian Chile. Public posturing and the formal stands of individual parties can be set aside in the negotiation process in an off-the-record context. According to Soffia, who often monitors and transcribes committee debates for internal congressional

Fifth, the ability of legislators to circumvent restrictions on legislative budgetary action gave them more power and influence in the legislative process than a literal reading of the 1925 constitution suggests. While the Congress was not allowed to propose new spending that was not included in the national budget, it often proposed additional expenditures, citing a future annual budget as the source of funds to finance them.[20] What is more, before the reforms of congressional budgetary authority, legislators' demands were often incorporated in national budgets before and during committee and mixed committee stages, escaping the view of analysts who were trying to determine the extent of legislative power.

Finally, the norms of informal interaction among legislators and between legislators and representatives of the executive branch reinforced a dynamic of compromise. The bars, restaurants, and cafés of Santiago were often the arenas in which critical issues of the day were discussed, questions were resolved, and deals were struck, as were the city residences and vacation homes of political elites. By the time legislation came to the floor, previous "understandings" had often already been worked out among legislators and between the Congress and the executive branch. Despite the undemocratic and "smoke-filled room" image depicted here, these informal interactions and exchanges were part of the glue that held working coalitions and the political system together. From interviews with legislators who served before the military government, it is clear that this atmosphere of informality and comfortable negotiation also has been undermined by simmering hostilities that are the products of the military regime. The spartan (yet simultaneously ostentatious) characteristics of the Congress building itself, located far from the locus of political activity in Santiago, and the modern technical demands of legislating, have also undermined this informal yet functional dynamic.

Therefore, though the Congress was not the sole institution on which Chilean democracy was built and maintained, it was central to the functionality of the political system and performed a variety of roles. Given the nature of the Chilean party system, Congress provided an arena for the flexible negotiation of national policy and ideological questions, moderated by the pragmatism necessary to meet local particularistic demands, the satisfaction of which was key to reelection and advancement within the political system and party organizations.

---

use, public and private discourse is often quite distinct, and important agreements have been reached in this less charged atmosphere. Interview, Valparaíso, April 27, 1993.

20. Weston H. Agor, *The Chilean Senate* (Austin: University of Texas Press, 1971), 9.

Congress, the Party System, and the Crisis of 1973

This pattern of cooperation came to an end with the events of the 1960s and 1970s. It is undeniable that the demise of Chilean democracy has its fundamental roots in a larger historical process of class polarization complicated by economic crisis and international intervention.[21] However, the polarization of the system was exacerbated by underlying transformations that loosened the glue that held the political and party system together. Rather than any one of these phenomena causing the demise of Chilean democracy, as certain scholars have suggested, their simultaneous evolution created a series of strains that made traditional individual and institutional responses less effective than was the case historically. However, given that the principal focus of Chapters 5 and 6 is institutional, more stress will be placed on the transformation in the dynamic relation between the president, the party system, and the Congress that helped lead to the crisis of democracy.[21]

In terms of the party system, the decline in popular support for the pragmatic Radical Party, and that party's replacement by the Christian Democrats as the premier party of the Center, brought forth a new dynamic of interparty competition that transformed the pattern of coalition formation in the country. Convinced that they would be a new force in politics, and bolstered by their spectacular performance in the congressional elections of 1965, the Christian Democrats were confident that they could successfully "go it alone" in the presidential election of 1970. Analysts have suggested, perhaps unfairly, a certain arrogance in the attitudes and policy prescriptions of the Christian Democrats during this period. However, there were also some powerful political consequences in terms of the party's core constituents, which made coalitions with the Right or the Left problematic. These are a function more of the historical moment than of the arrogance of the Christian Democrats. In particular, the party's unwillingness to openly confront the popular threat posed by the Left made the Right skeptical

21. The best studies of the dynamics of regime breakdown in Chile are Arturo Valenzuela, *The Breakdown of Democratic Regimes: Chile*; Paul Sigmund, *The Overthrow of Allende and the Politics of Chile* (Pittsburgh: University of Pittsburgh Press, 1977); and Manuel Antonio Garretón and Tomás Moulián, *Análisis coyuntural y proceso político: Las fases del conflicto en Chile* (San José, Costa Rica: Editorial Universitaria Centroamericana, 1978).

22. For an analysis of the role of the Congress during the Popular Unity government, see Julio Lavín Valdés, "El papel del Congreso Nacional en el gobierno de la Unidad Popular," *Revista chilena de derecho de la Universidad Católica de Valparaíso* 10 (1986): 304–24, and Juan E. Garcés, *Revolución, congreso y constitución: El caso Tohá* (Santiago: Editorial Quimantú, 1972).

about the intentions and true colors of the Christian Democrats. Similarly, the Left viewed the party as having a halfhearted and politically motivated position on the increasing demands for far-reaching social transformation in the country.[23] For the Christian Democrats, allying with ideological neighbors on either side would dilute their message of democratic reformism based on Christian principles and undermine their core bases of support. This reality upset the traditional pattern of coalition formation built around centrist parties.

What is more, the reforms of 1943 and 1970 discussed in Chapter 1 sharply proscribed legislative power, especially in regard to the clientelistic exchanges that had become the political currency of cooperation within the political system. While attempts had been made to legally limit these types of exchanges in the interests of budgetary integrity, most had failed. Unlike earlier reform efforts, the reforms of 1970 succeeded in definitively ending these practices by widening the scope of presidential power. The president's right of exclusive initiative to propose laws having to do with economic and social issues was expanded, and the Congress was strictly limited in the proposal of "*legislación miscelánea*," which had provided members with a powerful tool for securing the passage of clientelistic and pork-barrel legislation.[24]

Indeed, even before the 1970 reforms, the government of Eduardo Frei acted to eliminate personalistic legislation in practice (which it viewed as inefficient and wasteful), vetoing all but a few of the amendments and miscellaneous laws submitted by legislators.[25] The 1970 reforms, then, institutionalized legislative weakness through a de jure and de facto elimination of miscellaneous legislation by allowing only amendments that dealt with the *idea matriz* (central concept) of a bill.

Thus, along with opportunities for congressional initiative in economic and social policy, many of the opportunities for informal bargaining disappeared. Particularistic exchanges that had helped to stem the complete ideological centrifugation of the party system in the past were banned at the very time when the drives of polarization created by domestic and international

23. A number of political considerations made it difficult for the Christian Democrats and the Right to form a coalition in 1970. See Tomás Moulián and Isabel Torres, "La problemática de la derecha política en Chile, 1964–1983," in *Muerte y resurrección: Los partidos políticos en el autoritarismo y las transiciones del cono sur*, ed. Manuel Antonio Garretón and Marcelo Cavarrozzi (Santiago: FLACSO, 1989), 335–93.

24. For an analysis of the 1970 reforms, see Eduardo Frei et al., *Reforma constitucional 1970* (Santiago: Editorial Jurídica, 1970).

25. Valenzuela and Wilde, "Presidential Politics and the Decline of the Chilean Congress," 207.

transformations were at their strongest. Small favors ceased to be translated into larger agreements, and ideological issues came to dominate political discourse.

The 1970 election of Salvador Allende with only a plurality of the vote in a three-way presidential race could not have come at a worse time. Lacking a broad coalition in Congress, Allende could not institute the transformational agenda that he felt Chilean society demanded. And his status as a double minority president left him without a majority for passage of significant legislation. However, more serious in terms of regime stability in Chile, the opposition also lacked sufficient votes to successfully initiate and carry out impeachment proceedings.

Increasingly extraconstitutional actions both in the Congress and by the president led to suspicion and distrust, which intensified the already serious social and party-system polarization. International protest activities contributed to a revolutionary atmosphere in the country and spurred internal popular activities. Political parties took advantage of domestic political movements, seeking to mobilize their supporters and exacerbating an already explosive situation. The high cost of failing to maintain ideological integrity led to increased party polarization and maximalist positions. Ideological outbidding eventually outstripped the political system's ability to respond, raising the stakes for all political actors involved. The locus of political activity moved from time-honored, yet increasingly moribund, institutions to the streets, and eventually, to military garrisons.

Executive Strength and Legislative Weakness in Postauthoritarian Chile

This chapter has argued that the gradual expansion of executive power at the cost of congressional prerogatives had some problematic repercussions for regime stability in Chile. However, what are the consequences of the continued evolution of the expansion of executive power within the framework established by the 1980 constitution, given some of the transformations and continuities in Chilean politics and society discussed in the previous chapters? Given the party moderation and "de-ideologicalization" of the Chilean party system discussed in Chapter 4, is the Congress as central to the workability of the democratic system as it was in the past? To answer these questions, it is important first to analyze the significance of the new limited role for Congress established by the 1980 constitution.

Analysts of legislative politics long ago abandoned unifunctional analyses of legislatures as simply lawmaking bodies.[26] The influence and role of legislatures in actual lawmaking, suggested by the term "legislature," varies from country to country depending both on formal legal precepts and on the actual norms of the legislative process. However, scholars have underscored that legislatures can influence politics in other ways, given the multifunctional roles they play.

It is clear from the discussion above that the Chilean legislature indeed played a multifunctional role within the political system. In addition to its lawmaking function, it also provided an effective arena for articulation of various interests and for conflict resolution, which in turn performed an important legitimizing role for the Congress and for democracy in general. The 1980 constitution places important limits on the ability of Congress to continue to perform all these functions.[27] What are the consequences of these limitations?

Lawmaking

Because the president has the capacity to so thoroughly control the legislative process, the Congress has become much less relevant to the legislative process, defined in its most narrow sense as lawmaking. If the Congress fails to approve the budget, it automatically becomes law, giving the president effective decree power. In terms of other types of legislation, the president has the ability to exercise a negative veto on what the Congress considers. It is true that the president must seek the approval of Congress, in order to pass legislation, but the president can exercise control of the most important legislative questions by employing the many faculties granted to the

26. The most important early works analyzing the multifunctional roles of legislatures include S. H. Beer, "The British Legislature and the Problem of Mobilizing Consent," in *Lawmakers in a Changing World*, ed. E. Frank (Englewood Cliffs, N.J.: Prentice Hall, 1966), 30–48; Robert Packenham, "Legislatures and Political Development," in *Legislatures in Developmental Perspective*, ed. A. Kornberg and L. Musolf (Durham, N.C.: Duke University Press, 1970), 521–82; and J. Blondel, *Comparative Legislatures* (Englewood Cliffs, N.J.: Prentice Hall, 1973).

27. These functions are based loosely on those identified by Packenham. In his Brazilian case study, Packenham identifies ten functions performed by the legislature in addition to "lawmaking." They are not discussed separately here because they really overlap to a greater extent than suggested by Packenham, and some do not apply as much to Chile. See Packenham, "Legislatures and Political Development," 521–37.

executive by the 1980 constitution. Presidential urgencies can be used to continually "bottle up" the legislative process and effectively prevent consideration of legislation originating in the Congress. The president can also force Congress to consider only executive initiatives during extraordinary sessions.

The proscriptions placed on legislators in terms of the types of legislation they can initiate make it difficult for legislators to propose bills of any significance. Almost all significant legislation involves some type of expenditure, or deals with a social or economic question of the type described in Article 62 of the constitution, which outlines the president's areas of exclusive initiative.

For example, during the 1993 legislative session an opposition senator sought to present a bill to the Congress that would allow women to determine when state-sanctioned maternity leave would be taken. Currently, the law establishes certain periods for prepartum and postpartum leave. Though not modifying the established period for maternity leave, this bill would have let women themselves decide how much time to take before and after the birth of their child. Nonetheless, upon review by the appropriate legislative committee the introduction of the bill was ruled unconstitutional and therefore inadmissible—because it dealt with "social security," an area in which the executive has exclusive initiative.[28]

The president's urgency prerogatives further undermine the ability of legislators to have their legislation enacted. One deputy lamented that one of his proposals had been accepted by a Chamber committee but that its discussion had been pending for three years and three consecutive legislative sessions, given that it had consistently been moved down to a lower level on the agenda as executive urgencies were moved ahead of it. He was convinced that the legislative period would end without the committee considering a piece of legislation that he deemed important both for his district and for the country as a whole.[29]

The designation of urgency by the executive also upsets the rhythm of work in Congress and creates discontinuity in the consideration of individual proposals. While a committee is studying a particular project in depth, an urgent executive proposal often arrives without previous notice and forces delay in the discussion of the original project. By the time the original proposal is again ready for consideration, much of the initial deliberation

28. Off-the-record interview, Valparaíso, 12 May 1993.
29. Off-the-record interview with Concertación Deputy, Valparaíso, 15 April 1993.

and study must be repeated in order to refamiliarize committee members with the most important aspects of the proposed legislation.

One of the legislature's principal lawmaking functions is to improve legislation through collective deliberation. The greater the number of actors with input on a particular piece of legislation, the more thoughtful and comprehensive it will be when it becomes law. However, the president's control of the legislative agenda limits the effectiveness of the legislature as a deliberative body.

One Christian Democratic deputy recounted how Aylwin rammed through Congress laws regulating coal subsidies (an important piece of the president's legislative agenda). The deputy contended that, given the president's designation of urgency, legislators were given only ten days to consider this important, complicated, and rather large bill. The Congress lacked the time to do an in-depth study of the issue or to engage in significant debate concerning the pros and cons of the specific articles of the bill. When the laws, as designed by the president, took effect and proved to be unworkable, Congress was forced to again legislate on the same issues in order to fix the mistakes in the original proposal. The deputy argued that if the Congress had been given enough time to properly debate and study the issue, it would not have been forced to relegislate and would have saved a great deal of time and work.[30]

Finally, while in the preauthoritarian period legislators could achieve their legislative goals by circumventing many of the limitations placed on them in terms of particularistic legislation and the national budget, this is no longer the case.[31] The 1980 constitution is much less ambiguous in its wording concerning the legislative processes for budgetary and fiscal matters than the original text of the 1925 constitution. Empirical evidence makes clear that legislators respect the letter of the law in terms of the origination and amendment of this type of legislation, to a much greater extent than their preauthoritarian counterparts.

These limitations on lawmaking capacity have some important consequences. They affect both the quality of legislation and the ability of the Congress to act as a check on presidential power. Given fixed terms of office, presidents feel an understandable urgency in promoting their legislative agendas.

30. Interview with Deputy Andrés Palma, Valparaíso, 2 June 1993.
31. Agor discusses ways in which limitations placed on legislators were circumvented in the past. In terms of the budget, the Congress escaped the limitation on proposing new spending without indicating a source for funding by simply designating a future annual budget as the source. See Agor, *The Chilean Senate*, 9–10.

It makes sense that presidents would use every tool at their disposal to guard against perceived inaction. But this urgency may lead to elaboration of ill-conceived or poor-quality legislation given a lack of due consideration. In addition, the legislative process is not only intended to provide for the input of a wide range of opinions when elaborating bills. Congress is also supposed to check and correct legislation, to ensure that presidents do not exceed their legal authority or political mandate in proposed bills.

In interviews with a sample of deputies that reflected the partisan distribution of the Congress, 100 percent of opposition members and 96.7 percent of government members agreed that presidential urgencies both negatively affect the quality of legislation and limit deputies' representative capacities. What is more, 86 percent of legislators interviewed felt that, when given the opportunity, the Congress had improved the quality of executive initiatives, in terms of both content and legislative technique. The limitations placed on legislators in terms of time and access to information outlined in Chapter 1 further limit the ability of the Congress to act more forcefully and decisively to improve legislation.

Interest Representation and Articulation

The restricted spheres of action and influence of legislators limit their ability to carry out their functions of interest representation and articulation, both narrowly and widely considered. From a national perspective, the current limitations on how the Congress undertakes its most basic representative functions are especially serious in a country with a multiparty system. Because presidents are likely to be elected with a minority of the vote,[32] the winner-take-all characteristics of the presidency, combined with congressional weakness, can prevent the real interest representation of the majority of citizens who are not partisans of the president. This limitation on representation is compounded by the exclusionary tendencies of the parliamentary electoral system mentioned earlier and explored in greater detail in the next chapter. Certainly, every political system excludes certain political options, and indeed functional political systems must aggregate interests—everyone cannot win. However, unlike in the United States, Great Britain, or other countries with

32. Though a presidential second-round election was instituted according to the 1980 Constitution, in many ways this type of election represents a "manufactured majority." The significance of the second-round election to the support bases of presidents will be discussed in greater detail in the next chapter.

two-party systems, in multiparty systems exclusion is more serious, because more people do not win when a minority party can dominate democratic institutions in ways that it usually cannot in two-party systems.

Interest representation in democracies is based on the principle that societies are composed of distinct groups that have diverse values, demands, and legitimate sectoral interests. Demands are met and agreements are reached through negotiation and bargaining between these sectors, which are considered equals. However, congressional weakness creates an uneven playing field and limits the sectoral scope of interest articulation and representation. The ability of political elites to successfully achieve goals in the institutional realm helps prevent the use of extrainstitutional avenues. Similarly, yet on a distinct level, democratic legitimacy depends both on political efficacy and on the ability of most sectors of society to make themselves heard within the political system.

In terms of interest representation more narrowly considered, the 1980 constitution achieves what earlier constitutions and attempts at reform failed to accomplish: the end of clientelistic and particularistic legislation.

When combined with circumscribed congressional action on issues of national importance, these limitations put legislators in a difficult position with regard to their constituents. Even though the National Congress was closed for almost seventeen years, a certain public vision of the traditional role of the legislature persists at the constituent level. Logrolling and satisfying particularistic demands were key functions of legislators in the preauthoritarian period. In addition, in a unitary system like Chile's, the central government, rather than local or municipal authorities, was to a great extent responsible for allocating resources. One of the few ways for constituents to lobby successfully for change was to appeal directly to the most visible and accessible agent of the state: their deputy. Deputies could facilitate the satisfaction of demands, because they were able to expedite requests in an overburdened bureaucracy with limited resources.

In Chile's reconstituted democracy, constituents often continue to expect that their deputy or senator can deliver favors or intervene regarding jobs, benefits, pensions, streetlights, funding for a community or youth center, or other types of particularistic demands. Although municipal authorities were reestablished in June 1992 and therefore many such requests should now be referred to the municipality, the electorate often expects a legislator to be able to satisfy these demands. One Christian Democratic legislator underscored this point by contending that the electorate seems to perceive deputies as "*alcaldes grandes*" (big mayors), not national representatives.[33] Confirming this perception, a staff member for a Concertación deputy estimated that of all the correspondence he receives from constituents, only 5 percent of it has anything to do with legislative issues at the national level. The other 95 percent consists of requests for jobs, scholarships, increases in pensions, or problems related to lighting, roads, sewers, and water.[34]

Certain deputies have attempted to define their role in campaign literature more clearly. A Renovación Nacional deputy wrote effectively in a campaign pamphlet: "There is some confusion regarding the work of deputies and mayors. The work they do is quite different. A deputy debates laws and acts as an oversight and check on government action. On the other hand, mayors and the town council administer the resources of the municipality. For example, it is the function of the mayor and not a deputy to fix a street, provide lighting for a neighborhood, or worry about parks, municipal education, etc."[35]

Despite his disclaimer, the deputy still lists at the end of the pamphlet all the actions he has taken with regard to each of these particularistic issues on behalf of constituents. Almost all campaign literature lists the concrete actions taken by deputies in relation to these types of issues, even though most of these requests should be referred to the municipality. Thus, despite widespread misinterpretation of the role of deputies, and clear efforts to clarify that role, it is still politically necessary and expedient to take action on the personal requests of constituents.

Constituents may not be aware that because of the limitations imposed by budget restrictions, exclusive executive initiative, and presidential urgencies, the range of actions that legislators can take on these proposals is much more limited than in the past. Members usually recommend action in the form of an "*oficio*" (request for information) sent to the ministry involved in the issue, or directly intervene with an appeal to municipal government authorities. Neither of these avenues guarantees substantive results in resolving the issue or satisfying the demand.

Given the widespread public image of what a deputy is supposed to do, and that Chamber members are unable to point to an effective record in influencing legislation on national issues, they have a strong incentive to attempt to satisfy personalistic constituent demands in exchange for support

33. Interview with Deputy Eugenio Ortega, Valparaíso, 31 March 1993.
34. Interview with Eduardo Barros González, Valparaíso, 2 April 1993.
35. See Campaign brochure issued by Alberto Espina "Rindo Cuenta: 1990–1993." Translation by the author.

in future elections. Nonetheless, contemporary constitutional proscriptions about including articles not germane to the *"idea matriz"* (central concept) of legislation, and other limitations outlined here, eliminate the ability of legislators to provide "pork" and contribute to the public's belief that the legislators and the Congress are ineffectual or uncaring. In essence, the political currency of negotiation and interest representation has been undermined.

This is not to suggest that the type of particularistic spending that existed in the past in Chile should now be permitted. Indeed, all but one of the legislators interviewed for this study were opposed to granting Congress additional latitude in the area of particularistic spending, given its potentially pernicious effects on the integrity of the national budget.[36] However, it is important to acknowledge that these policies were functional, and the inability of legislators to undertake them within the framework of current law represents a further curtailment of the tools legislators have to effectively represent constituents and to extract concessions and negotiate with the executive branch in the interests of their district. What is more, there is a fine line between interest representation and satisfaction of personalistic demands. Representation and the satisfaction of demands, particularistic or not, are two of the principal functions of legislators in democratic systems.

Congress as an Arena for Negotiation, Interest Aggregation, and Conflict Resolution

One of the most important consequences of the limited role the legislature plays in the Chilean political process is the loss, or at the very least a decreased profile, of an important arena for negotiation and interest aggregation. Why is this significant when, as Chapters 3 and 4 suggested, there is an underlying consensus within the political system in regard to the most important issues?

Weston Agor points to the historical importance of the Congress as an arena for compromise. He contends that scholars tended to underestimate

36. Chile is not the only country in the world where these types of pork-barrel policies have acquired a bad name. Nonetheless, clientelistic legislation never really resulted in the extravagant spending excesses that these legislators, and some of the legislation's critics, have suggested. For a discussion of this point, see Valenzuela and Wilde, "Presidential Politics and the Decline of the Chilean Congress," 211.

the power of Latin American legislative institutions because of an excessive reliance on formal-legal analysis and a limited understanding of the informal norms and empirical realities that affect how legislatures function. He argues that the Chilean Congress was a key arena for helping to maintain consensus in Chile's multiparty system, given that it was one of the few Chilean political institutions in which every sector of Chilean society was represented.[37] The role of Congress as an arena for interbranch and interparty negotiation is still crucial. Chile's multiparty system is alive and well. Thus, Agor's contention has just as much validity today as it did in the preauthoritarian era. Congress remains the only institution in which the full range of political options can be represented.

However, the role of Congress as an arena for negotiation is limited in a number of ways. First, many legislative leaders who were interviewed for this study, and especially those who had served in Congress before the coup, pointed to the preauthoritarian dynamic of informal negotiation both within Congress and between it and the executive, as a positive element that the political system now lacks. While this is certainly a reflection of a degree of nostalgia, members did point to some concrete elements that have contributed to such a development. Often cited as reasons for the transformed informal mechanisms of interaction were the hectic schedules of members, complicated by the sense of isolation and the need for additional travel between the capital, Congress, and members' home districts, given the inconvenient location of the Congress in the port of Valparaíso. However, the most important reason cited was that deputies do not have the tools to engage in informal negotiations, given the weakness of the legislature.

Second, and more important, is that without the type of coalition that has existed since the beginning of the Chilean transition, opposition parties within Congress would have little voice in the political direction of the country. In this context, the limited power of the legislature and of individual legislators diminishes the importance of the assembly as an arena for negotiation. Given the limitation on spheres of legislative action, there is little left to negotiate, and legislators have few tools to employ in areas where negotiation is possible. What is more, they come to the bargaining table with little leverage and with established limits on what they can demand in exchange for providing support for executive initiatives.

<hr>

37. Agor, *The Chilean Senate*. Although this reality was not transformed by the reforms of 1943 and 1970, the potential for full representation of all party sectors within Congress was surely limited with the adoption of the binomial electoral system, the significance of which will be more fully analyzed in the next chapter.

The wide political range of forces represented in the Congress (especially in a multiparty system), as opposed to the winner-take-all nature of the presidency, means that there is a more diverse set of actors involved in the negotiation process. If presidents are provided with a more dominant role in the legislative process than the Congress itself, this process of negotiation may be attenuated by the decree or urgency powers of the president. However, in situations in which the president must negotiate instead of decree, a more diverse and complex set of sectoral and party interests can be incorporated into both the national dialogue and actual bills, making legislation more acceptable and legitimate to a broader range of political sectors.

There are really two axes of conflict in the executive-legislative equation: one centering around party differences and one that deals with institutional interests. While the former is certainly more significant for our understanding of interbranch politics than the latter, it is important to recognize that the Congress as an institution has a certain institutional identification and interests, and an agenda of its own. That is to say, there are times when Congress may seek to satisfy its own goals in opposition to the president, attaching less importance to party labels. This is especially the case in terms of urgency powers, the prompt answering of *oficios*, and respect for amendments and changes made to legislation by Congress. Congressional weakness thus also undermines the ability of Congress to force consideration of its institutional agenda in the face of executive domination.

Comparative and theoretical work on presidential systems supports these conclusions. In their cross-national study of presidentialism, Matthew Shugart and John Carey find that political systems characterized by very powerful presidents, especially in terms of legislative prerogatives, have less successful records of democratic longevity than other types of presidential systems.[38] For these scholars, stronger legislative branches can serve "as arenas for the perpetual fine-tuning of conflicts," while strong presidents often seek simply to avoid conflict and impose their own will.[39]

Numerous case studies also confirm a strong correlation between presidential strength in the legislative arena and problems of democratic governability and political efficacy.[40] It is precisely the weaker presidential systems (in terms of legislative prerogatives) that have had more success in sustaining democracy. This theoretical finding is particularly relevant in the

38. Shugart and Carey, *Presidents and Assemblies*, 148.
39. Ibid., 165.
40. See especially the volume edited by Shugart and Mainwaring, *Presidentialism and Democracy in Latin America*.

Chilean case, given the extraordinary legislative powers of the president. Indeed, Shugart and Mainwaring rank the Chilean president highest in Latin America when it comes to legislative prerogatives.[41]

Legitimation Function

In the preauthoritarian period, the Congress performed a critical legitimating function through representation of a wide range of political sectors and the satisfaction of demands. Though not unquestioned, the overall legitimacy of the political system was bolstered by congressional legitimacy, given that political parties across the spectrum had some input in the formulation of national policy, legislation, and budgetary priorities.

The current limits placed on congressional latitude undermine the ability of the Congress to perform this legitimizing function in both latent and manifest terms.[42] In terms of latent legitimization, the negative public view of Congress undermines the legitimacy of democracy in general, because one of the principal institutions of democracy is seen as unnecessary and/or ineffectual. In terms of manifest legitimization, the inability of Congress to play a substantive role in the legislative process undermines the ultimate legitimacy of law, given that a majority of sectors in society do not participate in the formulation of legislation. This further weakens the already questionable integrity of the institutional and legal framework inherited from the authoritarian regime.

Though not definitive measures of the legitimacy of the institution, preliminary indications are that the public has little confidence in, or understanding of, the Congress. The overall evaluation of Congress as an institution is quite low. In a survey conducted in December 1992, only 14 percent of those surveyed rated Congress as an institution in which they had "much confidence." Indeed, Congress trailed Catholic bishops, ministers of government, and even high-level officials of the armed forces in the public's expression of trust in Chile's diverse groups and institutions.[43]

Survey data also demonstrate that the public is not exactly sure what Congress or their representatives actually do, and has a negative estimation

41. Ibid. (especially the introduction and conclusion).

42. Though his discussion is based on the Brazilian case, Robert Packenham provides a useful discussion of the legitimizing functions of legislatures that can be applied more generally. The terms "latent" and "manifest" are used here in the same sense in which Packenham applies them. See Packenham, "Legislatures and Political Development."

43. Centro de Estudios Públicos—Adimark, "Encuesta de opinión pública," January 1993. These survey data do not differ significantly from the public evaluation of legislative

Table 5.1. Comparative evaluation of deputies and the executive branch, 1992

	Deputies %	Executive %
They are doing it well.	21.9	55.1
They are doing it badly.	11.6	15.4
Not exactly sure what they are doing.	59.6	19.7
No response.	6.9	9.8
Total	100	100

SOURCE: Participa, "Estudio sobre la democracia y participación política," Informe Segunda Medición 1992, Santiago, Chile, April 1993, 31–36.

NOTE: More recent data on the same subject lacks comparable validity because the wording and structure of the question were changed and only one year of subsequent data even with this rewording is available.

N = 1,503 for both surveys.

of the performance of the institution. This contrasts markedly with respondents' approval rating of the executive branch, or "the government." In a survey conducted in 1992, interviewees were asked: "With respect to the deputies that represent your district, which phrase best describes what you think in terms of how they are doing their work?" Next they were asked: "And now, in terms of the government, how would you say that it [the Executive branch] is doing its work?" Table 5.1 compares the responses.

Clearly, respondents are more familiar with actions of the executive branch. More significant than the high level of approval for the executive branch is the fact that 59.6 percent of respondents are not sure exactly what their representatives, or deputies, do. This lack of understanding has implications not only for the legitimacy of Congress but also for the very legitimacy of representative government. While constituents may have a vague idea that they should contact their deputy if they have a problem, their rudimentary understanding of what legislative representation is supposed to be makes it difficult for members of Congress to effectively perform the representative role their constituents expect. This failure to perform effectively may leave constituents disgruntled and dissatisfied with the functioning of democratic institutions in general.

---

institutions in other Latin American countries. In a certain sense, then, they may be interpreted as a critique of legislatures in particular rather than a criticism of the Chilean legislature per se. However, by most accounts the Chilean legislature historically was a more efficacious and legitimate body than its counterparts in the region. Thus, its very similar evaluation as an institution may indeed be a signal that Chile's Congress is becoming more like that of the country's neighbors.

Frustration with the performance of the Congress as an institution is also apparent. While approval ratings for the president were consistently high throughout the first administration, the general approval rating of Congress has been quite low since the first survey was made in 1991. The surveys asked interviewees in 1991, 1992, and 1993 if they agreed with a number of statements regarding the Congress. Table 5.2 summarizes the results.

In a 1997 survey in which respondents were asked to rate how fifteen distinct institutions were fulfilling their role in society, the Congress rated third from last, after unions and political parties. The armed forces and the police received significantly better evaluations than Congress did, even though crime was consistently designated as one of the country's top problems in public-opinion surveys. Even Chile's in many respects malfunctional judicial system rated slightly higher than the Congress.[44]

Given the relatively recent reestablishment of democratic institutions in the country, it is troubling to see so little confidence in the Congress. Although that development is a worldwide phenomenon, it is especially problematic in situations in which democracy has not yet been completely consolidated. Institutions in nations that are redemocratizing lack the resilience that the more-consolidated democracies have to help them deal effectively with public mistrust and disgust.

Although a simple strengthening of the Congress would not automatically enhance the legitimacy of the political system, improvements in the representative and legislative capacity of Congress could at least rehabilitate its tarnished image and contribute to increased confidence in democratic institutions in general. It would also increase the institutional capacity of Congress, giving it the power to stand up to presidents who are determined to control the legislative process, without giving the Congress a significant consultative role.

Conclusion

The process of democratic transition in Chile has consistently demonstrated the willingness of elites representing the entire range of sectoral and party

44. Adimark, "Estudio de opinión pública Adimark" (Santiago: Adimark, April 1997). The percentages cited were of the institutions that received a rating of 5, 6, or 7 on a scale of 1 to 7. Congress' rating was 36.4 percent, compared with the armed forces at 63.1 percent, the police at 62.1 percent, and the judiciary at 36.6 percent.

Table 5.2. Public evaluation of legislative functions, 1991–1993 (% of sample that agreed with statements)

Statement	Year		
	1991	1992	1993
The Congress is functioning well.	54.7	43.0	44.2
Members of Parliament only worry about people at election time.	54.8	74.7	74.1
There needs to be more contact between the people and Congress.	79.8	85.5	82.5
Laws do not help people like me.	40.9	44.4	37.3

SOURCES: Participa, "Estudio sobre la democracia y participación política," Informe Segunda Medición 1992, Santiago, Chile, April 1993, 31–36; Participa, "Los chilenos y la democracia," Informe 1993, Santiago, Chile, 1994, 60.

interests to negotiate and pragmatically reach agreements. Nonetheless, an institutional framework that squelches particular voices and limits popular representation mitigates against maintaining this dynamic of cooperation. This is the case at the very time when, as previous chapters demonstrate, all significant political sectors are willing, and indeed predisposed, to attempt to reach agreements.

Whether the controversial issues still facing society, and some of the potential problems of democratic governability that emerge as they are addressed, can be resolved within a context in which the arenas, incentives, and tools for negotiation are absent is still questionable. Nagging socioeconomic inequality, political disagreements, and unresolved social questions, as well as ongoing political conflicts, cannot be mediated with the involvement of only those sectors who benefit from electoral and institutional engineering or by virtue of having simply captured the presidency. Given the combination of interparty agreement on basic issues and multipartism, the optimal formula for conflict resolution is not exclusion, but rather inclusion of the full range of political options within democratic institutions. This formula has worked for Chile in the past, except in situations characterized by domestic and international ideological confrontations, situations that are unlikely in the future.

In a multiparty context where no one party can garner a majority, congressional weakness concentrates effective political power in an office that is not necessarily representative of a wide spectrum of political options in Chile. No political system represents the interests of all, and interest aggregation is a necessary feature of democratic systems. Beyond a purposively constructed consociational regime, it is difficult to imagine a government characterized by complete inclusion across the political spectrum. However, there are degrees of exclusion, and when they are very extreme the process of interest aggregation itself may cease to function without adequate representation and tools for negotiation. The exclusionary characteristics of Chile's exaggerated presidential system (especially in cases of double minority presidencies) and the potentially unrepresentative characteristics of its electoral system can make the conflict-dampening process of interest aggregation more difficult.

Congressional weakness in essence encourages opposition parties to use the few tools at their disposal more strongly. Thus, in a paradoxical way congressional weakness, and the lack of incentives for negotiation that it creates, makes Congress stronger where it can do the most damage. When parties do not have the strength to win through negotiation, they have incentives for obstructionism, through the withholding of votes and attempts to derail the legislative project of the president at any cost. If legislators are given a significant role in policy making and agreements are negotiated and not forced, all legislators have a stake in the success of policy. With negotiation, those policies would be acceptable to a wider range of political forces. If legislators play a significant role in negotiations, they ultimately have some responsibility for legislation that leaves the chambers. Thus, they would be more likely to defend legislation rather than simply attempting to shoot down the president.

In addition to the theoretical and comparative work that points to the difficulties associated with extremely strong presidents, there is empirical evidence that Chilean elites are not satisfied with the framework for executive domination. Of the deputies interviewed for this study, 94 percent representing governing parties considered executive domination of the legislative process a negative feature of the Chilean institutional structure. Ninety-two percent of opposition deputies agreed. Many also agreed that presidents have tried members' patience in the use of presidential faculties, and that Congress will be less willing to tolerate as dominant an executive once the threat of an armed incursion is less serious. Deputies and senators consistently pointed to the special context of the transition, which has served to modify the behavior of the Congress and make it more likely to tolerate executive domination.

However, congressional weakness is not the only impediment to a continuing dynamic of compromise and ultimately to democratic governability. Each negative feature of the institutional structure discussed here is reinforced by other aspects of the overall framework for democracy, and primarily the parliamentary electoral system. Chapter 6 examines other features of the institutional framework that both support exaggerated presidentialism and intensify some of its negative characteristics.

6

ELECTORAL AND LEGAL CONSTRAINTS TO INTERBRANCH COOPERATION AND DEMOCRATIC GOVERNABILITY

Interbranch relations are not conducted in a political vacuum. The incentives for cooperation within and between the executive and the legislature are not only a function of the relative strength of each. Executive/legislative relations are undertaken within the complex web of institutions and legal norms that form the overall framework for democratic government. This relationship is even more complex in Chile than in most democratic systems, given the many "authoritarian enclaves" embedded within the postauthoritarian institutional framework.[1]

The full constellation of institutional variables has a profound effect on the incentive structure of governing elites and on the potential workability of the distinct ways in which executive/legislative relations are structured. Different sets and combinations of these variables can make presidentialism a more stable and workable alternative, a reality that only recently has received sufficient attention in the literature analyzing presidential and parliamentary systems. There is a tendency to focus on the type of institutional arrangement in a broad sense, without sufficient differentiation between

---

1. "Authoritarian enclave" is a termed coined by Garretón. See his *The Chilean Political Process*.

the distinct functional dynamics of presidentialism and parliamentarism produced by the influence and intervention of other institutions and legal precepts.[2]

This chapter will analyze how the incentives for interbranch cooperation are limited not only by congressional weakness but also by the constitutional and legal framework in which Congress is embedded and operates. It will underscore how this framework has the potential to create problems of democratic governability and political efficacy because it further undermines the already limited incentives for interbranch cooperation and undercuts the ability of the Congress to perform the multifunctional roles outlined in the previous chapter and to act as an arena for negotiations.

Juan Linz and Arturo Valenzuela point to *doble minoría* presidents as one of the most problematic aspects of Latin American presidentialism. Given the combination of multipartism with presidential systems, the predominant political configuration in Latin America, presidents are often elected with only a plurality of the vote and without a legislative majority; hence, they are minority presidents in two ways. For these scholars, and others, this is the aspect of presidentialism that has often led to deadlock and immobilism and contributed to the instability of Latin American presidential government.[3]

Scott Mainwaring and Matthew Shugart depart from this view, which has become the conventional wisdom concerning the perils of presidentialism, by arguing that the problems of presidentialism do not emerge as a result of minority presidents per se, but rather situations in which a president's party lacks a "sizeable legislative contingent."[4] Presidents, they contend, need to

---

2. Shugart and Carey's book is an important exception to the general dearth of works on distinct institutional combinations. See Shugart and Carey, *Presidents and Assemblies*. Work on the relationship between electoral laws and the workability of distinct types of institutional combinations has also blossomed in recent years, with important books like Mark Jones's *Electoral Laws and the Survival of Presidential Democracies* among a few others. However, like most studies in the same vein, these are cross-national in focus, lacking in-depth analyses of particular cases. In this sense, this study intends to contribute to this literature through an in-depth analysis of a particular case. Its findings confirm many of those of the works cited above. What is more, even of the cross-national studies cited, few have systematically attempted to explore the significance of this network of institutions in relation to socioeconomic and political variables. This is certainly the case for analyses of Chile, but it also applies to other presidential systems.

3. Juan Linz and Arturo Valenzuela, eds., *The Failure of Presidential Democracy: The Case of Latin America*, vol. 2. See also Mainwaring, "Presidentialism, Multipartism, and Democracy."

4. Scott Mainwaring and Matthew Shugart, "Conclusion: Presidentialism and the Party System," in *Presidentialism and Democracy in Latin America*, ed. Mainwaring and Shugart, 394.

rely not necessarily on a legislative majority but rather on a significant core party around which working coalitions can be built. They argue that without this core party, and especially within the context of highly fragmented party systems, many of the perils of presidentialism identified by Linz and Valenzuela are indeed valid. This is the case because fragmented multipartism makes it more difficult for presidents to build governing coalitions where a stable dominant party often does not exist. The Brazilian political system provides a textbook example of these difficulties.[5]

Both Linz and Valenzuela's and Mainwaring and Shugart's observations are significant for the Chilean case. While Christian Democrats Patricio Aylwin and Eduardo Frei could rely on a majority *coalition*, it is important to bear in mind that their party received only 26.0, 27.1, and 22.3 percent of the vote, respectively, in the 1989, 1993, and 1997 elections for the Chamber. What is more, in 1993, it did so in a situation of unprecedented popularity for the party's retiring president. The Christian Democratic Party is by far the largest and most popular party in Chile, yet in two of the last three elections it received a little more than one-quarter of the vote, and its share of the vote in legislative elections decreased for the 1997 elections. What is more, as the PPD and PS have repeatedly stressed, the total vote of the two parties of the left in 1997 surpassed that received by the Christian Democrats. Thus, given the current dynamic of party competition, and the uncertainty in coalition formation that it produces, it is quite likely that future presidents may not be able to rely on sizeable legislative contingents of their own parties, let alone majorities.[6] The conduct of interbranch relations since the return of democracy has been facilitated by presidents' ability to rely on a governing coalition. What is more, the binomial electoral system will continue to provide incentives for forming electoral coalitions. However, though both major coalitions have proven solid in recent years, there certainly remains the potential for the reemergence of Chilean parties' historical tendencies to distance themselves from unpopular presidents in times of crisis, disagreement, or political infighting.

5. On this reality, see Scott Mainwaring, "Dilemmas of Multi-Party Presidential Democracy: The Case of Brazil," in *Presidentialism and Democracy in Latin America*, ed. Shugart and Mainwaring; and Timothy Power, "Politicized Democracy: Competition, Institutions, and 'Civic Fatigue' in Brazil," *Journal of Interamerican Studies and World Affairs* 33 (Fall 1991): 75–112.

6. While the Christian Democratic Party is well institutionalized and relies on a great deal of popular support, Chilean political history provides numerous examples of how such parties have seen their fortunes precipitously decline. This is particularly the case for parties of the Center. For an excellent discussion of this phenomenon, see Timothy Scully, *Los partidos del centro y la evolución política chilena* (Santiago: CIEPLAN, 1992).

In this sense, then, the most important consequence of the combination of multipartism with exaggerated presidentialism in the Chilean case is that the problem of *doble minoría* presidents, a historically difficult facet of the Chilean institutional structure, has not been attenuated and is not likely to be in the near future. But certain features of the current institutional and legal framework—including the parliamentary electoral system, the timing and sequencing of elections, and whether a second-round presidential election is employed—make minority presidents even more likely. In the Chilean case, the constellation of these variables encourages the election of *doble minoría* presidents, creating additional obstacles to interbranch cooperation.

In addition, instead of encouraging stability, as military reformers envisioned, the parliamentary electoral system has the potential to create serious impediments to interbranch cooperation and democratic consolidation, given its exclusionary and volatile characteristics.

Finally, the "semiautonomous" bodies, and other institutional innovations of the outgoing military regime that form part of the overall framework for presidential government, are also important obstacles to cooperation and to the long-term consolidation of a successful, efficacious, representative democracy.

The Binomial Electoral System and Minority Presidents: Exclusion and Volatility[7]

Despite significant theoretical and empirical evidence to the contrary, certain analysts of electoral theory contend that majority/plurality electoral systems spell increased stability.[8] Plurality systems are considered to enhance governability by stemming party fragmentation, thus making it more likely that a president will be able to rely on a majority in parliament. Given this dynamic, plurality electoral systems are said to facilitate the legislative

---

7. Portions of this section appeared previously in Peter Siavelis, "Electoral Reform and Democratic Stability in Chile: The Political Consequences of the Adoption of a Plurality Electoral System in a Multi-Party Context" (paper presented at the Annual Meeting of the American Political Science Association, New York, September 1–4, 1994).

8. Majority and plurality systems are distinct in terms of the requirements to win an election. Although the Chilean system is really a plurality system (despite its two-member districts), it will also be referred to as "majoritarian" because it belongs to the generic category of electoral systems that have majoritarian tendencies and characteristics.

process, leading to more coherent policy. In addition, plurality formulas are lauded for their superior ability to produce continuity in government, avoiding the abrupt shifts often created by the exigencies of coalition formation in proportional representation (PR) systems.[9]

Nonetheless, a careful analysis of the binomial electoral system shows that many of these contentions are not valid in the Chilean case, particularly given the nature of the party system and the demonstrated inability of the electoral system to transform it.

First, it is doubtful that such a direct relationship exists between electoral formulas and the party system. There is mounting evidence that the transformational effects attributed to electoral systems are often counterbalanced or superseded by other variables, such as the strength and breadth of social cleavages.[10]

Second, on the continuum between majoritarian and PR electoral systems, Chile falls much closer to the former, given its small district magnitude. Nonetheless, the reality that it is not a pure majoritarian system gives it somewhat unique properties, even though analysts often attribute to it the characteristics and purported benefits of pure majoritarian systems.[11] The operational characteristics of the Chilean system are really much more complex and will have distinct effects, depending on the party context of the country at a given moment.

Given the contemporary party context of the country, the electoral system has encouraged the formation of two large and relatively stable coalitions. This should not lead one to believe, however, that Chile is a two-party system or that these coalitions are immutable. Neither should one conclude that the binomial system has somehow automatically created the extant pattern of competition and that it guarantees similar incentives for consensus and coalition formation in the future. Given a change in the contemporary

9. The debate about the superiority of certain types of electoral system has indeed been a long and controversial one. For classic statements on the problems with proportional representation and the superiority of plurality systems, see Carl Friedrich, *Constitutional Government and Politics*, 4th ed. (Waltham, Mass.: Blaidsdell, 1968), chap. 15, and F. A. Hermens, *Democracy or Anarchy? A Study of Proportional Representation* (Notre Dame, Ind.: University of Notre Dame Press, 1941). For more recent contributions to this debate, see Arend Lijphart, "Constitutional Choices for New Democracies," *Journal of Democracy* 2 (Winter 1991): 72–84, and Guy Lardeyret, "The Problem with Proportional Representation," *Journal of Democracy* 2 (Summer 1991): 30–36.

10. See Siavelis, "Continuity and Change in the Chilean Party System."

11. Misperceptions like these are evident in Rabkin, "Redemocratization, Electoral Engineering, and Party Strategies in Chile, 1989–1995," and Guzmán, "Reflexiones sobre el sistema binominal."

coalition pattern, the binomial system has the potential to create obstacles to interbranch cooperation and democratic governability for three principal reasons: (1) While the binomial system encourages preelectoral coalition formation and enhances the prospects for building working congressional majorities for presidents, it by no means guarantees them; (2) the binomial system has the potential to significantly underrepresent parties and even entire ideological tendencies in the Congress; (3) the electoral system has the capacity to produce a great deal of volatility in congressional composition.

Coalition Formation and Governing Majorities

Though designed to do so, the binomial system does not necessarily increase the likelihood that presidents will be able to rely on congressional majorities. The first two postauthoritarian presidents—Christian Democrats Patricio Aylwin and Eduardo Frei—were elected with a majority of the popular vote and have been able to rely on a majority coalition in the Congress. However, while both these presidents have been able to rely on the support of a majority *coalition* in Congress, the actual percentage of seats of the Christian Democratic Party in the Chamber of Deputies has been only 32.5, 30.8, and 32.5 percent, respectively, for each of three legislative sessions of each of the presidents' terms.[12]

The Christian Democrats are by far the largest and most popular party in Chile. However, just as in the preauthoritarian period, there are currently four or five significant parties in Chile and none can claim majority status (see Chapter 4).[13] Given this reality, the binomial system has not transformed the inherent need of Chilean political parties to negotiate and form coalitions in order to produce majority government. That is a problem that, some believed, the adoption of a plurality electoral system would solve by automatically producing two major parties.

Given the success of coalition formation, the first two postauthoritarian presidents have been able to avoid executive/legislative conflict and deadlock. However, to a great extent this reality is due more to the contextual features of the transition, and to the constellation of party coalitions it produced,

12. Because legislative and presidential elections are not concurrent, President Frei has served during two legislative terms characterized by a distinct party composition in each of the chambers.

13. See Chapter 4 for definitions of party relevance. In addition, these parties are relevant not only in the terms defined here but also in Sartori's terms, as having "coalition" and "blackmail" potential. Sartori, *Parties and Party Systems*, 121–24. Certain other parties could also be considered relevant, but five clearly are, according to most accepted criteria.

than to any inherent mechanical characteristic of the binomial system (a reality that is explored in depth in Chapter 2). With a breakdown of the current pattern of coalitions, the binomial system does not make it more likely that a president will be able to rely on a legislative majority, principally because the functional dynamic of the party system has not been transformed. Given this reality, many other features of the institutional framework also mitigate against the election of presidents with significant legislative contingents.

The Binomial System and Underrepresentation

With the continued existence of Chilean multipartism, the parliamentary electoral system has the capacity to significantly underrepresent parties, and even broad coalitions, from representation in the National Congress. Because to win a seat in a congressional district a party must poll at least 33.4 percent of the vote of the two largest parties or alliances, a party or coalition that does not reach this threshold in its level of national vote will be left significantly underrepresented or, more seriously, will be denied legislative representation. Of course, with distinct patterns of party competition and distributions of vote across districts, these thresholds vary. With more parties, the threshold for winning seats will be lower. However, even with more parties and with heightened competition, electoral thresholds persist, and would remain difficult to cross, given the dispersion of votes in a context of multiparty competition, and the reality that there are only two seats per district. Small, nonaligned parties have already been barred legislative representation in recent elections. But more important, assuming there is a reemergence of a three-bloc pattern of competition, entire political currents can be significantly underrepresented in, or completely shut out of, the Congress despite receiving a great deal of electoral support.[14]

Even if the current pattern of bipolar competition continues, a poor electoral showing by the Right, in which it receives less than 33.4 percent of the vote across districts nationally, would have disastrous electoral consequences. It would leave a significant political sector without an institutional

---

14. This argument is more fully developed in Arturo Valenzuela and Peter Siavelis, "Ley electoral y estabilidad democrática." A series of electoral simulations demonstrate the exclusionary characteristics of the electoral system with small percentages of transfers in the vote. For a more complete and varied set of simulations that test the functioning of a moderate proportional representation system against that of the binomial system, see Siavelis, "Nuevos argumentos y viejos supuestos."

voice and signify an end to the *democracia consensual* that has characterized Chilean politics since the end of the authoritarian government.

The exclusionary tendencies of the electoral system further undermine the
already limited ability of Congress to act as an arena for solving problems
and mediating political conflict in the country. Because certain parties can be
potentially barred from representation in Congress, their institutional voice
and bargaining power are limited, and extraparliamentary political action
becomes more attractive. Granted, as demonstrated in previous chapters,
the stakes of the game of Chilean politics have significantly lowered because
there is now a certain degree of consensus on fundamental issues. However,
analyses of democracy must also move beyond issues of stability to address
the efficacy and representative capacity of political institutions. Electoral
limits on representation exact a price in both these areas. In these regards,
supporters of the binomial system may have been excessively sanguine concerning the positive outcomes it produces, given its recent and very brief
history. With the passage of time, perhaps some of the long-term costs associated with the system will become apparent. In any case, it cannot be
denied that the incentives for coalition formation have been enhanced, compared with the preauthoritarian period. While there are strong incentives for
succeeding in forming coalitions, success in doing so may be far more transitory than it has appeared in this special post-transitional context.

Why would negotiations fail, or coalitions fall apart, when there are
strong incentives to maintain them? The answer to this question is complex
and depends on the pattern of partisan competition. However, it lies both in
the process of coalition formation itself and how this process occurs in the
context of eroding support for a government.

First, because there are only two seats available in each congressional district, the number of rewards for coalition participation is limited. Significant
political capital and time are spent cobbling coalitions together. Each party
and each alliance is forced to engage in a frenzied and time-consuming negotiation process to determine the number of candidates each party will be
allowed to present in elections, and in which districts they will be presented.

These negotiations can take the form of epic, time-consuming and dis-
tracting political struggles. During an interview with one deputy when the
slates for the 1993 legislative elections were being negotiated, the deputy
received five telephone calls from five different leaders of the component parties of his coalition. After instructing the author to turn off the tape recorder,
and stressing that anything substantive said in the course of the telephone calls
was strictly off the record, he proceeded to argue the virtues of a particular

candidate, contending that he should run in a district farther north, given his lack of support in the south.[15] The person with whom the deputy was speaking countered that he doubted the candidate could win in the north on his own, but contended that in the south he could at least put the coalition's list over the top and ensure the victory of his coalition partner in the district. This particular candidate was the subject of all the telephone calls, during which the deputy told conflicting stories and professed contradictory opinions concerning the electoral potential of the candidate. The opinions expressed, of course, were all part of strategic posturing that depended on the party credentials of the person to whom he was speaking.[16] During the entire conversation no mention was made of the candidate's relationship to his constituents or whether as a deputy he would be a suitable representative for his district.

With a PR electoral system, thresholds would be much less important. Though coalition formation would still be attractive, and perhaps necessary (given that most reforms propose district magnitudes between three and five), there would be a more flexible set of rewards to aid in coalition formation. There is no guarantee that, in the future, the incentives for undertaking the types of difficult negotiations outlined above will exist, or that they will be successful. Indeed, there may be disincentives to do so, depending on the partisan situation, the popularity of presidents, and the relative sequencing of presidential and parliamentary elections.

Second, and related to the above consideration, the Concertación has been most threatened at times when arguments over electoral spoils and cabinet positions have emerged.[17] If electoral coalitions evaporate when a president is less successful than the two presidents Chile has had in the postauthoritarian era, the efficacy and representative capacity of the Congress will also experience a corresponding decline. In this less propitious atmosphere for negotiation, in which coalition partners are attempting to distance themselves from an unpopular or unsuccessful government, there are fewer incentives for reaching agreements on joint lists, and parties may be more tempted to "go it alone."

15. The deputy did give the author permission to recount the negotiations, provided no names or party labels were used.

16. Off-the-record interview, Santiago, 23 April 1993.

17. The periods leading up to presidential, legislative, and municipal elections have uniformly been characterized by threats and rumors predicting the breakup of the Concertación, principally over disputes involving candidatures. Even after elections, disagreements persisted over cabinet assignments.

This makes the election of minority presidents more likely, given the timing and sequencing of legislative and presidential elections (discussed below), and especially if parliamentary elections are to occur near the end of a presidential term. The party of an unpopular president can easily lose electoral support going into legislative elections and be left with little or no support in Congress. A president may be left in a particularly precarious situation if the level of support of his or her party or coalition falls below 33 percent (or the corresponding threshold, depending on the pattern of party competition).

A concrete (though of course purely hypothetical) example will make the significance of this scenario clearer. In 1999, the most pressing issue facing the Concertación was the choice of a common presidential candidate. PS-PPD candidate Ricardo Lagos was designated as the standard-bearer for the 1999 presidential election with the strong opposition of some sectors within the Christian Democratic Party. Given the success of the Concertación in the lead-up to the elections, the alliance is likely to hold, and if survey data is correct, Lagos is likely to become president.[18] If the Lagos government falters or dramatically loses support, the parties of the Center will have a strong incentive to distance themselves from the president's party in order to improve their electoral appeal, for both municipal and mid-term legislative elections, not to mention the next presidential election. This will be a particularly strong temptation for the Christian Democrats should the parties of the Right react to a Socialist president by becoming more extreme. Preliminary reactions of many politicians on the Right have tended toward very ideological discourse and suggestions of movement toward the Right in reaction to the candidacy of Lagos. The Christian Democrats would have a strong incentive in this case to also move toward the Right in order to attract voters on the moderate Right.

If the parties of the Center present a separate parliamentary list for the 2001 congressional elections that results in dramatic gains for the Right

18. This contention does not rule out the possibility of the crumbling of the Concertación alliance, especially given that congressional elections will not be concurrent with the presidential elections of 1999. A concurrent congressional election creates more incentives for widespread support of a single coalition candidate for president given the impracticality of presenting two presidential candidates and each party also presenting a single parliamentary list, not to mention the perception of divisiveness it would create. Conceivably the Christian Democrats and the parties of the Left could be tempted to present presidential candidates of their own. Nonetheless, Lagos is the front-running candidate, and the Christian Democrats do have an incentive to avoid a repeat of the debacle of 1970, when the party entered the election as the "premier" Chilean political party and finished with a humiliating third-place showing in the presidential elections.

and the Center at the cost of the Left, the president would be left without a majority, or possibly with little support, in Congress. With four years of his term remaining, Lagos would be isolated, leading a moribund government with a high probability of executive/legislative deadlock. Policy formation would come to a standstill, undermining political efficacy. Each issue, even minor ones, would become politicized as members prepare for future elections and seek to pass the litmus test of opposition to the sitting government.

In essence, despite the assertions of electoral reformers, the fact remains that only two congressional seats are available in each district, in a country that is characterized by four or five parties. Coalition formation in the last three elections provided for relatively proportional representation for most parties, but without it certain parties would certainly have been significantly underrepresented in Congress, which can help lead to the election or creation of minority presidencies.

Electoral Volatility and Minority Presidencies

The binomial electoral system can produce a great deal of volatility in the composition of Congress, enhancing the probability of minority presidencies and making the electoral value of potential coalition partners uncertain. When compared with majority/plurality electoral systems, PR systems have a reputation for producing more abrupt changes in coalitional configurations, given their sensitivity to shifts of partisan identification within the electorate. However, in a multiparty system the thresholds established by the binomial system can produce more volatile results and enhance the probability that presidents will lose support midway through their terms. Because electoral thresholds are so important, a small transfer of votes or change in electoral support may mean a great deal for the parliamentary fortunes of a particular party, while a great change or transfer of votes may mean nothing, depending on a party's proximity to a certain threshold level. This sensitivity is more serious under the binomial formula because the system establishes two electoral thresholds, compared with the single one that exists in pure plurality systems.

Electoral simulations in an article published by this author explore the consequences of readopting a proportional representation system in Chile and demonstrate the functional dynamic of the binomial electoral system when compared with a moderate PR system. The PR system employed for the simulations was the one detailed in a reform proposal made by the Aylwin government.[19] It would have created district magnitudes ranging between three and five by combining several currently existing districts. Seats would have been distributed according to the d'Hondt formula.

To avoid having the peculiarity of a particular data set affect the results, three separate sets of electoral returns were used in the simulations: the 1989 congressional election, the 1992 municipal election, and an average of the two.

In all, more than thirty simulations were undertaken, with distinct distributions of the vote and distinct patterns of coalitions. In almost all cases, the binomial system proved much more volatile than the moderate PR system, and in no case did the magnitude of volatility of the PR system in any simulation even approach that of the binomial system. Transfers of the vote of approximately 7 percent resulted in shifts in party congressional composition of up to 28 percent when the binomial system was employed.[20]

Is this sensitivity to small changes in electoral support a general characteristic of the binomial system, or is it just a function of the relative threshold levels of the parties selected for the above simulations? Sets of simulations using two, three, and four bloc alliance patterns confirm that this volatility is not simply a function of this particular coalitional configuration, but rather universal in situations in which parties and coalitions are near crucial thresholds.

It is also important to underscore that the volatile tendencies of the binomial system do not arise only when there is a change in coalition patterns. A simple change of a few percentage points in the relative level of support for a party can result in sweeping changes at the parliamentary level and ultimately lead to its exclusion, with all the negative consequences this entails for democratic governability.[21] On the other hand, with the proportional

19. The proportional representation simulations employ the electoral system proposed by the government outlined in the message of the President of the Republic, No. 66-324, presented on June 5, 1992. The reform proposal involves legislative redistricting that would decrease the number of electoral districts from 60 to 45. Because the redistricting does not change the fundamental administrative division of the country, it was relatively easy to account for the redistricting in the simulations. The redistricting only entails the combination of electoral districts that already exist. Therefore, in the districts that were combined to form new districts the individual votes for each party are also combined. For a complete text of the presidential message outlining the electoral reforms in their entirety, see El Mercurio, 10 June 1992, C4.

20. For the simulations and a discussion of their results, see Siavelis, "Nuevos argumentos y viejos supuestos."

21. For an in-depth discussion of this point, see Valenzuela and Siavelis, "Ley electoral y estabilidad democrática."

system such a party would retain parliamentary representation with a proportional reduction in its strength, until it reached the much lower threshold of exclusion characteristic of most proportional systems.

In this sense, the binomial system may not be sensitive to large changes in the relative percentage of votes but can be extremely sensitive to small ones. Thus, control of the Congress can abruptly shift from one ideological sector to another with small shifts in the vote. This can create problems of policy coherence and—more serious if a president loses significant legislative support—executive/legislative deadlock.

The volatile tendencies of the binomial system also add a great deal of unpredictability to the coalitional calculations of parties. No party can be sure of the significance of a shift in electoral support, or evaluate the necessity or potential value of coalition partners. The advantage of the proportional system is precisely that it is proportional, and changes at the electoral level translate into analogous changes at the parliamentary level, be they large or small. Parties can better predict what a coalition partner is worth based on its level of national support.

What types of conclusions can be drawn from these results? It is clear that a moderate PR system would introduce two important characteristics that the binomial system indisputably lacks. A moderate PR system would be much less sensitive to electoral change, and actually moderate changes at the parliamentary level when there is a transfer of votes. In every proportional simulation, when there was a change in the relative electoral strength of coalitions there were no drastic fluctuations at the parliamentary level.

A moderate PR system would also introduce an element of predictability by standardizing the coalition value of each party so that changes at the parliamentary level would reflect the percentage of votes that a party contributes to a coalition. In simulations of the PR system, the percentage of seats gained with transfers of vote was always much closer to the percentage of actual votes transferred, no matter which coalition was the recipient of those votes. Alternatively, the binomial system makes the same votes worth different amounts for different coalitions, resulting in a great deal of volatility. The simulations demonstrate that a transfer of 7 percent of the vote from one coalition to another can mean anywhere from an 8 percent increase to a 28 percent increase in parliamentary seats (and potentially more, given unexplored or distinct coalitional formations), depending on the distribution of votes and a particular party's proximity to the thresholds the binomial system establishes. However, with the proportional system the same transfer of votes always means an increase of around 7 percent or less in parliamentary seats, an amount that is much closer to the actual percentage of the vote transferred.

One could argue that proportional representation, of course, also has a downside, especially in presidential systems. In every electoral system there is a inherent conflict between representation and stability. Complete representation of every political option within the legislature would have negative consequences for governability, both in Chile and in many other countries. What is more, this study has repeatedly pointed to the difficult combination of presidentialism and multipartism, and the permissive qualities of proportional representation are empirically linked to the creation and maintenance of multiparty systems. Nonetheless, the representation-stability dilemma is many times a false one, because in highly divided societies it is often representation that can help ensure stability by giving significant political actors a stake in the democratic game. What is more, in countries already characterized by multipartism it is unlikely that a change in the electoral system can put the multiparty genie back in the bottle. In the formative stages of party-system development, proportional representation is surely associated with a multiplication of parties. Nonetheless, in Chile multipartism continues to exist with the binomial system, and it is questionable whether a moderate PR system would even lead to the multiplication of parties. A moderate PR system would still prevent the proliferation of small parties but provide all the benefits set out here (as well as those discussed in more detail in the final chapter).

The Timing and Sequencing of Presidential and Parliamentary Elections

Literature on the timing and sequencing of elections and the effect of distinct electoral formulas on democratic governability has proliferated in recent years. Theorists have recognized that it is impossible to isolate the effects of executive and assembly elections on each other. Their relative timing and sequencing has an important effect on dynamics of the party system, the likelihood that presidents will be able to rely on majorities in the legislature, and the prospects for cooperation between the executive and the legislature.[22] The method of presidential election has also been recognized as significant in affecting the outcome of these variables.[23]

Part of the formula for presidential domination set out in the 1980 constitution was the establishment of an eight-year presidential term.[24] The designers of the constitution contended correctly that an extended presidential term would provide for stability and continuity in policy-making. Nonetheless, the lengthy term of office for Chilean presidents would have created a number of serious problems. Because it is exceedingly difficult to remove an unpopular or ineffective president, the eight-year term would have provided little flexibility in the face of a governmental crisis.[25]

What is more, constitutional designers chose an eight-year term in order to synchronize elections better. Before 1973, presidential elections were held every six years and legislative elections every four, making nonconcurrent elections quite frequent. Constitutional designers contended that retaining a four-year legislative election cycle and adopting an eight-year presidential term would make elections concurrent half the time and avoid the disruption caused by the continuous cycle of elections that characterized the preauthoritarian period. The traditional nonconcurrence of elections in Chile made for a country that was perpetually *"en campaña"* (a state of affairs that recent unfortunate institutional reforms has re-created).

In February 1994 the Chilean Congress overwhelmingly approved a reduction in the presidential term of office from eight to six years. Though intended to enhance flexibility by allowing for earlier removal of an unpopular president through electoral processes, the reform creates other, perhaps more serious, problems, given the timing and sequencing of presidential and legislative elections. While the term of office for the president was changed, the terms of office for members of the Senate and the Chamber remained the same. The former are elected for a period of eight years, while the latter serve for four.

22. See Mark Jones, *Electoral Laws and the Survival of Presidential Democracies*; Shugart and Carey, *Presidents and Assemblies*, chaps. 9–12; and Matthew Shugart, "The Electoral Cycle and Institutional Sources of Divided Presidential Government," *American Political Science Review* 89 (June 1995): 327–43.

23. Matthew Shugart and Rein Taagepera, "Plurality Versus Majority Election of Presidents: A Proposal for a 'Double Complement Rule,'" *Comparative Political Studies* 27 (October 1994): 323–48.

24. President Patricio Aylwin served only a four-year term, in keeping with the transitional framework set out in the 1980 constitution.

25. In comparative cross-national terms, the eight-year Chilean presidential term was quite long. For a discussion of the importance of flexibility in this regard, see Arturo Valenzuela, "Party Politics and the Crisis of Presidentialism in Chile," 137–43.

The most recent reform, thus, makes it even more likely that presidents will face a hostile Congress, because elections will be held concurrently less often. Instead of every eight years, congressional and presidential elections will now be held concurrently every twelve years.[26] In essence, reformers solved one problem and created another that is more serious.

If a president is elected with the support of a coalition of parties in addition to his or her own in parliament, and proves ineffective or dramatically loses support, other parties of the coalition have an incentive to distance themselves from the president in preparation for mid-term elections. Thus, a minority presidency is created, even though the president may have been initially elected with the support of a legislative coalition. The need to differentiate oneself from the president's party creates incentives for obstructing the president's legislative agenda.

In addition, the incentives for noncooperation by coalition members become even stronger as parliamentary elections approach. Parties that once formed a part of an unpopular president's coalition will have more to gain by undermining rather than cooperating with the president. In this situation, these parties have a strong incentive to present separate parliamentary lists. With numerous electoral lists, the exclusionary tendencies of the parliamentary electoral system make it even more likely that the president will have little legislative support following the election. The president can easily be transformed into a minority president if his or her party fails to poll the percentage of votes across districts nationally in order to cross crucial electoral thresholds. This is even more likely because no individual party in Chile has been capable of garnering more than 30 percent of the national vote since the return of democracy.

Nonconcurrent elections also increase the frequency of elections, the significance of which is not often discussed by scholars of Latin American electoral politics. Given that municipal races are not always concurrent with either presidential or legislative elections, the current electoral timetable means that an election that is national in scope will occur, on the average, every 1.7 years.[27] The frequency of elections can further undermine the incentives for executive/legislation cooperation and conflict resolution. Elections heighten campaign rhetoric, politicize even relatively minor issues,

26. Under the eight-year formula, all deputies and half the senators were elected every four years. Therefore, every four years congressional and presidential elections would have coincided, but there would also have been one mid-term congressional election.

27. For a discussion of this issue and a comprehensive timetable of future Chilean elections, see Instituto Libertad y Desarrollo, *Temas públicos*, series, no. 133, 5 March 1993.

and serve as constant tests of popular support for the government.[28] Legislators have a strong incentive to abandon a government that fails these frequent tests, as they turn their sights on future presidential and parliamentary elections.

This reality creates an additional, problematic paradox. While increasing politicization on the elite level, continuous elections often result in apathy and disgust at the level of voters. Thus, this perpetual cycle of elections creates a political class of perpetual campaigners, and potentially a weary and disillusioned electorate.

There is preliminary empirical evidence of growing disillusionment with electoral processes in the country. While voting is obligatory in Chile, registration is voluntary.[29] There are stiff financial penalties for not voting, yet there is no penalty for not registering. A growing number of young people, especially, are opting out of the required registration process; more than one million young people who reached the legal voting age of eighteen between the parliamentary elections of 1993 and 1997 chose not to register. These nonregistrants are not counted among the growing percentage of those who refuse to participate or who cast blank or null ballots. This suggests that participation is decreasing more precipitously than deteriorating turnout statistics already confirm.

Among those who do register and vote, the number of null and spoiled votes has grown steadily. Voters who choose not to vote for any candidate can leave their ballots blank, destroy them by voting improperly, or invalidate their ballot by writing obscenities or messages on it. The number of null votes reached an all-time historical high of 13.54 percent for the 1997 Chamber of Deputies election, and blank votes totaled 4.22 percent.[30] Table 6.1 demonstrates this declining participation.

The percentage of null votes was highest in the very important Fifth Region, reaching 19.36 percent of the total. Several commentators noted that if the "null vote" forces presented candidates, they would have been successful in garnering "null" members of Congress in a few districts, despite the electoral system's thresholds.[31]

28. Elections in Chile, despite ideological transformations, are still all-consuming affairs. No wall is left unpainted, banners are hung from every available stationary object (and a good number of mobile ones), and parties engage in intense and vocal public campaigning. There is an environment of intense politicization for weeks before elections.

29. This somewhat nonsensical system is currently under debate. Members of the Congress are debating a reform that would make registration obligatory and voting voluntary.

30. *El Mercurio*, 14 December 1997, D14.

31. Ibid.

Table 6.1. Blank and null votes and abstentions in Chilean parliamentary elections, 1988–1997 (percentages)

Election	Year	Null	Blank	Abstentions
Plebiscite	1988	1.30	.90	2.69
Presidential	1989	1.40	1.10	5.28
Senators	1989	2.90	2.10	5.28
Deputies	1989	2.68	2.37	5.28
Municipal	1992	3.06	5.86	10.20
Presidential	1993	3.68	1.85	8.71
Senators	1993	4.92	3.45	8.71
Deputies	1993	5.29	3.35	8.71
Municipal	1996	7.95	3.02	12.14
Senators	1997	12.57	4.37	NA
Deputies	1997	13.54	4.22	NA

SOURCE: *El Mercurio*, 12 December 1997, A1.

NA = Not available.

The consistent increase in the number of votes cast for the Communist Party also suggests growing disillusionment. The incongruity between support for the party in public-opinion polls and in elections suggests that the Communist vote represents something of a protest vote. These developments, of course, represent more than weariness from continuous elections. However, the perpetual politicization and constant electioneering that results certainly contribute to disillusionment.

Finally, cross-national evidence supports many of the arguments advanced here concerning nonconcurrent elections. As asserted, party fragmentation is problematic for the ability of presidents to sustain legislative majorities. One of the most significant findings of Shugart and Mainwaring's cross-national study of presidentialism, as it relates to the Chilean case, is the tendency of nonconcurrent elections to contribute to party-system fragmentation.[32] Their theoretical conclusions support the contention made in Chapter 4 that the effective number of parties in Chile will remain about the same, at least for the short and medium terms. This is especially true given that the purported reductive effects of the binomial system have not yet materialized and are not likely to in the near future. Continuing fragmentation makes it less likely that presidents will be able to rely on sizeable legislative contingents during future governments.

Shugart's cross-national study of election timing in presidential systems also suggests an additional difficulty with nonconcurrence. He finds that

32. Mainwaring and Shugart, "Conclusion," in *Presidentialism and Democracy in Latin America*, ed. Mainwaring and Shugart.

party seat shares of presidents tend to increase in early-term elections but decline as time goes on. Thus, given nonconcurrence and the lengthy term of the Chilean president, one might expect some difficulty for presidents in maintaining legislative majorities, particularly when elections are held late in their terms.[33] Similarly, Mark Jones finds that concurrent elections are one of the best ways to help ensure that presidents will be able to rely on sizeable legislative contingents.[34]

Presidential Second-Round Elections and *Doble Minoría* Presidents

A major step taken by constitutional reformers in an attempt to avoid the problem of presidents elected with a minority of the vote was the establishment of a second-round runoff election between the two highest-polling candidates in the event that a president does not receive a majority of the vote. The majority rule for presidents does not really solve the problem of minority presidents, but rather manufactures a majority where one might not exist.[35] In fact, a majority system may encourage candidates to enter a race that they cannot possibly win, in an effort to force a second round. Shugart and Taagepera find that majority runoff rules tend to be associated with a higher average number of effective presidential candidates than plurality election rules.[36] What is more, the result of the second round might simply produce the election of the candidate that is least objectionable to most of the electorate, as opposed to that preferred by a plurality of voters.[37] Linz is correct in noting that a mandate won in the first and second round represents two distinct types of majorities. The runoff victory is probably not

33. Shugart, "The Electoral Cycle and Institutional Sources of Divided Presidential Government."

34. Mark Jones, *Electoral Laws and the Survival of Presidential Democracies*, 103–18.

35. Douglas Rae uses the term "manufactured majorities" to refer to those majorities artificially produced by the electoral system. See Rae, *The Political Consequences of Electoral Laws*, 74–77.

36. Shugart and Taagepera, "Plurality Versus Majority Election of Presidents."

37. This problem is not simply a theoretical one. There have been many cases in which the second-round winner did not poll highest in the initial presidential election. A dramatic example of this scenario was Alberto Fujimori's 1990 victory over Mario Vargas Llosa in a second-round presidential election in Peru.

one that is supported by a coherent coalition or party, and it is most likely a negative majority.[38]

Even if the second round helps to ameliorate the problems of legitimacy and presidential stature that the election of presidents with small pluralities can cause, it does nothing to eliminate the second component of the *doble minoría* predicament: presidents without a congressional majority.

In fact, the possibility that presidents might serve with legislative minorities is increased by the practice of second-round elections. First, second-round elections often lead to the formation of temporary alliances, but after the presidential election there is little incentive for coalition members to continue to support the president. If a president who received only a plurality were chosen in the Congress, as in the past, at least he or she would be aware of the political alliances that resulted in his or her election and the importance of maintaining them. By giving a presidential candidate a majority of the popular vote, election with the use of a second round may cause presidents to interpret their mandate as an expression of the support of the majority of the electorate and make them less appreciative of the importance of congressional coalitions.

Second, the majority rule essentially means that in some cases the presidential and legislative elections are no longer concurrent, even in years when they are supposed to be. The second part of the two-round election will take place after the composition of Congress has already been determined. In this case, while the president may be a representative of the party that is least objectionable to a majority of voters, the Congress may be composed of members of the parties the electorate prefers, again making executive/legislative deadlock more likely and creating problems of democratic governability.

Jones's cross-national study finds a strong negative association between the use of the majority runoff formula and the likelihood of presidents having party majorities or near majorities.[39] What is more, Shugart and Carey's findings support contentions made here concerning the reality that majority runoff systems can in themselves create nonconcurrence even when concurrence exists. They find that in systems with majority runoff there is not much difference in the effective number of parties between systems that employ concurrent versus nonconcurrent electoral cycles.[40]

38. Juan Linz, "Democracy: Presidential or Parliamentary. Does It Make a Difference?" (unpublished manuscript), 1991.
39. Mark Jones, *Electoral Laws and the Survival of Presidential Democracies*, 90.
40. Shugart and Carey, *Presidents and Assemblies*, 223.

"Autonomous" Powers, Interbranch Cooperation, and Democratic Governability

The 1980 constitution provides for a series of nonelected bodies that also affect the prospects for interbranch cooperation. Though designated as "neutral" and "autonomous," the constitutional roles of the armed forces, the National Security Council, and the Constitutional Tribunal were established with an eye to ensuring the integrity of the constitution and the security of the nation, by preventing irresponsible actions of capricious majorities. However, because these institutions are "above" democratic authorities, each affects the legislative process to varying degrees, and all undermine the legitimacy of democratic institutions by transferring ultimate decision-making power outside the bounds of democratic institutions or authorities designated by them.

Perhaps the most questionable feature of the 1980 constitution in terms of limits on democratic authorities is the "unremovability" of high-level officials of the armed forces by the president.[41] This provision of the constitution guaranteed General Pinochet and other members of the governing junta their posts throughout the process of transition, and put limits on the range of choices democratic authorities had with regard to military appointments, promotions, and dismissals. This was a serious issue in the immediate post-transitional period because it allowed military authorities to exercise veto power over government policy, directly or through institutions in which members of the armed forces are influential. Though less important today, the insularity of military authorities from decisions made by democratically elected authorities has not ceased to be significant. Certain analysts, perhaps rightly, consider the tutelary role of the armed forces, and particularly the threat of armed incursion, to have been moderating features in the immediate post-transition period by acting as a rein on civilian authorities in their efforts to undertake far-reaching and potentially destabilizing reforms. However, there are no precedents for this type of role for the military in any system that is commonly accepted as a democracy. What is more, the success of democratic consolidation depends on the legitimacy of institutions and on

41. Article 93 of the *Constitución Política de la República de Chile* states: "The Commanders in Chief of the Army, Navy and Air Force, and the General Director of the Carabineros shall be appointed by the President of the Republic from among the five senior generals who have the qualifications required by the respective institutional statutes for such posts. They shall serve in their posts for four years, may not be reappointed for a new term of office and shall not be subject to removal from their posts."

the policies they produce. The continued role of the military as the final arbiter on major issues, and the inability of the president to control military appointments, limits the range of options that elected and civilian authorities have and undermines the legitimacy of democratic institutions.

Something similar can be said about the National Security Council (CSN—Consejo de Seguridad Nacional). The undemocratic nature of its composition and the vagary of its role as an institution charged with "making known its concerns" on any issue that "might affect national security," grant it wide purview in determining the issues on which it chooses to rule. The CSN also institutionalizes military power and the vested interests of the Right within what is supposed to be an autonomous institution. This increases the potential for interbranch conflict, given the military's role as a fourth branch of government with which the other three branches must reckon. What is more, the two members that the CSN appoints to the Constitutional Tribunal allow it to have an effect on the legislative process, albeit indirectly.

While the roles of the armed forces and the National Security Council are primarily significant in terms of "macro-political" concerns like legitimacy, the Constitutional Tribunal has more of an effect on the everyday legislative process and on executive/legislative relations. Constitutional tribunals exist in Spain, Italy, France, Germany, and many other nations around the world. However, in Chile the composition of the tribunal, and the laws regulating its performance, its spheres of action, and its potential for politicization, provide important impediments to interbranch cooperation.[42]

As noted in Chapter 1, the composition of the Constitutional Tribunal, for the most part, is determined by nonelected officials. Only two of its seven members are named by democratic authorities (one of the two is designated by the Senate and is thus not appointed by a totally democratic body). The tribunal's current membership is dominated by Pinochet appointees. In this sense, though the tribunal is meant to be an "autonomous body" there was a clear political intent in its formation and in determining its membership. Given this reality, the legitimacy of the decisions made by the tribunal will be questionable until it is composed solely of those appointed by civilian

42. For a discussion of some of these issues, see Programa de Asesoría Legislativa, "Ficha legislativa No. 167, Proyecto de reforma constitucional: Tribunal Constitucional," 8–12 June 1992. Page 57 of this document outlines the laws regulating the designation of the Constitutional Tribunals of each country cited. In every case it is democratic authorities or institutions that are viewed to be "above politics" (i.e., the king, or a nonpartisan president) which have a greater voice in determining the membership of the Tribunals.

authorities. Even in situations where the tribunal's decisions might be based on a strict reading of the constitution, members will always be open to charges of obstructionism and playing politics. What is more, in each of its successive decisions, the body is seen by many as defending an unpopular and illegitimate constitution.

In order for an autonomous body regulating the constitutionality of legislation to function well, it must be accepted by all parties as a fair and legitimate arbiter. But because this is not the case in Chile, legislators and the executive are tempted to challenge its rulings, increasing the likelihood of conflict between the tribunal and democratic authorities. With a tribunal designated by popularly elected leaders, the integrity and legitimacy of its decisions would be enhanced and more likely to be accepted by Congress and the president. Its rulings would be more acceptable to a wider range of political sectors, thus enhancing the tribunal's role as a check on both branches of government and facilitating the legislative process.

Judicial review is an acceptable and, some would say, necessary component of a democratic system. What is more, many countries, most notably France, also have constitutional tribunals that are similar to Chile's in terms of their authority. However, in the Chilean case the ultimate functional significance of the tribunal depends on its level of activism and on the evolution of its role within the constitutional system.[43]

If it chooses to do so, the tribunal can create bottlenecks in the legislative process and sow the seeds of interbranch conflict. The tribunal is only required to make decisions within thirty days on a number of specific issues. In terms of ordinary laws and rulings on constitutionality, there is no deadline for tribunal decisions. The Chamber of Deputies can demand that the tribunal consider the constitutionality of any presidential decrees or instructions issued within the bounds of the president's regulatory powers (*potestad reglamentaria*), with the agreement of only one-quarter of its membership. While the tribunal considers the constitutionality of many types of laws and constitutional amendments automatically as part of a regular legislative *trámite* (step), members of the Chamber can present questions regarding the constitutionality of any type of legislation at any time, granting them the ability to delay or even head off legislation before it gets too far. Opposition legislators therefore have the power to obstruct presidential initiatives by forcing them into the tribunal at every stage of consideration.

---

43. The French case confirms this contention. The Constitutional Council in France currently plays a much different and more important role than its designers intended.

The tribunal can further obstruct initiatives by delaying its decisions.[44] On other issues, such as those judging the constitutionality of initiatives that originate within the legislature, the tribunal can be equally obstructive if it has political reasons for doing so.

The Constitutional Tribunal has been relatively cooperative with the first two democratic governments, taking measured and limited actions in its rulings. However, in crisis situations, in cases of presidential decrees where policy decisions might be more controversial, or if the traditionally competitive pattern of party politics reemerges in Chile, the tribunal can act as an effective bloc against government and legislative initiatives, encouraging deadlock and immobilism. What is more, its rulings can provide ammunition and tools for an obstructionist opposition that is bent on undermining governments for politically motivated reasons.

In terms of the potential for politically motivated decisions, the tribunal has a precedent for becoming quite politicized. It was created in 1970, as a final constitutional arbiter to prevent adoption of unconstitutional laws and decrees. However, its effectiveness was undermined by a loss of legitimacy because of perceived ideological motives behind its decision-making during the crises of the Allende years. Thus, though the recent activities of the tribunal have not yet contributed to serious interbranch or macro-political conflict, its activities and decisions have, like those of other institutions and political actors, been shaped profoundly by the democratic transition and may change in the future.

Conclusions

This chapter has argued that several aspects of the presidential system not specifically related to the relative powers of the president or Congress can profoundly affect the incentives for interbranch cooperation and democratic governability.

Despite the intentions of military authorities to introduce a complete package of institutional reforms aimed at engendering stability, important institutional obstacles to interparty and interbranch cooperation remain.

---

44. The Tribunal was accused of acting that way in judging the constitutionality of modifications to the laws on regional government. See "Diputados discuten y votan las modificaciones a la Ley Regional," *El Mercurio*, 16 November 1992, C2.

The most important error military reformers made was to assume that the dynamic of multiparty competition in Chile could be transformed. Because it has not been transformed, the most severe obstacle to interbranch cooperation, that of *doble minoría* presidents, has not been eliminated. Indeed, the timing and sequencing of elections and related electoral legislation make *doble minoría* presidents even more likely. What is more, while the binomial system creates incentives for coalition formation, given the timing and sequencing of elections and the complicated nature of alliance formation, these coalitions are likely to erode in the context of poor performance by presidents, especially those who are far into their terms.

While *doble minoría* presidencies certainly existed in the past, they did so in an environment in which there were other arenas for negotiation and mechanisms to encourage conflict resolution and interbranch cooperation, principally centered in the National Congress. But many of these arenas and conflict-dampening mechanisms no longer exist. The combination of minority presidents and limited incentives for conflict resolution sets the stage for serious interbranch conflict, with all of the negative consequences that entails for democratic governability.

From a wider perspective, the potentially exclusionary characteristics of the electoral system also undermine the legitimacy and the representative capacity of the political system. The best way to resolve conflict in Chile is to have the complete range of political options represented within democratic institutions. This helps to discourage potentially destabilizing extra-institutional activities, and the disillusionment that could result when important sectors of the electorate do not have the ability to affect governmental decision making.

In addition, the "autonomous" powers created by the 1980 constitution further complicate executive/legislative relations by allowing the use of a series of potentially obstructionist and questionably legitimate tools that usurp the authority and legislative capacity of both the Congress and the president. The authority of these autonomous powers transforms the traditional venue for conflict resolution in Chile. Instead of interbranch negotiations leading to agreement, a series of bodies that are not subject to the authority of civilians can intervene to make binding decisions throughout the legislative process.

Thus, the entire institutional framework in which exaggerated presidentialism is embedded further undercuts the already limited incentives for interbranch cooperation created by the imbalance of power between the president and Congress. It is Chile's complete postauthoritarian institutional package, and the overall framework of its particular brand of presidentialism, rather than presidentialism per se, that provide the most important constraints to democratic consolidation.

7

CONCLUSIONS

Theoretical Observations and the Necessity of Reform

Despite the potential for Chile's exaggerated presidential system and the framework in which it is embedded to encourage interbranch conflict and problems of democratic governability and political efficacy, the success of the Aylwin and Frei administrations demonstrates that presidentialism can, given certain circumstances, work well in Chile. However, the success of the first postauthoritarian democratic administrations was fundamentally a function of the context of the process of democratic transition, which served to mute conflict and create a pattern approaching a de facto consociational government in Chile.

The point of departure for understanding the need for institutional reform in Chile is the recognition that the positive contextual features that in large part helped to determine the success of the transition process are indeed transitional. Chile is and will continue to be a country characterized by a multiparty system, and important programmatic and political differences between Chilean parties remain. What is more, the country is still characterized by profound and important divisions and has not faced a major economic or political crisis. In the future, latent conflicts are likely to become more manifest as the many important unresolved issues buried by the transition process come to the fore.

Given all these realities, the most pressing need is to create institutional mechanisms that encourage cooperation among Chile's numerous parties and between the branches of government in the future, despite some of the disincentives created by certain problematic features of the country's presidential system. It is also essential to adopt measures that will encourage institutionalization and maintenance of the pattern of *democracia consensual* that characterized the Aylwin administration and to a lesser extent the Frei government.[1]

Certain institutional and legal changes would help improve the prospects for political efficacy and democratic governability by making the institutional framework for democracy more congruent with the socioeconomic and political context of the country. There are three important first steps necessary to achieve this goal.

First, the balance of power between the branches of government must be transformed, either through a change in the configuration of executive/ legislative relations or through significant reforms to the presidential system as it currently exists. In the past, the ability of presidents and the Congress to reach accords through interbranch and interparty negotiation in Congress put relations between the branches of government at the center of wider conflict resolution within the political system. This dynamic was possible because Congress had the ability to engage in meaningful negotiations with the president through a combination of rewards and sanctions. Thus, in order for a similar and still necessary dynamic to develop, congressional prerogatives must be widened to provide incentives for both branches to negotiate and reach agreements.

Several proposals for a "semi-presidential" or "premier presidential" system have been advanced to achieve the conflict dampening goals outlined above.[2] Indeed, a legislative special commission was created to study the question of the most appropriate way to structure executive/legislative relations in the country. Rejecting a pure parliamentary system, the Special

---

1. In terms of the arguments of this study (and as argued more explicitly below), the Frei administration has indeed been characterized by less of a sense of consensual democracy and by the emergence and strengthening of latent conflict.

2. The frequent misgrouping of all systems with a president and a prime minister together as "semi-presidential" is often misleading. Shugart and Carey contend that though the Weimar Republic, Sri Lanka, and Portugal are often characterized as simply "semi-presidential," their real characteristics, and particularly the formal balance of powers between the president and premier, bring them closer to what they define as "president-parliamentary." Indeed, the Chilean "Parliamentary Republic," though alternately described as parliamentary and semi-presidential, is really much closer to Shugart and Carey's definition of "president-parliamentary," given that there was dual responsibility of the cabinet to both the president and the

Commission concluded that the adoption of a semi-presidential form of government would be the most appropriate and workable option for Chile.[3]

However, given the unlikelihood of fundamental regime reform in the near future, this chapter focuses on how presidentialism, as it currently exists, can be improved. The most important facet of reform is to strengthen Congress in order to reestablish its role as an effective lawmaking body that is capable of representing parties across the political spectrum. A strengthened Congress would allow the institution to be the arena for compromise and negotiation between parties and between the branches of government that it once was.

Second, for Congress to assume this role additional reforms to many aspects of the entire institutional framework are necessary. These reforms should be aimed at enhancing the representative capacity of Congress to ensure that all significant parties are represented, and at decreasing the likelihood of executive/legislative deadlock. In this vein, it is necessary to reform the parliamentary and presidential electoral system, the timing and sequencing of elections, and the role of the "semi-autonomous" institutions created by the 1980 constitution. In addition to enhancing the prospects for interbranch cooperation, reform in these areas would add a measure of increased legitimacy and enhanced efficiency to the democratic system.

Finally, it is important to capitalize on the lessons provided by the Aylwin administration and enact measures that encourage institutionalization and maintenance of the existing pattern of *democracia consensual* by reinforcing the aspects of the administration that facilitated interparty and interbranch cooperation.

However, before embarking on a discussion of individual reforms, a few qualifications are in order. Analysts of Chilean politics have pointed to the positive role that the controls established by the 1980 constitution played in

---

assembly. For a definition of each of these mixed forms of government and a discussion of its significance, see Shugart and Carey, *Presidents and Assemblies*, chap. 4.

3. See Cámara de Diputados de la República de Chile, "Informe de la comisión especial de estudio del régimen político chileno," adopted 9 May 1990. For a useful general discussion of semi-presidential systems, see Giovanni Sartori, *Comparative Constitutional Engineering* (New York: New York University Press, 1994), 121–35. For additional discussions concerning the possibility of introducing a premier-presidential or semi-presidential system in Chile, see Humberto A. Noguiera, *El régimen semipresidencial, ¿Una nueva forma de gobierno democrático?* (Santiago: Editorial Andante, 1986), and, by the same author, "El régimen semi-presidencial: Una alternativa viable al presidencialismo en Chile," in *Reformas al presidencialismo en América Latina: Presidencialismo vs. Parlamentarismo?* ed. Comisión Andina de Juristas (Caracas: Editorial Jurídica Venezolana, 1993), 103–31, and Giovanni Sartori, "Ni presidencialismo ni parlamentarismo," in *Cambio de régimen político*, ed. Oscar Godoy (Santiago: Ediciones Universidad Católica, 1992), 37–56.

preventing any one sector from imposing its will on another. The constitution established clearly delineated limits on both civilian and military authorities and prevented immediate and potentially destabilizing constitutional reform. While many of the so-called authoritarian characteristics of the 1980 constitution served as moderating features within a pacted transition, the long-term consolidation of democracy depends on elimination of the institutional vestiges of authoritarian rule. This is the case both because the controls on civilian authorities have proven to be unnecessary and because the long-term legitimacy of the democratic system depends on elimination of a political role for nonelected authorities.

What is more, all the reforms outlined here fit into the realm of the possible and realistic. For each of the reforms outlined below, there are historical and constitutional precedents on which they can be based. Many political elites have accepted the idea that reform is necessary and that the complete consolidation of democracy cannot take place without efforts to fully democratize the political system. Many recognize that the current institutional framework is inappropriate for contemporary Chilean society. One deputy, echoing the very hypothesis of this study, contended that the institutional framework designed by the outgoing military regime "does not correspond to contemporary political reality."[4] Another argued that, while the current institutional framework was useful in mediating conflicting interests in the context of a pacted transition, "in the long-term it has the capacity to sow more deeply the seeds of conflict hidden by the transition."[5]

Finally, this chapter does not intend to suggest that without reforms there will be a return to the violence and polarization of the 1970s. Advocates of parliamentary regimes point to the tendency of presidential regimes to produce executive/assembly deadlock and military incursions into politics. While this is certainly a serious and plausible effect of inappropriate institutional design, as scholars move to study Latin American political systems in the period of democratic consolidation it is perhaps more important at this juncture to analyze the functioning of democratic systems in qualitative terms. That is, in addition to problems of macro-democratic governability and military interference in politics, the lack of congruence between institutions and society can also create less dramatic, but more common and likely, possible problems. These include drifts in policy-making, decreased govern-

4. Interview with Deputy Octavio Jara, Valparaíso, 13 April 1993. Translation by the author.
5. Off-the-record interview with PPD deputy, Santiago, 28 April 1993. Translation by the author.

mental efficiency, problems of political representation, and a dwindling confidence in political institutions.[6]

How, then, can institutional reforms improve the qualitative performance of Chile's democratic system in order to enhance political efficacy and prevent the development of more serious problems of democratic governability?

The President and Assembly: The Balance of Power

There is a sophisticated understanding of the significance of institutional arrangements for democratic governability among Chilean political elites. Many of the subjects interviewed for this study, citing sophisticated theoretical arguments of the need for reform, had obviously read the literature on institutional arrangements in Chile.

Interviews with members of the Chamber and the Senate confirm strong support for institutional change in the country, especially among Concertación legislators. Of all the deputies sampled, 57 percent opted for semi-presidentialism, with presidentialism and parliamentarism following at 33 percent and 10 percent respectively. Though support for adoption of a semi-presidential regime was highest among deputies of government parties, about 42 percent of opposition members also supported this option (among the opposition, 58 percent supported the maintenance of a presidential regime, while support for the adoption of a parliamentary regime was nil).

Thus, despite strong theoretical arguments in the academic literature for adopting a parliamentary form of government in Chile, there is limited elite support for such an option, and for a number of reasons the prospects are not good. What is more, notwithstanding the recognized benefits of the premier-presidentialism system and significant support for regime reform among members of the Concertación, several obstacles make adoption of such a regime in Chile unlikely.

First, the Right is not inclined to reform the constitution at all, because many of the sector's leaders view a strong presidency as an antidote to the

6. There is increasing discussion of this problem in the academic and popular literature on Latin American politics. O'Donnell considers Chile a success story in his discussion of delegative democracy. However, in a post-transitional context, and given the strength of the Chilean president and weakness of the Congress, Chile has the potential to develop many of the negative characteristics identified by O'Donnell. See Guillermo O'Donnell, "Delegative Democracy," *Journal of Democracy* 5 (January 1994): 55–69.

party-dominated politics that existed for much of Chile's history.[7] Many also see the 1980 constitution as one of the most important positive legacies of the authoritarian regime and contend that the reconstituted and reformed presidential system has not been given sufficient time to prove its effectiveness. In addition, supporters of the presidential option cite tradition as an important element, contending that Chileans have a long history of presidentialism that forms a fundamental component of the country's political culture.[8] This is reinforced by the bad name that parliamentarism and mixed forms of government have, because of their erroneous association with the turbulent period in Chilean history known as the "Parliamentary Republic" from 1891 to 1925.[9]

Polling data also suggest that the public is not nearly as concerned with constitutional reform as political elites are. In a 1997 public-opinion survey, out of fifteen possible choices "constitutional reform" ranked second to last after "infrastructure" as "problems to which the government should dedicate more effort to solve." Only 2.8 percent of those surveyed ranked constitutional reform as one of their first three choices.[10]

However, the most important impediment to institutional reform in Chile is the combination of high legislative quorums established for reform of the

7. Despite these assertions, there is some support for the idea of regime reform on the Right, albeit limited (see below). The author also noted an additional though difficult-to-measure correlation between the age of interviewees and their views on institutional reform. Older legislators tended to defend presidentialism more strongly, while younger members were more open to the idea of regime reform.

8. Interviewees often also stressed the importance of the tradition of Chilean presidentialism, noting that parliamentarism is really a "foreign" political arrangement (without recognizing that "Chilean presidentialism," as well as most of its Latin American counterparts, was an institutional arrangement based on ideals and logic drawn directly from the Constitution of the United States and its precursor documents—for example, James Madison, *The Federalist*).

9. The term "parliamentary republic" is really a misnomer, because the regime that existed in this period was not a pure parliamentary system. Rather, the regime was characterized by shared cabinet responsibility to the Congress and the president, a configuration that created extreme problems of cabinet instability and democratic governability. What is more, under the 1891 arrangement, parliament did not elect the prime minister, and the president could not dissolve the Chamber of Deputies. Furthermore, a modern party system did not exist throughout this period, a reality that has an important impact on how distinct institutional arrangements function. For a discussion of this period, see Fernando Pinto Lagarrigue, *Balmaceda y los gobiernos seudo-parlamentarios* (Santiago: Editorial Andrés Bello, 1991), and Hernán Ramírez Necochea, *Balmaceda y la contrarrevolución de 1891* (Santiago: Editorial Universitaria, 1969).

10. CEP-Adimark surveys including the possible response "constitutional reform" began only in 1997, so comparative data, or data tracing the evolution in opinion toward the issue of constitutional reform, are difficult to find. See Centro de Estudios Públicos, "Estudio nacional de opinión pública No. 7" (Santiago: Centro de Estudios Públicos, December 1997–January 1998).

constitution, and two consecutive Senates in which the government has lacked a majority. With each successive government, the probability of fundamental regime reform decreases as the interests of political actors become increasingly embedded in maintaining the status quo.

Reformed Presidentialism: Making Chilean Presidentialism Work

Because fundamental institutional change in Chile is unlikely, it is important to analyze ways that the extant presidential system can be improved. Despite the recognized problems with presidentialism, its potential for success in Chile, unlike many other Latin American countries, is enhanced by certain characteristics of the country's party system. Matthew Shugart, Scott Mainwaring, and others have underscored the problematic consequences of the combination of presidentialism and fragmented multipartism, characterized by malleable, undisciplined parties.[11] Unlike those in Brazil, Ecuador, Peru, and Bolivia, Chilean parties are relatively well disciplined and characterized by strong party organizations. While the Chilean party system remains fragmented despite the efforts of military reformers to encourage integration, the moderately disciplined and institutionalized nature of Chilean parties provides a potentially more workable context for presidentialism.[12] Given the strength of party organizations, party leaders can better wield control and maintain the necessary discipline to negotiate and maintain coalitions. The potential workability of Chilean presidentialism is also enhanced by the ideological renewal of all major political parties.

Despite this potentially positive party context, continuing multipartism still requires mechanisms for reducing interparty conflict and encouraging interbranch cooperation. Bearing in mind the importance of differentiating between types of presidentialism, which has been repeatedly stressed throughout this study, several reforms to the presidential system that now exists in Chile could help temper some of its negative characteristics. The most urgent reform is to reestablish the equilibrium between the executive and legislative branches by strengthening the powers of the Congress.

11. See Scott Mainwaring and Matthew Shugart, "Presidentialism and Democracy in Latin America: The Debate," and Mainwaring, "Dilemmas of Multi-Party Presidential Democracy," both in *Presidentialism and Democracy in Latin America*, ed. Mainwaring and Shugart.
12. On the institutionalization of the Chilean party system, see Scott Mainwaring and Timothy Scully, introduction to their edited volume *Building Democratic Institutions*. It is extremely difficult to arrive at measures of party discipline in Chile, because until very recently no records that detailed how individual members voted were kept or published. These conclusions are based on interviews with members of the Chamber of Deputies and the Senate.

This work, supported by the comparative findings cited throughout, has argued that democratic systems characterized by extremely strong presidents, especially in terms of legislative powers, tend to be less durable. Yet the probable causes of such a phenomenon have not been explicitly discussed here, in the work of Shugart and Carey, or in other works with a similar focus.[13] The arguments advanced below set forth some tentative reasons why systems with very strong presidents may be less durable. While one could argue that these conclusions are based on the particularities of the Chilean case, they are instructive in terms of wider comparative theory building.

First, and as shown in previous chapters, in the years between the promulgation of the 1925 constitution and 1973, the Congress progressively lost prerogatives and influence through reforms granting the president increased powers. While these reforms limited the latitude of all legislators, members of the governing parties at least retained the influence that usually came with membership in a governing coalition. However, it was the legislators of opposition parties who most suffered. While in the past they could negotiate and extract limited concessions from the executive branch, the restrictions imposed by constitutional reform undercut their authority and eliminated the tools at their disposal to effectively negotiate and achieve legislative or broader political goals. Thus, the role of the legislature as an arena for opposition expression was undermined. If opposition forces are continually denied a voice in the national political dialogue and limited in their influence over the actions of the executive, achieving party goals through democratic means and through negotiation is likely to become a less attractive option. As Giovanni Sartori has convincingly argued, substantive participation within the institutions of democracy fosters their acceptance.[14]

Second, a strong Congress reduces the majoritarian tendencies of presidential government that have often precipitated executive/assembly conflict and have in many cases led to democratic breakdown. With a stronger Congress, a president is forced to negotiate both policy and the legislative agenda. Presidents must allow consideration of proposals that originate in the legislative branch, both from sectors supporting the president and from opposition members. Actual legislation may not be the preferred option of any one sector, but rather a middle ground that is tolerable for a greater number of sectors across the party spectrum in Congress. This reinforces the

13. Shugart and Carey, *Presidents and Assemblies*.
14. Sartori, *Parties and Party Systems*, 139.

notion that the Congress also has a popular mandate that is no less legitimate than that of the president, though it is based in distinct party options. Juan Linz has underscored how the problem of dual legitimacy can play out with unhappy consequences. The reality that both the president and the legislature can claim a popular mandate, he argues, is a recipe for conflict between the branches of government and ultimately serious crisis.[15] Linz does not discuss explicitly the possibility that a more even distribution of power between the executive and legislative branch might provide political actors with an incentive to solve conflicting legitimacies by compromise and creatively combining distinct democratic mandates through negotiation.

Similarly, because a stronger Congress effectively forces negotiations between the branches of government and between parties, the legislature becomes the natural arena for conflict resolution. If a president is forced to seek out congressional approval for the most significant and controversial legislation, the president's party must engage other parties in discussions on potential solutions to conflict.

There are a number of ways without significant modifications to the constitution or other statutes that the powers of the Congress can be reinforced. First, the faculty to jointly set legislative urgencies in collaboration with the executive branch can be returned to the Congress, as was the case according to the constitution of 1925. If there is widespread agreement in Congress that an initiative of its own is important, the executive cannot single-handedly delay or prevent its consideration. Congress could deny a presidential request for urgency consideration if the president proves obstructive in permitting urgency declarations for legislative initiatives.

In addition, with the power of urgency declaration, Congress would have more time to better debate, study, and alter presidential initiatives. This would give Congress increased influence, ultimately producing higher quality and more universally acceptable legislation. Members of Congress could induce the executive to include parliamentary proposals into executive policy by making approval of a presidential urgency contingent upon their incorporation. It is Congress, and not the presidency, that is the deliberative body charged with evaluating, debating, and amending legislation. Members of Congress clearly have a more accurate understanding of how long it takes to undertake this process effectively than the president does. One of the most important roles of Congress is to improve legislation

---

15. Juan Linz, "Presidential or Parliamentary Democracy: Does It Make a Difference," in *The Failure of Presidential Democracy*, ed. Juan Linz and Arturo Valenzuela, 6–8.

through collective deliberation. Therefore it needs the time and capacity to do so.

Another way to reinforce the role of Congress in setting the legislative agenda would be to end the traditional division between ordinary and extraordinary legislative sessions, thus eliminating the presidential prerogative to determine the materials that can be considered during the latter. This would give the Congress additional time to consider initiatives that its own members have proposed.

The balance of power between the branches of government can also be made more equitable by giving the Congress an increased voice in the areas in which the executive now has exclusive initiative. In interviews with a sample of forty-three legislators reflecting the party distribution of seats in the two chambers, only one member contended that the Chamber of Deputies should have the right of exclusive initiative for the national budget.[16] Deputies agreed that the Chamber's latitude in budgetary matters should not be widened. Members of Congress recognize that the clientelistic, log-rolling policies of the past had a pernicious effect on the economic well-being of the country. Though contributing a measure of democratic stability in the past through the satisfaction of demands, ultimately these types of expenditures helped lead to a wider dynamic of distrust for politicians and to a bloated state sector.

However, the current limitations on Congress' areas of initiative extend beyond the realm of particularistic spending and include issues of national budgetary priorities and large-scale social questions that affect the entire country. A reform of the budgetary process could proscribe the proposal of particularistic spending and initiatives involving wage policy, while returning to the Congress some initiative in the area of social policy at the national level and allowing Congress to make transfers between categories of national spending.

The role of the Congress in the national political process can also be bolstered by eliminating limitations on the origination of bills dealing with such national issues as maternity leave, working conditions, management-labor relations, and collective bargaining. With these reforms, Congress could play an enhanced role in determining national priorities without falling victim to populist temptations. Giving Congress a voice in these issues would increase the representative capacity of legislators and enhance the legitimacy of the legislature in the eyes of constituents. Rather than simply detailing a series of

16. Off-the-record interview with PPD Deputy, Santiago, 28 April 1993.

oficios that they have submitted, members of the Congress would have a real role in elaborating and influencing legislation on the national level.

Finally, reform in all these areas requires that the balance of power in terms of information and staff between the executive and the assembly be made more equal. In order to initiate quality bills and to perfect and influence bills that originate in the executive branch, the assemblies must have increased access to information and expert advisors. However, there is strong political resistance to increasing the budgets of individual members to provide for larger staffs. Improvements can be made without increased expenditures. There is a great deal of overlap in the services provided to individual members by the Offices of Information of the Chamber and the Senate and the Library of Congress.[17] Streamlining these three bodies, and consolidating into one office the areas in which they overlap, would provide additional funds for more focused and specific informational resources. In addition, a team of professional, permanent, nonpolitical appointees with subject-specific expertise for each of the legislative committees could provide the specialized information and counsel necessary for members to make informed judgments concerning the main issues and fundamental questions that are pertinent to each piece of legislation.

What is more, rather than simply transferring faculties from one branch to another, it is also important to enhance the power the legislative branch already has, especially in the area of oversight. While Congress has the powerful ability to initiate impeachment proceedings against government officials, this course of action can and should be employed only in extreme cases. Beyond impeachment, the Congress has few tools to perform its oversight function. Enhanced powers of *fiscalización* (oversight) for the Congress can better enable it both to act as a check on presidential power and to stem corruption, without having to resort to extreme measures like censure and impeachment.

First, the *oficio* system clearly needs to be reformed in order for it to perform a real oversight function. For the *oficio de información* and the *oficio de fiscalización*, it is important to establish a time limitation and a sanction for members of the executive branch who do not provide deputies with

---

17. The Offices of Information of the Chamber and of the Senate produce general reports of legislative statistics that could easily be done by one body. Individual parties and party sectors also have access to "think-tanks" that provide information identical to that of the Offices of Information. In addition, the questions of individual members submitted to the Offices of Information are often referred to the Library of Congress. There is no reason that these requests cannot simply be submitted directly to the Library.

significant, detailed, and explicit responses to their requests for information. The commission appointed to study the Organic Law of Congress in 1989 eliminated a sanction of three months' job suspension that previously existed for consistent unresponsiveness to congressional *oficios*. A sanction of this type would transform the utility of *oficios*, forcing both the executive and the legislative branches to take them more seriously.

Second, investigative commissions must be reformed, but reform in this area is even more complicated than in the case of the *oficio* system, given the use and abuse of investigative commissions as political instruments and the questions of ministerial responsibility they often raise. A possible solution to this problem would be to continue to allow the formation of legislative commissions with multiparty representation. However, in order to avoid their politicization, legislation could dictate that committee members must come to agreement on a single conclusion, rather than coming up with a minority opinion and a majority opinion. If differences prove irreconcilable, the Contraloría General de la República could intervene to consider the commission's report and render a binding opinion. The Contraloría had a long tradition of political independence in the preauthoritarian period. It was an important bulwark of the legalism that was a defining feature of the Chilean political system. With a director appointed for life from within the court system, this universally respected body was charged with auditing public accounts, ruling on the constitutionality of executive decrees, and advising government officials on the constitutionality of laws.[18] If the respect accorded the Contraloría in the past can be resurrected, the Contraloría could be an effective arbiter of disputes when legislative commissions cannot come to agreement. At the same time, it could rule on whether judicial proceedings should be initiated against those found responsible for wrongdoings in the reports of legislative commissions, providing the possibility of sanctions and a powerful check on executive action.

Reform of the Framework for Chilean Presidentialism

The full conflict-resolving potential of Congress, and the creation of incentives for interbranch cooperation, can be realized only through additional

---

18. On the Contraloría General de la República, see Enrique Silva Cimma, *Derecho administrativo chileno y comparado* (Santiago: Editorial Jurídica, 1969).

reforms in areas that are not specifically related to the relative strength of the branches of government. These include electoral reform, measures to institutionalize the informal patterns of cooperation characteristic of the Aylwin administration, and changes in the structure and function of the so-called semi-autonomous institutions.

Electoral Reform

It is widely accepted in the academic literature that presidentialism functions best when the executive can rely on a legislative majority, or at the very least a substantial legislative contingent. However, presidential forms of government are also based on the principle of checks and balances and on the congressional oversight of executive action. The goal of any electoral reform should be to balance these two principles—that is, to devise an electoral framework that will be more likely to result in the election of presidents with legislative majorities but that also allows for a flexible alternation of shifting majorities.

The electoral system, both presidential and parliamentary, is an extremely important variable that influences the capacity of the political system to achieve both goals. By shortening the presidential term and making all legislative elections concurrent with presidential elections, it is more likely that a president will be able to rely on a legislative majority of his or her own party or coalition of parties, or at the very least, a sizeable legislative contingent. A presidential term of four years would allow concurrent elections without altering the existing cycle of legislative elections. In addition, a four-year term would decrease the winner-take-all nature of the presidential election and allow an incompetent or unpopular president to be removed and replaced more easily and sooner by popular election.[19] Though members of a coalition may still attempt to distance themselves from the president's party when approaching an election, the electorate would have the responsibility to determine whether this course of action was a wise one. Former coalition members would be either elected along with their presidential candidate or immediately sanctioned for disloyalty to the previous president.

A shorter presidential term would also provide increased incentives for coalition formation and maintenance, because a shorter term brings the

19. Another alternative would be to shorten the terms of deputies to three years and the terms of senators to six years, making half of the legislative elections concurrent with presidential elections. Nonetheless, a reform of this type is unlikely in view of the significant public and elite opposition to increasing the frequency of elections.

expectation of governing closer to coalition members and provides a more flexible formula for intracoalitional negotiation of presidential candidacies. The potential for alternation among parties of presidential candidacies, combined with the increased flexibility of a shorter term, would enhance the prospects for maintaining a viable governing coalition. Indeed, and as noted in Chapter 2, the high-stakes nature of competition for the presidency has already begun to create problems of coalition maintenance for the Concertación.

Eliminating the second-round presidential election would also decrease the chances that a president would serve with a legislative minority, by ensuring that the definitive presidential election is concurrent with the congressional election and by discouraging party fragmentation. While instituting such a reform alone may not do much to ease the problems of minority presidents, undertaking it along with the complete package for electoral reform suggested here would certainly make the election of minority presidents less likely.

However, eliminating the second round, one could argue, fails to address the very reason that second-round elections were adopted: to avoid the election of presidents with small pluralities of the vote. Given the extent of party institutionalization and discipline in the country, it is less likely that presidents would be elected with small pluralities than would be the case in party systems like Brazil's or Ecuador's (had the countries not also adopted the two-round ballotage system). Nonetheless, the disadvantages of a second-round system can be reduced by adopting a "double complement rule" or by establishing a threshold above which presidents would not be subject to majority runoff.[20] In terms of balancing optimal results and the electorate's ability to understand the system, the latter solution is probably the most desirable, with a threshold of about 40 percent.

---

20. Costa Rica employs a threshold system, as did Peru between 1963–68. In Costa Rica the threshold is 40 percent, and in Peru it was one-third of the votes. Matthew Shugart and Rein Taagepera propose adoption of a "double complement rule," or a formula that is derived as the arithmetic average of majority runoff and plurality criteria, in order to balance the advantages and disadvantages of each type of system. With such a rule, the candidate that finishes first would not be subject to a majority runoff if the shortfall from a majority of the second-place candidate is more than double the first place candidate's shortfall from a majority. See Shugart and Taagepera, "Plurality Versus Majority Election of Presidents." While one could argue that this somewhat confusing system could function quite well in a society capable of understanding some of the operational intricacies of the binomial system, its mathematical advantages are outweighed by its disadvantages in terms of the public's ability to understand it. A simple threshold rule would be much easier to understand, and thus, more likely to be accepted.

Reform of the current parliamentary electoral system is also necessary for decreasing the probability that there will be minority presidents and for enhancing incentives for coalition formation and interbranch cooperation. However, interviews with legislators revealed that electoral system change was the one reform issue on which there were the most significant differences of opinions between government and opposition legislators. One hundred percent of the government deputies interviewed for this study favored adoption of a proportional representation (PR) system, while 75 percent of the opposition supported maintaining the binomial system. However, these results should be interpreted with a great deal of caution. Debates in the press reveal that the positions of parties in regard to electoral reform are profoundly shaped by the particular political moment and the results of public-opinion survey data. At times, members of the government coalition have supported the maintenance of the binomial system, while important party players on the Right have advocated reform, often depending on each sector's proximity to the electoral thresholds established by the binomial system. What is more, after three elections the Concertación has realized that if the fortunes of the Right wane, the alliance could achieve an unprecedented legislative majority and find itself in a position to engage in far-reaching constitutional reform. At the same time, the parties of the Right have realized that without significant gains in support they are unlikely to govern in the near future. This has led to something of a reversal of opinion, with some on the Right realizing that a proportional representation system could encourage disintegration of the Concertación, given that each of its major parties would be tempted to present separate parliamentary lists. This could conceivably split the Concertación's vote and provide an important benefit for the Right, both in terms of legislative seats and in terms of its potential to place a candidate in the presidency should the Center and the Left split over the issue of a common presidential standard-bearer.

Despite these transitory political considerations, a proportional representation system would provide important benefits in terms of long-term democratic governability. Such a system would enhance the conflict-resolving capacity and legitimacy of Congress by ensuring that all significant political sectors have a voice in the national political dialogue. It would avoid both the dramatic shifts in parliamentary representation and the exclusionary propensities of the current binomial system. However, the proportional representation system adopted should be a moderate type with relatively small district magnitudes. Even the legislators interviewed who favored the adoption of a PR system underscored that they do not suggest simply returning to the electoral system that existed before 1973. Most agreed that the permissiveness of the system encouraged the proliferation of parties and made coalition formation difficult. Every legislator interviewed for this study, when coming out in favor of the adoption of a PR system, contended that it should be a moderate one. A proportional representation system with district magnitudes ranging between 3 and 6 would provide for effective representation of the most significant parties of the government and opposition, but avoid hyperproportionality in the representation of smaller parties who could engage in legislative blackmail.[21]

Sartori contends that a party opposition will be more likely to behave responsibly if it has some expectation that it will govern or participate in governing coalitions in the future.[22] In this sense, party systems have the capacity to integrate irresponsible opposition into the realm of democratic politics. The mechanism he identifies as best able to play this role is a PR electoral system.[23] Proportional representation gives smaller parties the opportunity to participate, and participation fosters acceptance of the political system.

Yet this work has shown that the Chilean binomial electoral system not only has the potential to bar participation of small nonaligned parties, but also can exclude entire ideological currents.

A moderate PR system would be less likely than the binomial system to exclude a democratic opposition. Under the rules of the binomial system, an electoral sweep of the president's party in a legislative election can easily result in complete exclusion for other parties. In the event that a party receives 20 percent of the vote of the two largest coalitions nationally, under the binomial system it would be significantly underrepresented in Congress, while with a proportional system it would garner approximately 20 percent of the seats in the National Congress. Single-party domination is unhealthy in a country like Chile, where no party option can consistently garner a majority. What is more, this work has repeatedly underscored the negative consequences of exclusion when a political system is faced with the challenge of resolving controversial and difficult problems.

In mechanical terms, a proportional representation system can be easily instituted without significant legislative redistricting or a dramatic increase

21. This argument is more completely developed in Siavelis, "Nuevos argumentos y viejos supuestos."
22. Sartori, *Parties and Party Systems*, 139.
23. Ibid., 141.

in the number of legislators serving in Congress. Existing legislative districts could be combined, and the number of deputies only moderately increased.[24]

Moderation and disciplined competition are also more likely with careful selection of the type of electoral list. Chile was the first, and one of the few, countries in Latin America to employ an open-list electoral system. Open-list proportional representation gives voters the opportunity to vote for particular candidates, rather than distributing seats to winning candidates on the basis of the order in which they appear on preestablished party lists. Open-list systems therefore tend to give more power to the voter, but they also tend to undermine party discipline because the party loses the powerful tool of rank-ordering candidates. In spite of Chile's pre-1973 open-list system, parties were historically disciplined and institutionalized. Nonetheless, in a effort to help ensure continued discipline and add a dose of moderation to the PR system, a closed-list system would help to further balance the interests of representation and stability.

Certain advocates of electoral reform have also suggested that establishing a minimal threshold for representation to Congress would help to limit party-system fragmentation and the blackmail capabilities of small parties.[25] However, in the Chilean case small district magnitude would obviate the need for a minimal threshold, because, in order to gain a seat, a party would have to get a relatively high percentage of support in a district. Given that no significant ethnically or religiously based parties are concentrated within particular geographical areas, and that support for parties across the political spectrum is relatively evenly distributed throughout the country, a minimum threshold is not really necessary.[26] Moderate magnitude provides a threshold that is strong enough to prevent the representation of small or extremist parties with blackmail potential.

This proposal to limit the access that very small and extremist parties have to Congress through moderate district magnitude does not contradict what has already been said about the importance of inclusion. Every electoral system must balance the dual challenges of representation and democratic

24. Aylwin's proposal for the adoption of a moderate PR system outlined in Chapter 6 combined districts in this way.

25. See, for example, José María Fuentes, "La alternativa proporcional con barreras de entrada: Un sistema electoral adecuado para Chile," *Estudios públicos* 51 (Winter 1993): 269–302.

26. While indigenous Mapuche communities are concentrated in the south of the country, particularly the ninth region, and have recently become more vocal, their small number and lack of economic resources and political organization have prevented the development of Mapuche-oriented political parties capable of achieving national representation.

governability. A moderate PR system would simply tilt this balance more toward representation. It would enhance the representative capacity of the political system by giving all significant political sectors a voice in Congress, but it would avoid some of the destabilizing consequences of hyperrepresentation. In essence, the design of the binomial system was guided by the questionable assumption that low district magnitude would enhance governability with a recognized but necessary cost in terms of representation. If the evidence presented in this study is correct, Chileans are paying a price in terms of representation without receiving the benefits of long-term stability and governability that this cost is supposed to underwrite. A moderate PR system both costs less in terms of representation and provides more in terms of stability.

Finally, any electoral reform should end the appointment of senators and eliminate the prerogative of lifelong Senate seats for former presidents. Among those interviewed for this study, 100 percent of government deputies supported the elimination of the "institutional" senators while only 33 percent of the opposition favored such an option. Nonetheless, responses to this question for the opposition are undoubtedly partially (if not primarily) determined by party political considerations and by the Right's desire to maintain a majority in the Senate. In addition to the costs to legitimacy exacted by the antidemocratic process for the designation of these senators, the "hangover" from previous presidents' appointments can help prevent presidents from obtaining a majority in the upper chamber. Arguably, the institution of nonelected senators was a useful moderating element within the context of the democratic transition. However, a role for the opposition could better and more legitimately be ensured by establishing a more proportional electoral system rather than a series of appointments made by authorities outside the legislative branch.

Similarly, though the appointment of former presidents to lifelong positions in the Senate is perhaps justifiable, given their ostensible experience in governing, giving presidents an afterlife in Congress both further strengthens an already exaggerated presidency and can conceivably tilt the balance of power in Congress and deprive successive presidents a majority in the legislature.

Institutionalizing Cooperation

Many of the roots of success of the Aylwin and Frei Administrations lie in the pattern of party competition that was characteristic of the transition period and are quite difficult to duplicate indefinitely. However, these post-authoritarian governments do provide certain lessons that can be applied by subsequent administrations. As suggested throughout this study, the Frei government has fewer of the characteristics of *democracia consensual* than the Aylwin administration and has been characterized by a less collaborative management style. While to a certain extent this is simply a result of distinct personalities and styles, this change is also a preliminary confirmation of many of the contentions of this study concerning a return to "politics as usual" as the urgency of the transitional period abates.

Nonetheless, the positive aspects of interbranch and interparty relations during both governments can be built upon and reinforced through efforts to institutionalize the formal and informal norms of interbranch and inter-party interactions.

In essence, both administrations provide ample evidence that constant and fluid contact between Congress and the president, and between parties (of both the government and the opposition), can help to attenuate interbranch conflict and lead to negotiated settlements. Structured interaction can also transfer the unfolding of controversial disagreements from the national media (which can in turn make them even more explosive) to the halls of government. Constant contact forces the moderation that comes from having to engage in face-to-face negotiations.

Although throughout the Aylwin and Frei administrations the coordination between the branches of government was undertaken by the Ministry of the General Secretary (SEGPRES), the constitution does provide for a minister whose sole function is managing relations between the government and Congress.[27] Though not employed by either administration, the appointment of such a minister consistently by subsequent administrations could serve to institutionalize a link between the executive and legislative branches. The appointment of a "Minister for Congress" could help to formalize and enhance the role already played by SEGPRES in interbranch relations.

Another way to encourage dialogue and compromise would be to institu-tionalize the periodic meetings between "political" ministers (especially the Ministry of the General Secretary) and the parliamentary commissions of each party. Periodic, bilateral meetings between ministers and the chairs of Chamber and Senate committees working in the same area would encour-age interbranch coordination, introducing an element of shared interests

---

27. *Constitución Política de la República de Chile*, Article 33.

and responsibility in the elaboration of legislation. While these types of meetings occurred throughout both administrations, there is no reason that they cannot be formalized within the *reglamentos* governing both chambers of Congress and the ministries. Without formal institutionalization, they become less important.

Indeed, this informal dynamic of cooperation and consultation already appears to be eroding, perhaps because it has not been institutionalized. The Frei government has been repeatedly criticized for not consulting with the member parties of the Concertación, especially with regard to cabinet changes and major policy initiatives.[28] The changes suggested here, combined with a stronger legislature, would most likely provide enhanced incentives for cross-branch and interparty negotiations.

Though the Aylwin administration did not engage in formal meetings between the government and the parliamentary commissions of the opposition, there are convincing reasons for also attempting to institutionalize these types of meetings, at the very least with the *jefes de bancada* of opposition parties. The institutionalization of formal contact gets elites used to discussing and negotiating important issues. If such a process has already become routine before controversial and divisive issues arise, it is more likely that those issues will be subject to a similar negotiation process.

The Reform of "Semi-Autonomous" Powers

There is certainly a potentially positive role for the semi-autonomous powers created by the 1980 constitution within the overall framework of Chilean democracy. However, the scope of their activities and the generation of their membership should be transformed in order for them to play a more effective, legitimate, and stabilizing role.

While the president has the ability to name high-level officials in the armed forces, they must be chosen from the five most senior officers, and once appointed they cannot be removed by democratic authorities. This limits the ability of the executive to sanction high-level military officials who defy presidential authority. What is more, it challenges the legitimacy of duly elected authorities given the veto power retained by military forces. Protests by military officials, like the *boinazo* of May 1993, continue, and the president has little latitude when it comes to punishing officers involved in such acts of insubordination. While overt acts of military insubordination have been waning, the existence of a "fourth branch" of government that

28. *La Tercera*, 3 August 1998, 1.

has veto power over the other three branches only complicates the process of conflict resolution. Civilian authorities must be assured that the agreements reached are binding and will not be subject to ultimate arbitration by the military.

The process of democratic transition forced a balancing act between military officials and the president. This was an unavoidable by-product of the mutual process of trust-building in the immediate postauthoritarian period. Military and civilian authorities consistently tested their bounds. The armed forces made their concerns known through limited public demonstrations of force, while civilian authorities attempted to rein in military authorities through media discourse and attempts to marshal public opposition to extraconstitutional military actions. These boundaries have been firmly established, and military leaders realize that there is little public support for a continuing political role for the armed forces. However, for complete institutionalization of Chilean democracy, civilian authority over the military must be definitively reestablished. The president's role as the commander in chief of the armed forces must be strengthened and consolidated, and the executive's right to appoint, remove, and determine the salaries of military officials restored. The "unremovability" of the generals now serving, however, should be maintained in the interests of avoiding immediate civil-military conflict, and the new measures should take effect as high-level officials retire.

Similarly, the role of the National Security Council in issuing edicts should be limited and its membership transformed. Although National Security Councils, or similar institutions, exist in many democratic nations, they do so in a context in which they are fully subordinate to the president, prime minister, or other democratic authorities. Security councils of this type can perform a vital role in coordinating the overall defense and security policy of nations. However, the National Security Council's ability to issue opinions on the country's internal affairs helps to perpetuate the tendency of the military to become involved in domestic politics and to continue to make public pronouncements on issues outside of its purview of authority. The council's membership should be expanded to include the president of the Chamber of Deputies, thus providing a clear majority for civilian authorities. The areas in which the council can intervene to make its opinions known should be restricted to issues affecting national defense and security, narrowly considered. Its latitude should be further limited by specifically proscribing the council from ruling or issuing opinions on domestic political events. While the National Security Council has been relatively reserved in the way it has employed its prerogatives, there is no guarantee that it will exercise such restraint in the future.

The role of the Constitutional Tribunal must be similarly reformed. These types of bodies perform fundamental oversight functions in many democratic systems, ensuring the constitutionality of legislation and acting as a check on the legislative and executive branches. However, in the Chilean case, the tribunal was appointed with clearly political motivations by non-elected authorities, creating both problems of legitimacy and potential problems of governability. Because civilian authorities question the motivations behind the decisions and rulings of the tribunal, it lacks the legitimacy it needs in order to exercise its role as a final arbiter on constitutional matters. With a more democratic composition, the tribunal could play a vital and stabilizing role in defending the constitution and exercising a much needed oversight function.

Thus, the Constitutional Tribunal should be retained and its essential prerogatives maintained, but generation of its membership should rest squarely with democratic authorities and, more precisely, with each of the three democratic branches of government. The three members of the tribunal currently drawn from the senior membership of the Supreme Court can continue to be appointed in the same way. The makeup of the Supreme Court will gradually change with successive appointments by democratic authorities. Given that membership of the National Security Council is not determined by democratic authorities, its role in appointing members of the Constitutional Tribunal should be eliminated. The council's right to appoint two members of the tribunal should be turned over to democratic authorities, with the president and the legislative branch each appointing an additional member. However, given the existence of designated senators (if they are not eliminated), the right of appointment should rest either in the Chamber of Deputies or in a plenary session of the Chamber and the Senate, to dilute the power of nonelected senators. Thus, three of the tribunal's members would be appointed by the Supreme Court, and two each would be appointed by the president and by Congress.

Theoretical Observations and the Future of Executive/Legislative Relations in Chile

Though fundamentally a case study, this analysis of executive/legislative relations in contemporary Chile supports some of the recent findings in the theoretical literature on institutional arrangements. At the same time, it has uncovered some potentially interesting theoretical propositions, which warrant future examination and testing.

Much of the academic debate concerning executive/legislative relations in Latin America has focused on the distinction between parliamentary and presidential regimes. Juan Linz, Arturo Valenzuela, and others have shown that the institutional configuration of executive/assembly relations is an important variable that affects prospects for democratic longevity.[29] By bringing the issue to the fore, they have made scholars realize that there has been insufficient focus in the literature on this important political variable.

Shugart and Carey take Linz and Valenzuela's analysis of institutional arrangements one step further by demonstrating that treating parliamentary and presidential regimes as polar opposites is incorrect.[30] They stress that there are numerous variables that differentiate presidential systems and affect the way they function, and that in fact some types of presidentialism may contribute to the prospects for democratic longevity better than others. For Shugart and Carey, the issue is not the mere existence of presidentialism, but the balance of power between the president and assembly, the question of who names cabinets, and other institutional characteristics, which also make a difference in terms of democratic governability. They suggest that presidential systems characterized by very strong presidents may have less successful records of democratic longevity. Much of the evidence presented here provides support for that conclusion.

However, this case study has taken the analysis of institutional arrangements one step further by uncovering how socioeconomic and political variables can affect the functional properties of particular institutional arrangements. This is the case in analyzing both the roots of the positive performance of the Aylwin administration and the potentially negative role that exaggerated presidentialism can play in a society that is characterized by enduring conflicts and persistent divisions.

In theoretical terms, this case study suggests that the issue of congruence may be more important than the theoretical literature has so far suggested. The characteristics of societies, socioeconomic divisions, and the nature and competitive dynamic of the party system all profoundly affect the workability of particular institutional arrangements. Thus, in empirical terms it is

29. For summaries of their arguments that have appeared in several places, see Juan Linz, "Presidential or Parliamentary Democracy: Does It Make a Difference," and Arturo Valenzuela, "Party Politics and the Crisis of Presidentialism in Chile."
30. Shugart and Carey, *Presidents and Assemblies*.

crucial that elites in democratizing polities carefully consider the characteristics of their societies when attempting to design or re-form the institutional framework for democracy. While this seems obvious and has been emphasized in some of the recent work on institutional design, what is less obvious and more difficult is to project the evolution of these variables over time, especially in societies where socioeconomic change is taking place at breakneck speed.

This case study also suggests that analysts of institutional arrangements may have focused too much on the distinction between parliamentary and presidential regimes, and on the relative balance of power between the branches of government. Other institutional variables, and the complete framework for democratic government, can profoundly affect the relative strength of presidents, the incentives for interbranch cooperation, and how particular institutional arrangements function.

In particular, this study provides evidence for the following theoretical propositions: First, too much has been made of the distinction between parliamentary and presidential systems without examining the distinct subtypes of parliamentarism and presidentialism. The key variable is not the mere existence of one type of institutional arrangement or another, but rather how it is designed, and how executive/legislative relations are actually structured. For example, in presidential systems one needs to ask: How powerful is the president? How powerful is Congress? What is the president's role in the legislative process? How much latitude does the president have in terms of vetoing bills, declaring urgencies, issuing executive decrees, or determining the nature of important legislative initiatives like the budget? How effective are presidents in the actual use of their faculties? Is there an imbalance in staff and informational resources between the two branches of government? Each of these variables affects both the dynamics and the workability of presidential systems.

There are badly designed presidential systems and badly designed parliamentary systems, depending on these and a number of other variables discussed below. The simple existence of presidentialism does not necessarily negatively affect the workability of a democratic regime, as some theorists have suggested. The balance of power between the president and the legislature can have a strong impact on policy coherence, interbranch relations, and democratic governability. What is more, the nature of the party system (and the distinct constellations of partisan and constitutional powers it produces), the complex formal and informal pattern of interbranch and interpersonal relations, and the ability of legislators to provide pork can also help override some of the problems of democratic governability that critics of presidentialism have identified.

Second, and related to the first point, analyses of presidentialism in Latin America have not focused sufficiently on how the entire framework of democratic government affects executive/legislative relations. The electoral system, the timing and sequencing of elections, and the existence of legal bodies outside the legislative and executive branches affect the prospects for cooperation and the potential workability of distinct institutional arrangements. Therefore, many of the criticisms leveled at presidentialism in the theoretical literature can be more, or less, serious obstacles to cooperation and democratic governability, depending on the particular constellation of legal and institutional variables in which presidential systems operate.

Third, while scholars have analyzed the importance of the relationship between party-system variables and institutional arrangements, there often seems to be an assumption, especially among those who advocate parliamentary systems, that party systems are static and immutable. They contend that parliamentary government is more suitable for multiparty systems, without allowing for variations in the operational dynamic of different types of multiparty systems. These scholars do not sufficiently take into account the effect of shifting political alignments and coalitional configurations, and that is a mistake. While there may be certain constants within national political systems, it is important to introduce a dynamic element into the analysis of the relationship between social structures and political institutions. What type of multiparty system exists? How much ideological distance is there between parties? How easy is coalition formation? And how is each of these issues affected by the parliamentary electoral system and the method of presidential election? How do constitutional and partisan powers of the president and assembly interact? Though an institutional arrangement may be workable in a particular time-dependent party-system context, a change in this context can create difficulties or make it distinctly unworkable. The goal should be to attempt to identify political institutions that are capable of responding and functioning within the long-term trajectory of the development of national party systems.

Finally, in the literature on presidentialism, not enough has been said about institutional arrangements and their relationship to noninstitutional variables. In rediscovering institutions, many theorists have overlooked the important contributions to the study of comparative politics made by scholars employing behavioral and society-based approaches. Distinct types of party systems, levels of economic development, and degrees of social conflict can produce a great deal of variation in how political institutions function, as can whether or not a country is in a process of democratic transition. These contextual variables, and how they affect the party system and incentive structure and decisions of individual actors, are more important than has been suggested. In particular, scholars need to analyze the question of the "fit" between institutions taken together and the socioeconomic and political context of the country. But analyses of fit involve some prediction, given the often rapid pace of socioeconomic change in developing societies.

In essence, the results of this case study suggest that critics of Latin American presidentialism are not wrong. However, many of their criticisms do not identify problems of presidentialism per se, but rather difficulties associated with certain types of presidentialism, within certain social and party-system contexts.

For Chile, although a parliamentary system may be a more workable option given the country's socioeconomic and political context, the prospects for fundamental regime reform become less likely with each successive government. The task now is to remedy some of the widely recognized inadequacies of the Chilean presidential system. By tilting the balance of interbranch power toward a more powerful Congress, engaging in reforms that enhance the representative capacity of the democratic system, and taking reform measures to make the election of minority presidents less likely, presidentialism can be a viable alternative for Chile. These reforms can help reestablish executive/legislative relations as the nexus for wider conflict resolution. While for the moment the apparent success of the first two postauthoritarian governments seems to mitigate against reform of the presidential system, the positive political and economic context of the country, which has been so important in encouraging governmental success, is by no means a permanent condition.

In the postauthoritarian period, Chileans succeeded in constructing the seemingly ever-elusive centrist coalition that many analysts identify as the element missing from Chilean politics throughout the 1970s and 1980s. Deep divisions and disagreements proved to be powerful impediments to the early advent of a democratic transition. This lack of consensus provided the military with an important pretense to remain in power and an eventual rationale for imposing constitutional controls on civilian authorities.

However, unlike any time in the country's history, in contemporary Chile there is sufficient consensus for parties and elites to cooperate in successfully confronting the socioeconomic and political challenges facing the country.

The transition process and the first several years of democratic government have revealed fundamental agreement concerning the most important economic and social questions. However, it has also become clear that as Chile enters the stage of democratic consolidation the moderating drives exerted by the process of transition have become less powerful. What is more, despite transformations in the last two decades, Chile remains a dynamic and complex society characterized by a multiparty system, multiple divisions, and a number of enduring socioeconomic challenges.

The key to success in the democratic transition was building a centrist consensus by incorporating the opinions and interests of all sectors across the political spectrum, even those of the opposition, in determining the postauthoritarian course of the country. Chile's contemporary democratic institutional framework has the potential to undermine the maintenance of consensus. Indeed, it encourages divisiveness by providing for consistent majority representation of minority opinions and illegitimate veto power. Through strengthening the Congress and limiting the latitude of executive authority, the consensus-building mechanisms of the transition process can be maintained by ensuring that all political sectors are incorporated within the national political and economic dialogue. Thus, Chile will be left with an institutional structure that better creates the incentives for cooperation among its diverse and multiple political parties, enhancing the legitimacy of both the National Congress and democratic institutions in general.

APPENDIX

This study is based primarily on field research undertaken by the author in Santiago and Valparaíso, Chile. Preliminary fieldwork was done between May and August 1990, but the bulk of the research took place between March 1992 and July 1993, including observation of formal debates, study of the legislative process, and interviews with political elites. Approximately seventy total interviews were undertaken. They varied in length from twenty minutes to four hours, with an average length of one hour and fifteen minutes. The interviews sought to arrive at a qualitative evaluation of how institutions affect choice from the perspective of political actors themselves. The interviews were designed to uncover how political actors perceive the legislative process and how institutional constraints affect their ability to perform their legal and empirical roles within it.

In the legislative branch, 25 percent of the membership of the Senate (N = 12/48) and the Chamber of Deputies (N = 30/120) was interviewed. Interviewees were selected to reflect the party distribution of seats in both chambers of the Congress. In addition, gender and age were also taken into account when determining the overall sample, to attempt to control for differences in points of view and responses that could potentially be a function of these variables. The small size of the population prevented the use of random sampling techniques.

Members of Congress were asked a series of open-ended questions. The rationale for such a method was based on the supposition that it is difficult to capture the true state of relations between the branches of government and the functional dynamics of Congress without significant qualitative evaluation. However, the questions were structured to also elicit concrete responses to allow for quantitative compilation of the results.

In addition to members of Congress, dozens of other officials in the legislative branch were also interviewed, including secretaries, staff, legislative aides, the directors of the Offices of Information of the Chamber and the Senate, and the Secretaries of Chamber and Senate Committees. In composing this sample, the party identification of interviewees was also taken into account.

In the executive branch, interviews were undertaken with high-level officials in four of the most important ministries, including the Ministries of the General Secretary of the Presidency, Finance, Interior, and Justice. Officials within the Ministry of Agriculture were also interviewed. In the executive branch, interviewees were also asked a series of structured questions very similar to those asked of officials in the legislative branch, though they were slightly altered in order to reflect the relative position of ministry officials within the legislative process. The most extensive series of interviews in the executive branch took place with officials and advisors within the Ministry of the General Secretary of the Presidency, which is charged with conducting interbranch relations and coordinating interparty coalitional relations.

Additional interviews were undertaken with people working in institutions associated in some way with the legislative process, but not working directly within it. These included the staffs of "think-tanks" of all partisan colors, and officials within the Library of Congress and the Center for Legislative Studies and Assistance (CEAL) at the University of Valparaíso.

This study is also based on more than thirty hours of observation of congressional debates, necessary to capture some of the norms of interaction between legislators and to get a handle on how the legislative process functions.

Finally, this work draws heavily on the academic literature on institutional arrangements, as well as other sources, including magazines, newspapers, party documents, and documentation of legislative activity produced by the Offices of Information of the Chamber of Deputies and the Senate.

REFERENCES

Secondary Works

Agor, Weston H. *The Chilean Senate.* Austin: University of Texas Press, 1971.
———, ed. *Latin American Legislatures: Their Role and Influence.* New York: Praeger, 1971.
Aguero, Felipe, Eugenio Tironi, Eduardo Valenzuela, and Guillermo Sunkel. "Voters, Parties, and Political Information: Fragile Political Intermediation in Post-Authoritarian Chile." Paper presented at the Twentieth International Congress of the Latin American Studies Association, Guadalajara, Mexico, 17–19 April 1997.
Aldulante, Adolfo, Angel Flisfisch, and Tomás Moulián. *Estudios sobre sistemas de partidos en Chile.* Santiago: FLACSO, 1985.
Allamand, Andrés. "Partido Renovación Nacional." In *Renovación ideológica en Chile.* Ed. Gustavo Cuevas Farren. Santiago: Universidad de Chile, 1993.
Andrade Geywitz, Carlos. *Reforma de la Constitución Política de la República de Chile.* Santiago: Editorial Jurídica de Chile, 1991.
Angell, Alan. *Politics and the Labor Movement in Chile.* London: Oxford University Press, 1972.
———. "Unions and Workers in Chile During the 1980s." In *The Struggle for Democracy in Chile,* rev. ed. Ed. Paul Drake and Iván Jaksic. Lincoln: University of Nebraska Press, 1995.
Arriagada, Genaro. "Después de los presidencialismos . . . ¿Qué?" In *Cambio de régimen político.* Ed. Oscar Godoy. Santiago: Ediciones Universidad Católica de Chile, 1992.
———. *El pensamiento político de los militares.* Santiago: CISEC, 1981.
———. *Pinochet: The Politics of Power.* Boulder, Colo.: Westview Press, 1988.
———. "El sistema político chileno: Una exploración del futuro." *Colección estudios* CIEPLAN 15 (December 1984): 171–202.
Barrera, Manuel. *Desarrollo económico y sindicalismo en Chile, 1938–1970.* Santiago: Centro de Estudios Económicos y Sociales, 1979.
Barrera, Manuel, and Samuel Valenzuela. "The Development of Labor Movement Opposition to the Military Regime." In *Military Rule in Chile.* Ed. Samuel Valenzuela and Arturo Valenzuela. Baltimore: Johns Hopkins University Press, 1986.

Barria Soto, Francisco. *El Partido Radical, su historia, su obra.* Santiago: Editorial Universitaria, 1957.

Barros, Eduardo. "El nuevo orden de partidos: Algunas hipótesis." *Estudios públicos* 38 (Fall 1990): 129–39.

Beer, S. H. "The British Legislature and the Problem of Mobilizing Consent." In *Lawmakers in a Changing World.* Ed. E. Frank. Englewood Cliffs, N.J.: Prentice Hall, 1966.

Bicheno, H. E. "Anti-parliamentary Themes in Chilean History: 1920–1970." *Government and Opposition* 7 (Summer 1992): 351–88.

Blondel, J. *Comparative Legislatures.* Englewood Cliffs, N.J.: Prentice Hall, 1973.

Boeninger, Edgardo. "Consolidation in Chile." *Journal of Democracy* 2, no. 3 (1991): 57–60.

Boynton, George, and Chong Lin Kim, eds. *Legislative Systems in Developing Countries.* Durham, N.C.: Duke University Press, 1975.

Braun, Guillermo Alfredo. *El Partido Radical y el Frente Popular.* Santiago: Editorial República, 1936.

Bravo Lira, Bernardino. *De Portales a Pinochet.* Santiago: Editorial Jurídica de Chile, 1985.

———. "Orígenes, apogeo y ocaso de los partidos políticos en Chile." *Política* 7 (July 1985): 9–42.

Brunner, José Joaquín, and Cristián Cox. "Dinámicas de transformación en el sistema educacional de Chile." In *Educación, equidad y competitividad económica en las Américas.* Ed. Jeffrey M. Puryear and José Joaquín Brunner. Washington, D.C.: INTERAMER, 1995.

Bulnes Ripamonti, Cristián. *Relaciones y conflictos entre los órganos del poder estatal.* Santiago: Editorial Jurídica de Chile, 1967.

Caivano, Joan. "Authoritarian Politics: The Dynamic Interplay Between a New Municipal Institutionality and Social Policies in Chile Under Pinochet." Master's thesis, Graduate School, Georgetown University, 1991.

Campero, Guillermo. *El movimiento sindical en el régimen militar chileno: 1973–1981.* Santiago: Instituto Latinoamericano de Estudios Transnacionales, 1984.

Campos Harriet, Fernando. *Historia constitucional de Chile.* Santiago: Editorial Jurídica de Chile, 1969.

Carrasco Delgado, Sergio. "Composición del Senado en Chile: Institución de los Senadores Designados." *Jornadas de derecho público* 20 (1990): 117–30.

Castañeda, Jorge. *Utopia Unarmed.* New York: Knopf, 1993.

Castañeda, Tarsicio. *Combating Poverty: Innovative Social Reforms in Chile During the 1980s.* San Francisco: ICS Press, 1992.

———. *Para combatir la pobreza: Política social y descentralización en Chile durante los '80s.* Santiago: Centro de Estudios Públicos, 1990.

Castillo Velasco, J. *Las fuentes de la Democracia Cristiana.* Santiago: Editorial del Pacífico, 1955.

———. *Teoría y práctica de la Democracia Cristiana chilena.* Santiago: Editorial del Pacífico, 1972.

Cavarozzi, Marcelo. "Patterns of Elite Negotiation and Confrontation in Argentina and Chile." In *Elites and Democratic Consolidation in Latin America and Southern Europe.* Ed. John Higley and Richard Gunther. New York: Cambridge University Press, 1992.

Cavarozzi, Marcelo, and Manuel Antonio Garretón, eds. *Muerte y resurrección: Los partidos políticos en el autoritarismo y las transiciones del cono sur.* Santiago: FLACSO, 1989.

Cea Egaña, José Luis. "Presidencialismo reforzado. Críticas y alternativas para el caso chileno." In *Cambio de régimen político.* Ed. Oscar Godoy. Santiago: Ediciones Universidad Católica de Chile, 1992.

————. *Tratado de la Constitución de 1980: Características generales, garantías constitucionales.* Santiago: Editorial Jurídica de Chile, 1988.

Cifuentes, Mercedes. "Health Care." In *Private Solutions to Public Problems.* Ed. Cristián Larroulet. Santiago: Editorial Trineo, 1993, 53–93.

Comisión Andina de Juristas. *Reformas al presidencialismo en América Latina: Presidencialismo vs. parlamentarismo.* Caracas: Editorial Jurídica Venezolana, 1993.

Comisión Económica para América Latina. *Panorama social de América Latina.* Santiago: CEPAL, 1997.

Comisión Económica para América Latina. *Statistical Yearbook for Latin America and the Caribbean: 1994 Edition.* Santiago: CEPAL, 1995.

Constable, Pamela, and Arturo Valenzuela. *A Nation of Enemies.* New York: Norton, 1991.

Coppedge, Michael. "District Magnitude, Economic Performance, and Party-System Fragmentation in Five Latin American Countries." *Comparative Political Studies* 30 (April 1997): 156–85.

Cruz-Coke, Ricardo. *Historia electoral de Chile.* Santiago: Editorial Jurídica de Chile, 1984.

Cuevas Farren, Gustavo, ed. *Renovación ideológica en Chile.* Santiago: Universidad de Chile, 1993.

Cumplido, Francisco. "Análisis del presidencialismo en Chile." In *Cambio de régimen político.* Ed. Oscar Godoy. Santiago: Ediciones Universidad Católica de Chile, 1992.

Dahl, Robert. *Polyarchy.* New Haven: Yale University Press, 1971.

Delano, Manuel, and Hugo Traslaviña. *La herencia de los Chicago boys.* Santiago: Ediciones del Ornitorrinco, 1989.

Diamond, Larry, Juan Linz, and Seymour Martin Lipset, eds. *Democracy in Developing Countries: Latin America*, vol. 4. Boulder, Colo.: Lynne Rienner, 1989.

————. *Politics in Developing Countries: Comparing Experiences with Democracy.* Denver, Colo.: Lynne Rienner Publishers, 1990.

Dinamarca, M. *La república socialista chilena: Orígenes legítimos del Partido Socialista.* Santiago: Ediciones Documentas, n.d.

Dow, Jay. "A Spatial Analysis of Candidate Competition in Dual Member Districts: The 1989 Chilean Senatorial Elections," *Public Choice* 97 (1998): 451–74.

Downs, Anthony. *An Economic Theory of Democracy.* New York: Harper and Row, 1957.

Drake, Paul. *Socialism and Populism in Chile.* Urbana: University of Illinois Press, 1978.

Drake, Paul, and Iván Jaksic, eds. *The Struggle for Democracy in Chile: 1982–1990.* Lincoln: University of Nebraska Press, 1991.

————. *The Struggle for Democracy in Chile*, rev. ed. Lincoln: University of Nebraska Press, 1995.

Durán Bernales, Florencio. *El Partido Radical*. Santiago: Editorial Nascimiento, 1958.

Duverger, Maurice. *Political Parties: Their Organization and Activity*, trans. Barbara and Robert North. New York: John Wiley and Sons, 1954.

Echaiz, R. L. *Evolución histórica de los partidos políticos chilenos*. Santiago: Editorial Francisco de Aguirre, 1971.

Eckstein, Harry. *Division and Cohesion in Democracy: A Study of Norway*. Princeton: Princeton University Press, 1966.

Edwards, Alberto, and Eduardo Frei. *Historia de los partidos políticos chilenos*. Santiago: Editorial del Pacífico, 1949.

Eyzaguirre, Jaime. *Historia de las instituciones políticas y sociales de Chile*. Santiago: Editorial Universitaria, 1967.

Falcoff, Mark, Arturo Valenzuela, and Susan Kaufman Purcell. *Chile: Prospects for Democracy*. New York: Council on Foreign Relations, 1988.

Faundez, Julio. "In Defense of Presidentialism: The Case of Chile 1932–1970." In *Presidentialism and Democracy in Latin America*. Ed. Scott Mainwaring and Matthew Shugart. New York: Cambridge University Press, 1997.

Ferreiro, Alejandro. "El congreso chileno." In *Poder legislativo en el cono sur*, vol. 1. Ed. Esteban Caballero and Alejandro Vial. Asunción: Centro de Estudios Democráticos, 1994.

Feuci, C. *The Chilean Communist Party and the Road to Socialism*. London: Zed Books, 1984.

Ffrench Davis, Ricardo. "Desarrollo económico y equidad en Chile: Herencias y desafíos en el retorno a la democracia." *Colección estudios CIEPLAN* 31 (March 1991): 31–52.

Fleet, M. *The Rise and Fall of Chilean Christian Democracy*. Princeton: Princeton University Press, 1985.

Fontaine Talavera, Arturo. "Significado del eje derecha-izquierda." *Estudios públicos* 58 (Fall 1995): 79–137.

Foxley, Alejandro. *Experimentos neoliberales en América Latina*. Santiago: CIEPLAN, 1982.

Frei, Eduardo, Gustavo Lagos, Sergio Molina, Alejandro Silva, Francisco Cumplido, and Enrique Evans de la Cuadra. *Reforma constitucional 1970*. Santiago: Editorial Jurídica, 1970.

Friedmann, Richard. *La política chilena de la A a la Z: 1964–1988*. Santiago: Editorial Melquiades, 1988.

Friedrich, Carl. *Constitutional Government and Politics*, 4th ed. Waltham, Mass.: Blaidsdell, 1968.

Fuentes, José María. "La alternativa proporcional con barreras de entrada: Un sistema electoral adecuado para Chile." *Estudios públicos* 51 (Winter 1993): 269–302.

Garcés, Juan E. *Revolución, congreso y constitución: El caso Tohá*. Santiago: Editorial Quimantú, 1972.

Garretón, Manuel Antonio. *The Chilean Political Process*. Boston: Unwin Hyman, 1989.

———. "The Political Opposition and the Party System Under the Authoritarian Regime." In *The Struggle for Democracy in Chile*, rev. ed. Ed. Paul Drake and Iván Jaksic. Lincoln: University of Nebraska Press, 1995.

Garretón, Manuel Antonio, and Tomás Moulián. *Análisis coyuntural y proceso político: Las fases del conflicto en Chile*. San José, Costa Rica: Editorial Universitaria Centroamericana, 1978.

Gil, Federico. *Los partidos políticos chilenos: Génesis y evolución.* Buenos Aires: Ediciones Palma, 1962.

———. *The Political System of Chile.* Boston: Houghton Mifflin, 1966.

Godoy, Oscar, ed. *Cambio de régimen político.* Santiago: Ediciones Universidad Católica de Chile, 1992.

———. *Hacia una democracia moderna: La opción parlamentaria.* Santiago: Ediciones Universidad Católica de Chile, 1990.

Grayson, G. *El Partido Demócrata Cristiano chileno.* Buenos Aires: Francisco de Aguirre, 1968.

Gutiérrez, Hernán. "Chile 1989: '¿Elecciones fundacionales?'" *Documento de trabajo, serie estudios públicos,* no. 3, FLACSO, Santiago, October 1990.

Guzmán, Eugenio. "Reflexiones sobre el sistema binominal." *Estudios públicos* 51 (Winter 1993): 303–25.

Heise, Julio. *Historia de Chile: El período parlamentario, 1861–1925.* Santiago: Editorial Andrés Bello, 1974.

———. *El período parlamentario.* Santiago: Editorial Universitaria, 1982.

Hermens, F. A. *Democracy or Anarchy? A Study of Proportional Representation.* Notre Dame, Ind.: University of Notre Dame Press, 1941.

Horowitz, Donald. "Democracy in Divided Societies." *Journal of Democracy* 4 (October 1993): 18–38.

Huntington, Samuel. *Political Order in Changing Societies.* New Haven: Yale University Press, 1968.

———. "Will More Countries Become Democratic?" *Political Science Quarterly* 99 (Summer 1984): 193–218.

IDEAS. *Manual del Congreso Nacional: Historia, funciones y atribuciones.* Santiago: IDEAS, n.d.

Instituto Libertad y Desarrollo. "Análisis cuantitativo del proceso legislativo." *Opinión sector político institucional,* no. P19 (December 1991).

International Labour Office. *Yearbook of Labour Statistics.* Geneva: International Labour Office, 1996.

Jobet, Julio César. *El Partido Socialista de Chile,* 2d ed. Santiago: Ediciones Prensa Latinoamericana, 1971.

Jones, Mark. *Electoral Laws and the Survival of Presidential Democracies.* South Bend, Ind.: University of Notre Dame Press, 1995.

———. "A Guide to the Electoral System of the Americas." *Electoral Studies* 14 (1995): 5–21.

Kornberg, Allan, Samuel Hines, and Joel Smith. "Legislatures and the Modernization of Societies." *Comparative Political Studies* 5 (1973): 471–91.

Laakso, Markuu, and Rein Taagepera. "Effective Number of Parties: A Measure with Application to Western Europe." *Comparative Political Studies* 12 (1979): 3–27.

Landsberger, H., and T. McDaniel. "Hypermobilization in Chile, 1970–73." *World Politics* 28 (July 1976): 502–41.

Lardeyret, Guy. "The Problem with PR." *Journal of Democracy* 2 (Summer 1991): 30–36.

Larraín, Hernán. "Democracia, partidos políticos y transición: El caso chileno." *Estudios públicos* 15 (Winter 1984): 111–15.

Larroulet V., Cristián, ed. *Private Solutions to Public Problems.* Santiago: Editorial Trineo, 1993.

Lavín, Joaquín. *Chile: Revolución silenciosa*. Santiago: Zig-Zag, 1988.

Lavín Valdés, Julio. "El papel del Congreso Nacional en el gobierno de la Unidad Popular." *Revista chilena de derecho de la Universidad Católica de Valparaíso* 10 (1986): 304–24.

Lechner, Norbert, ed. *Partidos y democracia*. Santiago: FLACSO, 1985.

Lijphart, Arend. "Constitutional Choices for New Democracies." *Journal of Democracy* 2 (Winter 1991): 72–84.

———. *Democracies: Patterns of Majoritarian and Consensus Government in Twenty-One Countries*. New Haven: Yale University Press, 1984.

———. *Democracy in Plural Societies: A Comparative Exploration*. New Haven: Yale University Press, 1977.

———. *Electoral Systems and Party Systems: A Study of Twenty-Seven Democracies 1945–1990*. New York: Oxford University Press, 1994.

Lijphart, Arend, and Bernard Grofman. Introduction. In *Choosing an Electoral System*. Ed. Arend Lijphart and Bernard Grofman. New York: Praeger, 1984.

Linz, Juan. *The Breakdown of Democratic Regimes: Crisis, Breakdown, and Reequilibration*. Baltimore: Johns Hopkins University Press, 1978.

———. "Democracy: Presidential or Parliamentary: Does it Make A Difference?" Unpublished manuscript, Yale University, 1991.

———. "Presidential or Parliamentary Democracy: Does It Make a Difference?" In *The Failure of Presidential Democracy*. Ed. Juan Linz and Arturo Valenzuela. Baltimore: Johns Hopkins University Press, 1994.

Linz, Juan, and Arturo Valenzuela, eds. *The Failure of Presidential Democracy*, vols. 1 and 2. Baltimore: Johns Hopkins University Press, 1994.

Lipset, Seymour Martin. "Some Social Requisites of Democracy: Economic Development and Political Legitimacy." *American Political Science Review* 53 (March 1959): 69–105.

Lipset, Seymour Martin, and Stein Rokkan. "Cleavage Structures, Party Systems, and Voter Alignments: An Introduction." In *Party Systems and Voter Alignments*. Ed. Seymour Martin Lipset and Stein Rokkan. New York: The Free Press, 1967.

Lovarría, A. *Chile bajo la Democracia Cristiana*. Santiago: Editorial Nascimiento, 1966.

Loveman, Brian. *Chile*. New York: Oxford University Press, 1979.

Lowenthal, Abraham, ed. *Armies and Politics in Latin America*. New York: Holmes and Meier, 1976.

Luders, Ralph. "Massive Divestiture and Privatization: Lessons from Chile." *Contemporary Policy Issues* 9 (October 1991): 1–19.

Lustig, Nora. *Coping with Austerity: Poverty and Inequality in Latin America*. Washington, D.C.: Brookings Institution, 1995.

Magar, Eric, Marc Rosenblum, and David Samuels. "On The Absence of Centripetal Incentives in Double Member Districts: The Case of Chile." *Comparative Political Studies* 31 (December 1998): 714–39.

Mainwaring, Scott. "Dilemmas of Multi-party Presidential Democracy: The Case of Brazil." In *Presidentialism and Democracy in Latin America*. Ed. Scott Mainwaring and Matthew Shugart. New York: Cambridge University Press, 1997.

———. "Presidentialism in Latin America: A Review Essay." *Latin American Research Review* 25, no.1 (1990): 157–79.

———. "Presidentialism, Multipartism, and Democracy: The Difficult Combination." *Comparative Political Studies* 26 (July 1993): 198–228.

Mainwaring, Scott, and Timothy Scully, eds. *Building Democratic Institutions: Party Systems in Latin America*. Stanford: Stanford University Press, 1995.

———. Introduction. In *Building Democratic Institutions: Party Systems in Latin America*. Ed. Scott Mainwaring and Timothy Scully. Stanford: Stanford University Press, 1995.

Mainwaring, Scott, and Matthew Shugart. Introduction. In *Presidentialism and Democracy in Latin America*. Ed. Scott Mainwaring and Matthew Shugart. New York: Cambridge University Press, 1997.

———. "Presidentialism and Democracy in Latin America: The Debate." In *Presidentialism and Democracy in Latin America*. Ed. Scott Mainwaring and Matthew Shugart. New York: Cambridge University Press, 1997.

———, eds. *Presidentialism and Democracy in Latin America*. New York: Cambridge University Press, 1997.

Maira, Luis, and Guido Vicario. *Perspectivas de la izquierda latinoamericana: Seis diálogos*. Santiago: Fondo de Cultura Económica, 1991.

March, James, and John Olsen. "The New Institutionalism: Organizational Forces in Political Life." *American Political Science Review* 78 (1984): 734–49.

Martínez, Javier, and Alvaro Díaz. *Chile: The Great Transformation*. Geneva: UNRISD, 1996.

Martínez, Javier, and Arturo León. *Clases y clasificaciones sociales: Investigaciones sobre la estructura social chilena, 1970–1983*. Santiago: Centro de Estudios del Desarrollo, 1987.

Martínez, Javier, and Eugenio Tironi. *Las clases sociales en Chile: Cambio y estratificación, 1970–1980*. Santiago: Ediciones Sur, 1985.

McDonald, Ronald H. *Party Systems and Elections in Latin America*. Chicago: Markham, 1971.

McDonald, Ronald H., and J. Mark Ruhl. *Party Politics and Elections in Latin America*. Boulder, Colo.: Westview Press, 1989.

Miranda, María Teresa. "El sistema electoral y el multipartidismo en Chile 1949–1969." *Revista de ciencia política* 4 (1982): 59–69.

Mitchell, B. R., ed. *International Historical Statistics: The Americas, 1750–1988*. Stockton, Calif.: Stockton Press, 1993.

Molinar, Juan. "Counting the Number of Parties: An Alternative Index." *American Political Science Review* 85 (December 1991): 1383–91.

Morse, Richard. "The Heritage of Latin America." In *Politics and Social Change in Latin America*. Ed. Howard Wiarda. Amherst: University of Massachusetts Press, 1974.

Moulián, Tomás. "Violencia, gradualismo y reformas en el desarrollo político chileno." In *Estudios sobre sistemas de partidos políticos en Chile*. Ed. Adolfo Aldunate, Angel Flisfisch, and Tomás Moulián. Santiago: FLACSO, 1985.

Moulián, Tomás, and Isabel Torres. "La problemática de la derecha política en Chile, 1964–1983." In *Muerte y resurrección: Los partidos políticos en el autoritarismo y las transiciones del cono sur*. Ed. Manuel Antonio Garretón and Marcelo Cavarozzi. Santiago: FLACSO, 1989.

Muñoz, Oscar, and Carmen Celedón. "Chile en transición: Estrategia económica y política." In *La política económica en la transición a la democracia*. Ed. Juan Antonio Morales and Gary McMahon. Santiago: CIEPLAN, 1993.

Nogueira, Humberto A. "El régimen semi-presidencial: Una alternativa viable al presidencialismo en Chile." In *Reformas al presidencialismo en América Latina:*

¿Presidencialismo vs. parlamentarismo? Ed. Comisión Andina de Juristas. Caracas: Editorial Jurídica Venezolana, 1993.

Nohlen, Dieter. *Enciclopedia electoral latinoamericana y del Caribe.* San José: Instituto Interamericano de Derechos Humanos, 1993.

————. *El régimen semipresidencial: ¿Una nueva forma de gobierno democrático?* Santiago: Editorial Andante, 1986.

Obando Camino, Iván Mauricio. "Observaciones acerca de la regulación de la ley de presupuesto en la Constitución Política de 1980 y sus normas complementarias." *Jornadas de derecho público* 23 (1993): 120–55.

————. "El papel de las comisiones mixtas en el procedimiento legislativo." *Revista de derecho de la Universidad Católica de Valparaíso* 14 (1991–92): 343–68.

O'Donnell, Guillermo. "Delegative Democracy." *Journal of Democracy* 5 (January 1994): 55–69.

O'Donnell, Guillermo, and Phillipe Schmitter. *Transitions from Authoritarian Rule: Tentative Conclusions About Uncertain Democracies.* Baltimore: Johns Hopkins University Press, 1986.

Packenham, Robert. "Legislatures and Political Development." In *Legislatures in Developmental Perspective.* Ed. A. Kornberg and L. Musolf. Durham, N.C.: Duke University Press, 1970.

Palma Zúñiga, Luis. *Historia del Partido Radical.* Santiago: Editorial Andrés Bello, 1967.

Partido Socialista de Chile. *Declaración de principios.* Santiago: Partido Socialista de Chile, 1998.

Piedrabuena R., Guillermo. *La reforma constitucional.* Santiago: Ediciones Encina, 1970.

Pinto Lagarrigue, Fernando. *Balmaceda y los gobiernos seudo-parlamentarios.* Santiago: Editorial Andrés Bello, 1991.

Power, Timothy. "Politicized Democracy: Competition, Institutions, and 'Civic Fatigue' in Brazil." *Journal of Interamerican Studies and World Affairs* 33 (Fall 1991): 75–112.

Prado Valdés, José Miguel. *Reseña histórica del Partido Liberal.* Santiago: Imprenta Andina, 1963.

Pye, Lucian, and Sidney Verba, eds. *Political Culture and Political Development.* Princeton: Princeton University Press, 1965.

Rabkin, Rhoda. "Redemocratization, Electoral Engineering, and Party Strategies in Chile: 1989–1995." *Comparative Political Studies* 29 (1996): 335–56.

Rae, Douglas. *The Political Consequences of Electoral Laws.* New Haven: Yale University Press, 1971.

Ramírez Necochea, Hernán. *Balmaceda y la contrarrevolución de 1891.* Santiago: Editorial Universitaria, 1969.

————. *Origen y formación del Partido Comunista de Chile.* Santiago: Editorial Austral, 1965.

Rehren, Alfredo. "Organizing the Presidency for the Consolidation of Democracy in the Southern Cone." Paper Presented at the Seventeenth International Congress of the Latin American Studies Association, Los Angeles, 24–27 September 1992.

Saffirio, Eduardo. "El sistema de partidos y la sociedad civil en la redemocratización chilena." *Estudios sociales* 82 (1994): 63–103.

Sanfuentes Carrión, Marcial. *El Partido Conservador: Doctrina y convenciones*. Santiago: Editorial Universitaria, 1957.

Sartori, Giovanni. *Comparative Constitutional Engineering*. New York: New York University Press, 1994.

———. "Ni presidencialismo ni parlamentarismo." In *Cambio de régimen político*. Ed. Oscar Godoy. Santiago: Ediciones Universidad Católica, 1992.

———. *Parties and Party Systems: A Framework for Analysis*. Cambridge, England: Cambridge University Press, 1976.

Scarpaci, Joseph. *Primary Medical Care in Chile: Accessibility Under Military Rule*. Pittsburgh: Pittsburgh University Press, 1988.

Scott, Robert. "Mexico: The Established Revolution." In *Political Culture and Political Development*. Ed. Lucian Pye and Sidney Verba. Princeton: Princeton University Press, 1965.

Scully, Timothy. *Cleavages, Critical Junctures, and Party Evolution in Chile: Constituting and Reconstituting the Center*. Ph.D. diss., Graduate Division of Political Science, University of California at Berkeley, 1989.

———. *Los partidos del centro y la evolución política chilena*. Santiago: CIEPLAN, 1992.

———. "The Political Underpinnings of Economic Liberalization in Chile." Unpublished manuscript, The Kellogg Institute of the University of Notre Dame, 1994.

Scully, Timothy, and J. Samuel Valenzuela. "De la democracia a la democracia: Continuidad y variaciones en las preferencias del electorado y en el sistema de partidos en Chile." *Estudios públicos* 51 (Winter 1993): 195–228.

Shepsle, K., and B. Weingast. "Institutionalizing Majority Rule: A Social Choice Theory with Policy Implications." *American Economic Review* 73 (1983): 357–72.

Shugart, Matthew. "The Electoral Cycle and Institutional Sources of Divided Presidential Government." *American Political Science Review* 89 (June 1995): 327–43.

Shugart, Matthew, and John Carey. *Presidents and Assemblies: Constitutional Design and Electoral Dynamics*. New York: Cambridge University Press, 1992.

Shugart, Matthew, and Rein Taagepera. "Plurality Versus Majority Election of Presidents: A Proposal for a 'Double Complement Rule.'" *Comparative Political Studies* 27 (October 1994): 323–48.

Siavelis, Peter. "Continuity and Change in the Chilean Party System: On the Transformational Effects of Electoral Reform." *Comparative Political Studies* 30 (December 1997): 651–74.

———. "Electoral Reform and Democratic Stability in Chile: The Political Consequences of the Adoption of a Plurality Electoral System in a Multi-party Context." Paper presented at the 1994 annual meeting of the American Political Science Association, New York, 1–4 September 1994.

———. "Exaggerated Presidentialism and Moderate Presidents." Paper presented at the symposium Legislaturas en América Latina: Perspectivas Comparadas, Centro de Investigación y Docencia Económicas, Mexico City, 6–7 February 1998.

———. "Executive-Legislative Relations in Post-Pinochet Chile: A Preliminary Assessment." In *Presidentialism and Democracy in Latin America*. Ed. Scott Mainwaring and Matthew Shugart. New York: Cambridge University Press, 1997.

———. "Nuevos argumentos y viejos supuestos: Simulaciones de sistemas electorales alternativos para las elecciones parlamentarias chilenas." *Estudios públicos* 51 (Winter 1993): 229–67.

Sigmund, Paul. *The Overthrow of Allende and the Politics of Chile*. Pittsburgh: University of Pittsburgh Press, 1977.

Silva, Eduardo. "The Political Economy of Chile's Regime Transition: From Radical to Pragmatic Neo-Liberal Policies." In *The Struggle for Democracy in Chile*, rev. ed. Ed. Paul Drake and Iván Jaksic. Lincoln: University of Nebraska Press, 1995.

Silva Bascuñán, Alejandro. "El nuevo Congreso Nacional." *Jornadas de derecho público* 20 (1990): 103–16.

Silva Cimma, Enrique. *Derecho administrativo chileno y comparado*. Santiago: Editorial Jurídica, 1969.

Smith, Joel, and Lloyd Musolf, eds. *Legislatures in Development: Dynamics of Change in New and Old States*. Durham N.C.: Duke University Press, 1979.

Suárez, Waldino. "El poder ejecutivo en América Latina: Su capacidad operativa bajo regímenes presidencialistas de gobierno." *Revista de estudios políticos* 29 (September–October 1982): 109–44.

Tagle Rodrígues, Enrique. *Liberales y Conservadores*. Santiago, 1917.

Tapia Videla, Jorge. "The Chilean Presidency in Developmental Perspective." *Journal of Interamerican Studies and World Affairs* 19 (November 1997): 451–81.

Tapia Valdés, Jorge. *La técnica legislativa*. Santiago: Editorial Jurídica, 1966.

Tironi, Eugenio. *Autoritarismo, modernización y marginalidad: El caso de Chile 1973–1989*. Santiago: Ediciones Sur, 1990.

———. *Los silencios de la revolución*. Santiago: Editorial Puerta Abierta, 1988.

Tulchin, Joseph, and Augusto Varas, eds. *From Dictatorship to Democracy: Rebuilding Political Consensus in Chile*. Boulder, Colo.: Lynne Rienner, 1991.

United Nations. *Economic Survey of Latin America and the Caribbean 1995–1996*. Santiago: United Nations, 1996.

Valenzuela, Arturo. *The Breakdown of Democratic Regimes: Chile*. Baltimore: Johns Hopkins University Press, 1978.

———. "The Military in Power: The Consolidation of One-Man Rule." In *The Struggle for Democracy in Chile*, rev. ed. Ed. Paul W. Drake and Iván Jaksic. Lincoln: University of Nebraska Press, 1995.

———. "Orígenes y características del sistema de partidos en Chile: Proposición para un gobierno parlamentario." *Estudios públicos* 18 (Fall 1985): 88–154.

———. "Partidos políticos y crisis presidencial en Chile: Proposición para un gobierno parlamentario." In *Hacia una democracia moderna: La opción parlamentaria*. Ed. Oscar Godoy. Santiago: Ediciones Universidad Católica de Chile, 1990.

———. "Party Politics and the Crisis of Presidentialism in Chile." In *The Failure of Presidential Democracy*, vol. 2. Ed. Juan Linz and Arturo Valenzuela. Baltimore: Johns Hopkins University Press, 1994.

———. *Political Brokers in Chile: Local Government in a Centralized Polity*. Durham, N.C.: Duke University Press, 1977.

———. "The Scope of the Chilean Party System." *Comparative Politics* 4 (January 1972): 179–99.

Valenzuela, Arturo, and Peter Siavelis. "Ley electoral y estabilidad democrática: Un ejercicio de simulación para el caso de Chile." *Estudios públicos* 43 (Winter 1991): 27–87.

Valenzuela, Arturo, and Alexander Wilde. "Presidential Politics and the Decline of the Chilean Congress." In *Legislatures in Development: Dynamics of Change in New and Old States*. Ed. Joel Smith and Lloyd Musolf. Durham, N.C.: Duke University Press, 1979.

Valenzuela, Germán Urzúa. *Historia política electoral de Chile*. Santiago: Editorial Jurídica de Chile, 1986.

———. *Los partidos políticos chilenos*. Santiago: Editorial Jurídica, 1968.

Valenzuela, J. Samuel. *Democratización vía reforma: La expansión del sufragio en Chile*. Santiago: Ediciones del IDES, 1985.

———. "Labor Movements in Transitions to Democracy: A Framework for Analysis." Working paper no. 104, The Kellogg Institute for International Studies, Notre Dame, Ind., 1988.

———. "Orígenes y transformaciones del sistema de partidos en Chile." *Estudios públicos* 58 (Fall 1995): 5–78.

Valenzuela, J. Samuel, and Jeffry Goodwin. "Labor Movements Under Authoritarian Regimes." Monographs on Europe Series no. 5, Center for European Studies, Harvard University, Cambridge, Mass., 1983.

Valenzuela, J. Samuel, and Timothy Scully. "Electoral Choices and the Party System in Chile: Continuities and Changes at the Recovery of Democracy." *Comparative Politics* 29 (July 1997): 511–27.

Valenzuela, J. Samuel, and Arturo Valenzuela, eds. *Military Rule in Chile: Dictatorship and Opposition*. Baltimore: Johns Hopkins University Press, 1986.

Varas, Augusto. *Los militares en el poder: Régimen y gobierno militar en Chile, 1973–1986*. Santiago: FLACSO, 1987.

Varas, Augusto, Felipe Aguero, and Fernando Bustamante, eds. *Chile: Democracia, fuerzas armadas*. Santiago: FLACSO, 1980.

Vergara, Pilar. *Auge y caída del neoliberalismo en Chile*. Santiago: FLACSO, 1985.

———. "Changes in the Economic Structure of the Chilean State Under the Military Regime." In *Military Rule in Chile: Dictatorship and Oppositions*. Ed. J. Samuel Valenzuela and Arturo Valenzuela. Baltimore: Johns Hopkins University Press, 1986.

Villalobos R., Sergio, Osvaldo Silva, Fernando Silva, and Patricio Estelle. *Historia de Chile*. Santiago: Editorial Universitaria, 1974.

Wiarda, Howard. "Toward a Framework for the Study of Political Change in the Iberic-Latin Tradition: The Corporative Model." In *Corporatism and National Development in Latin America*. Ed. Howard Wiarda. Boulder, Colo.: Westview Press, 1981.

Walker, Ignacio. *Socialismo y democracia en Chile: Chile y Europa en perspectiva comparada*. Santiago: CIEPLAN, 1990.

Wilkie, James, ed. *Statistical Abstract of Latin America*, vols. 29 and 31. Los Angeles: UCLA Latin American Center Publications, 1995.

Government Documents

Cámara de Diputados de la República de Chile. Boletín de Sesiones. 9 April 1998.

Cámara de Diputados de la República de Chile. "Informe de la comisión especial de estudio del régimen político chileno." 9 May 1990.

Constitución Política de la República de Chile, 1925.

Constitución Política de la República de Chile, 1980.
Declaración de Principios de la Junta de Gobierno, March 1974.
Diario Oficial de la República de Chile.
Ministerio del Interior de Chile. "Informativo Elecciones 1993." Cómputo no. 4.
El Pronunciamiento Militar del 11 de Septiembre de 1973, 11 September 1973.
Proyecto de Modernización, Congreso Nacional de Chile. *Proceso legislativo chileno: Un enfoque cuantitativo.* Valparaíso: Proyecto de Modernización, Congreso Nacional de Chile, 1995.
Reglamento de la Cámara de Diputados de la República de Chile.
República de Chile, documents of the Dirección de Presupuesto, 1993.
Servicio Electoral de Chile, *Partidos políticos.* Santiago: Servicio Electoral de Chile, 1990.
———. Resultados Electorales, 1989, 1992, 1993, 1997.

Other

Adimark, Santiago. "Estudio de opinión pública Adimark." Santiago: Adimark, April 1997.
Centro de Estudios Públicos, Santiago. "Documento de trabajo No. 208." Santiago: Centro de Estudios Públicos, August 1993.
———. "Estudio de opinión pública." Documento de trabajo No. 136. Santiago: Centro de Estudios Públicos, August 1990.
———. "Estudio social y de opinión pública." Santiago: Centro de Estudios Públicos, June 1990.
———. "Estudio nacional de opinión pública No. 7." Santiago: Centro de Estudios-Públicos, December 1997–January 1998.
———. "Estudio social y de opinión pública." Santiago: Centro de Estudios Públicos, June 1993.
———. "Estudio social y de opinión pública." Santiago: Centro de Estudios Públicos, July 1993.
———. "Estudio social y de opinión pública." Santiago: Centro de Estudios Públicos, December 1993.
Centro de Estudios Públicos—Adimark. "Encuesta de opinión pública." Santiago: CEP-Adimark, January 1993.
Instituto Libertad y Desarrollo. *Temas públicos* series (periodic publications on issues of public interest).
Latin American Weekly Report. London: Latin American Newsletters Ltd.
Participa. *Estudio sobre la democracia y participación política.* Informe segunda medición, 1993. Santiago: Participa, 1993.
———. "Los chilenos y la democracia." Informe 1993. Santiago: Participa, 1994.
Political Risk Services, Inc. *Chile: Country Report.* 1993.
Programa de Asesoría Legislativa. "Análisis electoral: Resultados electorales y representación parlamentaria." Documento de trabajo 45. July 1992.
———. "Ficha legislativa no. 167, Proyecto de reforma constitucional: Tribunal Constitucional." 8–12 June 1992.
Salomon Brothers. "Chile: Receiving the Benefits of Structural Reform." *Emerging Markets Research: Latin America.* September 1992.

Newspapers and Magazines

The Chicago Tribune.
La Epoca (Santiago).
The Financial Times (London).
Hoy (Santiago).
El Mercurio (Santiago).
La Segunda (Santiago).
La Tercera (Santiago).
The Washington Post.

INDEX